D1003965

Value and distribution in capitalist economies

Value and distribution in capitalist economies

An introduction to Sraffian economics

LYNN MAINWARING

Lecturer in Economics
University College, Cardiff

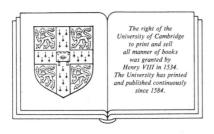

The right of the
University of Cambridge
to print and sell
all manner of books
was granted by
Henry VIII in 1534.
The University has printed
and published continuously
since 1584.

CAMBRIDGE UNIVERSITY PRESS

Cambridge
London   New York   New Rochelle
Melbourne   Sydney

Published by the Press Syndicate of the University of Cambridge
The Pitt Building, Trumpington Street, Cambridge CB2 1RP
32 East 57th Street, New York, NY 10022, USA
296 Beaconsfield Parade, Middle Park, Melbourne 3206, Australia

© Cambridge University Press 1984

First published 1984

Printed in Great Britain at the University Press, Cambridge

Library of Congress catalogue card number: 83-26228

British Library cataloguing in publication data

Mainwaring, Lynn
Value and distribution in capitalist economies.
1. Sraffo, Piero 2. Economics
I. Title
335.4'12   HB109.S/

ISBN 0 521 25904 5 hard covers
ISBN 0 521 27755 8 paperback

AN

TO MY PARENTS

Contents

Acknowledgements

Without the advice and painstaking criticism of Ian Steedman it is doubtful that this book would ever have been completed. Despite his heroic attempts to improve my logic and my English, many deficiencies surely remain. They are entirely the result of my own stubbornness. Thanks are also due to Geoff Harcourt, Jan Kregel, Heinz Kurz and Ray Rees for helpful comments and criticisms on various parts of the manuscript, and to Francis Brooke of Cambridge University Press for his encouragement and patience. I have had the benefit of the first-class typing services of Tricia Buckingham, Mavis Rees and Pat Watson. My wife, Ann, is probably as surprised as I am that this book is now in print. That it is is due, in no small part, to her enthusiasm and understanding.

Parts of chapters 7 and 9 draw on previously published essays in *Australian Economic Papers* and *Kyklos*, respectively. Permission to do so is gratefully acknowledged.

Preface

In the years that have elapsed since the publication of Piero Sraffa's *Production of Commodities by Means of Commodities* a number of books has appeared in which some aspect or other of his work is discussed. The more elementary of these rarely devote more than one or two chapters to the subject. For a deeper consideration it is necessary to turn either to Roncaglia's (1978) book, which assumes a familiarity with the subject to begin, or to several excellent but extremely mathematical works such as Abraham-Frois and Berrebi (1979) and Pasinetti (1977) and (1980). The books of Harris (1978) and Walsh and Gram (1980) are slightly less technical but still make little concession to the non-mathematical reader. There may be good reasons for this state of affairs. In a review of Pasinetti (1977), John Broome offered this advice: 'Newcomers to Sraffa would do well to take Pasinetti as their guide, since the use of mathematics gives Pasinetti a tremendous advantage over Sraffa in making himself understood' (Broome, 1978). A preference for the mathematical approach is not uncommon though it does tend to be confined to those who are relatively secure in their knowledge of algebra. I suspect that at least as common (especially among students) is a preference for less, and simpler, algebra, and more words. Perhaps it is because he does not use enough words that Sraffa has difficulty in making himself understood. His 'chiselled logic', to use Krishna Bharadwaj's phrase, may be as intimidating for beginners as Pasinetti's mathematics.

It is, of course, impossible to discuss Sraffa's economics without recourse to abstract reasoning of some sort. Nevertheless, Sraffa himself has shown that it is possible to explain the major issues without using advanced mathematical techniques (which, for present purposes, can be taken to include linear algebra and calculus). If it were possible to 'stretch out' Sraffa's own explanations and provide them with some background so that we do not, as Joan Robinson put it, 'plunge immediately into the argument without any preliminary discussion of assumptions and delimitation of topics', then we might avoid intimidation of either sort. It may also be helpful to provide a visual, more concrete expression of the arguments by the use of geometry. The object of this book is to provide such a treatment. The mathematical demands on the reader are that he or she should have an elementary knowledge (say O-level equivalent) of algebra, including an understanding of simultaneous equations and a familiarity with summation signs, and a predisposition toward the use of geometry, including a willingness to become acquainted with the geometry of vectors.

It should perhaps be made clear that, while Sraffa is the central character in this book, it is not exclusively about him. In the preface to *Production of Commodities by Means of Commodities** Sraffa makes it clear that the 'standpoint' of his book 'is that of the old classical economists from Adam Smith to Ricardo', and, in his Appendix D, he also notes connections with Quesnay, Torrens, Malthus and Marx. While it is not necessary to explore all of these connections to obtain a basic understanding of Sraffa's own ideas, some examination is certainly desirable. Of those named, Ricardo is arguably the most important in this respect. Over much of the period during which his ideas were developed Sraffa was also engaged in the editing of the *Works and Correspondence of David Ricardo*. It is only to be expected that Ricardo's writings had an important influence on Sraffa. We also have Sraffa's admission that his own ideas coloured his interpretation of important parts of Ricardo's work. An examination of this Sraffian reconstruction of Ricardo is helpful in providing a background against which to view *PC*. For that reason the first two chapters are devoted to a presentation of 'Ricardian' models of value and distribution.

Not only does Sraffa refer, in his preface, to the classical economists, he also says that '. . . others have from time to time taken up points of view which are similar to one or other of those adopted in this paper and have developed them further or in different directions from those pursued here'. Two writers he may have had in mind are Leontief and von Neumann. It is possible and, in my view desirable, to draw on the contributions of these economists to complement and supplement Sraffa's. This may not appeal to some purists but placing Sraffa's theory of value and distribution in the growth framework of the Leontief dynamic production model has proved particularly fruitful while fresh insights are being gained by a comparison of Sraffa with the highly generalised approach to competitive equilibrium of von Neumann.

The book is split into four parts. Part I provides the 'Ricardian' background. In the first chapter a model is constructed based on Sraffa's interpretation of an early attempt by Ricardo to develop a theory of profits. The second chapter explains the 'labour theory of value' which was the foundation stone of Ricardo's *Principles of Political Economy and Taxation*. It is not the purpose of this part to provide an historically accurate account

* Hereafter, abbreviated to *PC*.

of Ricardo. Rather it is to give the reader an opportunity to become familiar, in the context of relatively simple models, with certain fundamental ideas, concepts, definitions and, above all, with a particular perspective of real capitalist economies, which are to be found in the succeeding chapters.

Part II, which is the largest, develops the 'single-products' model in which each commodity is uniquely associated with a particular industry. Although in this part we use and re-evaluate ideas discussed in Part I, there is no logical continuity with what has gone before. In fact, chapters 3, 4, 6 and 7 run in close parallel with Part I of *PC*, beginning with an examination of a subsistence economy before analysing prices and distribution under capitalism. In addition to these Sraffian concerns, the Leontief growth model is explained in chapter 5 and the two aspects are fused together to obtain a fuller picture of the economy (chapters 5 and 8). This part concludes with an example of how this Sraffa–Leontief model can be applied to a particular problem; understanding the causes and consequences of international trade. Although the assumption of single-products industries only is quite unrealistic (more unrealistic than the reader may presently be aware), analytically this part is the core of the book and is essential to the understanding of the more sophisticated models of Part III.

Part III admits the possibility of 'joint production' in which several commodities may be produced by one industrial activity, or several activities may produce the same commodity. Joint production is not confined to a handful of minor agricultural processes like the production of beef and hide or corn and straw. Even the inclusion of modern multiple-product industries such as petrochemicals takes us only part of the way down the list. For joint production also includes all processes which use machinery; that is, just about every major process in the modern industrial economy. And that is not all. Processes which use land and other natural resources can also be regarded as joint-production activities. The unrealism of the models of Part II should now be appreciated. There is, however, a cost involved in pursuing realism: the analysis becomes much more involved. There is no doubt that the issues raised in Part III are much more complicated and are discussed at a higher level of abstraction than those in Part II. Although we stick by our promise not to use more than elementary algebra, the amount of that algebra becomes noticeably greater, especially in chapter 11 on fixed capital. Even so, the reader who has understood the basic principles of Part II should have no real difficulty with this. All that is necessary is to go a little more slowly. The only compensation I can offer is that I know of no other works where these issues are treated, even to the extent that they are here, without requiring of the reader a much greater knowledge of analytical techniques.

The last part draws together some loose threads and considers the significance of this type of theory and its relationships with other major schools of economic thought, particularly the Marxian and Walrasian schools.

At the end of each chapter there is a guide to further reading. These combine sources from which the present work has drawn and suggestions for going beyond what is included here. In compiling these guides I have tried to avoid the temptation of including everything of the slightest relevance. A shorter, more selective list of readings is probably of more use to the reader than an exhaustive bibliography.

In terms of coverage, it would be possible to obtain a rough parallel to this book (though on a much higher plane) by regarding Pasinetti's *Lectures in the Theory of Production* (written by him) and *Essays in the Theory of Joint Production* (edited by him) as a single two-volume work. It would, however, be misleading to imply that this book is simply a poor man's Pasinetti for, even here, there are important differences in the choice and treatment of the subject matter. Because Pasinetti may be regarded as a sort of 'radical orthodoxy', it is as well to point out these differences. It is unlikely that readers new to Sraffa will appreciate their significance and this is not the place to attempt to justify them. But it is important that warning should be given and that our position with regard to some important and controversial issues should be clearly stated at the outset. The following list may not be exhaustive but it does, I think, include the major differences.

(1) Sraffa emphatically asserts in the preface to *PC* that the assumption of constant returns is not necessary to those parts of his analysis which do not involve a choice of technique. I do not find Sraffa's justification for this assertion persuasive. To be perfectly clear, constant returns are assumed throughout this book.

(2) Sraffa's device of the 'Standard commodity' is widely regarded as the key to resolving certain outstanding problems in classical theory. One of these is Ricardo's unsuccessful search for an 'invariable measure of value'. My own view is that the search for an invariable measure of value is uninstructive and uninteresting. The Standard commodity has also been used to buttress Marx's theory of exploitation which in turn is based on the labour theory of value. I believe that Sraffa has rendered the labour theory of value obsolete and that, anyway, a theory of exploitation does not need these foundations. Consequently, this use of the Standard commodity also remains undiscussed. I am also of the opinion that the Standard commodity itself does not yield any significant results that could not be obtained without it. It may, however, aid the *understanding* of those results and so have value as a heuristic device. For that reason, and because of its importance in the literature, a discussion of this concept is included. I do, however, attribute much less importance to it than do Pasinetti and many other writers.

(3) The book contains no reference to the 'reduction to dated labour' discussed by Sraffa in chapter VI of *PC*. This is not to deny the potential usefulness of this procedure in certain circumstances. It is merely that the essential Sraffian results are already viewed from a number of perspectives and that the small gain in understanding does not justify yet another.

(4) The critique of naive neoclassical theory which reached its peak in the late 1960s was inspired by the publication of *PC*. These debates have been well recorded and little of interest has happened in the last ten years. Thus, without denying their importance, they are given only the briefest consideration.

Some of these issues are discussed further in Part III.

FURTHER READING

To avoid repetition an attempt has been made at the end of each chapter to list only those works which are especially relevant to that chapter. Some works of a more general nature are mentioned below. References are given to the name of the author or editor and the year of publication. An exception is Sraffa's *PC*, which is cited so often that this abbreviated form is more economical.

Useful introductions to *PC* are the review articles by Robinson (1961), Bharadwaj (1963) and Harcourt and Massaro (1964). Newman (1962) is both a review and a rigorous mathematical reformulation. Books (in English) which are devoted in large part to this subject are few and far between. Pasinetti (1977) and Abraham-Frois and Berrebi (1979) require a good knowledge of linear algebra. Walsh and Gram (1980), which aims to compare Sraffian theory with modern 'General Equilibrium' theory, also uses relatively advanced mathematics. On the same level is Schwartz (1961), who presents a model of the economy which in its essentials is the same as the Sraffa single-products system. Schwartz's independent contribution deserves to be more widely appreciated. Kregel (1971) may be a better starting point for non-mathematical readers. Broome (1983), which appeared shortly before this book was completed, covers a lot of the ground surveyed here. (It does, however, use slightly more advanced algebra.)

Collections of readings covering various aspects of the subject matter of this book are Harcourt and Laing (1971), Hunt and Schwartz (1972), Schwartz (1977) and, specifically on joint production, Pasinetti (1980).

Roncaglia (1978) is an excellent discussion of some of the conceptual issues arising out of *PC*. It also includes a list of Sraffa's published writings and a comprehensive bibliography of works (up to 1977) relating to all aspects of *PC*. See also, Bharadwaj (1978).

The classical economists mentioned by Sraffa in Appendix D to *PC* span a period of a little under a century. The major works of this school are Adam Smith's *The Wealth of Nations* of 1776 (Smith, 1961), David Ricardo's *Principles of Political Economy and Taxation* of 1817 (Sraffa and Dobb, 1952, Vol. I), T. R. Malthus' *Principles of Political Economy* of 1820 (largely reproduced with Ricardo's comments in Sraffa and Dobb, 1951, Vol. II), Robert Torrens' *An Essay on the Production of Wealth* of 1821, and Karl Marx's *Capital*, the first volume of which was published in 1867 (Marx, 1970). Francois Quesnay was the leading member of the preclassical French Physiocratic school. His *Tableau Economique* was published in 1758 (see Kuczinski and Meek, 1972) and is regarded as a forerunner of Leontief's input–output tables. For an introduction to the works of some of the leading classical economists, see O'Brien (1975) or Deane (1978) and, for a more detailed discussion in relation to theories of value and distribution, Dobb (1973). An evaluation of the contributions of Quesnay, Ricardo and Marx in relation to the Sraffa–Leontief model is given by Pasinetti (1977), chapter 1.

PART I

A reconstruction of classical value theory

A simple theory of distribution and prices

1 Social classes and shares in income

The division of society into classes is an essential feature of the writings of the classical economists. The three classes which they identified are the landlords, the capitalists and the workers or, as Ricardo chose to describe them, 'the proprietor of the land, the owner of the stock of capital necessary for its cultivation, and the labourers by whose industry it is cultivated'.[1] The land, the stock of capital and the potential for industrious labour are productive resources which, under capitalism, are subject to private ownership. The use of these resources gives individuals a claim on the product or income of society. Whether or not these claims have any moral or ethical foundation, they are backed by the social and legal institutions of capitalism. The shares of income received by landlords, capitalists and workers are referred to, respectively, as rent, profit and wages. It is often more interesting to consider these rewards in relation to the amount of each resource employed. Capitalists, for example, are not concerned to maximise profits irrespective of the amount of capital they devote to production. They are, rather, concerned to maximise profits per unit of capital, or the rate of profits. Landlords, similarly, are interested in rent per acre, and workers in wages per person per period, or the wage rate.

This tripartite division of society, together with the unique identification of landlords with rent, capitalists with profits and workers with wages, involve considerable simplification, probably more so for the modern capitalist economy than for the British economy of the early nineteenth century. Some political theorists of modern capitalism deny the existence of classes in the traditional sense; that is, of groups of individuals with common economic and social characteristics and pursuing common interests which may be opposed to those of other groups. Others would say that capitalist societies are divided, but that the number of classes far exceeds three. Miliband (1969), for example, considers the following as constituting separate classes: professional people, self-employed craftsmen and shopkeepers, 'cultural workmen' and those involved in running the state. Yet despite the blurring of the simple social divisions of the classical economists in modern capitalist countries, 'the principal form assumed by the 'relations of production' in these countries is that between capitalist employers and industrial wage-earners. This is one of the main elements of differentiation between advanced capitalist societies and collectivist societies on the one hand, and the pre-industrial societies of the 'Third World' on the other' (Miliband 1969, p.16). It would, at least, appear that the landlord as a distinct and powerful class is a casualty of a century and a half of capitalist economic development. This, perhaps, is because the modern landlord is also, often, an industrialist; and even when that is not the case, 'the proprietor of the land' and 'the owner of the stock of capital necessary for its cultivation' are likely to be one and the same person.

There is, therefore, something to be said for a two-class view: one class whose members' productive resources are largely confined to their own minds and bodies, and whose access to capital and land is limited; and another whose economic power rests in the ownership of assets either made by others or provided by nature and legally denied to others. This is not to argue that rent as a category of income does not require a separate analysis. It does so on the grounds that capital and land contribute to production in different ways. But the simple worker/capitalist division is sufficient to reflect the fundamental and highly unequal division of economic power in all capitalist societies.

Let us define society's *net product* (or *net income* or *social surplus*) as the difference between what it produces annually on the one hand, and, on the other, the subsistence requirement of the population and whatever is needed to make good the wear and tear (depreciation) of capital equipment and of the land. How precisely subsistence requirements are determined is not a clear-cut matter but that need not worry us here. Part of the net product may be used to finance the state, military expenditure, and cultural and religious activities. There is a rough correspondence between these activities and the list of 'lesser' classes given above. Deductions from the net product to finance these activities and so provide incomes for their associated classes can easily be considered within the general framework of our analysis. Since they do not add anything of significance to it they will be ignored. The other uses of the net product are for raising consumption above subsistence level and for providing net additions to the capital stock, that is, net investment. In the modern capitalist economy the state has an important rôle to play here. It can acquire part of the net product through taxation and it can disburse its proceeds in the form of social consumption (such as hospitals) and social investments (such as roads). It may contribute directly to industrial investment through the expansion of the nationalised industries. It also has the power to redistribute income and create legislation which favours one class or other, one activity or other. Yet despite its undoubted importance, analysis of the state's activities can again be superimposed on the analysis of pure capitalism and it, too, will be put aside. Ignoring the state then, the division of the net product between consumption and investment depends on the proportions which go to workers and capitalists. The rate of accumulation of capital is likely to be greater the larger is the share of profits in net product. Workers, on the other hand, are likely to use their share in the surplus mainly to supplement their subsistence wages. To what extent the net product should be directed to the pursuit of growth and to what extent to increase current consumption is an issue of great social importance. In capitalist economies its resolution depends on how the net product is distributed among its classes. 'To determine the laws which regulate this distribution, is the principal problem of Political Economy'.[2]

2 A 'corn-ratio' theory of distribution

In this section we shall develop a very simple theory of distribution using elements which have been derived from Ricardo. In his *Essay on the Influence of a Low Price of Corn on the Profits of Stock*,[3] of 1815, Ricardo integrates a theory of the determination of the rate of profits with a theory of rent due to Malthus. The theory of rent, in particular the notion of diminishing returns in agriculture, played a central rôle in the political arguments in which Ricardo was involved, especially in his concern to secure the importation of corn free of duty. But in his economic analysis rent was a secondary issue. The importance of Malthus' theory was that it enabled him to keep separate the analysis of rent and of the other two components. Thus when preparing his *Principles of Political Economy and Taxation* of 1817, Ricardo wrote of his 'getting rid of rent'[4] in order, as Sraffa puts it, 'to simplify the problem of distribution between capitalist and labourer'.[5]

As a consequence of his own investigations in the course of preparing the *Production of Commodities*, Sraffa says that a particular interpretation of Ricardo's *Essay* 'suggested itself as a natural consequence'.[6] This interpretation, or reconstruction, of the *Essay* he calls the 'corn-ratio' theory of profits.[7] As an exercise in the history of economic thought it has become the subject of some controversy. It is not our intention to enter that controversy. Our interest in the corn-ratio theory is that it provides us with the elements of a simple theory of distribution. The way in which we arrange these elements should not be regarded as an interpretation of Ricardo. Neither should it be regarded as an account of Sraffa's interpretation. The arrangement is made to suit our own purposes.

Consider an agricultural economy which produces just one commodity, corn. Production takes place in a yearly cycle from sowing to harvesting. There is no machinery in this economy; all the work is done by labourers.

The economy is capitalist in that the land is privately owned and the farmers hire labour in exchange for wage payments. The only non-labour input, or *means of production*, is the corn which is used for seed. Since corn is the only product, that too is the only consumption commodity. Suppose, then that L units of labour (measured in worker-years), together with a quantity of seed corn, c, combine to produce by the end of the year a quantity of corn, C. The process can be presented schematically:

Inputs		Outputs
Labour Corn		Corn
L $+ c$	$\longrightarrow$	C

Since the labourer lives entirely on corn this process can also be pictured in another way. Denoting the annual wage per worker as w (so many bushels of corn), we can combine the food-corn requirements wL, with the seed-corn, as follows:

Inputs		Outputs
$wL + c$	$\longrightarrow$	C

Thus both inputs and outputs are of the same single commodity.

As with Ricardo, it would be useful if we too could 'get rid' of rent. Rather than go through the theory of rent here and show how its analysis can be kept separate, we shall simply assume that rent is zero in our economy. (This itself implies that land is of uniform quality.) In that way we can, like Ricardo, concentrate on the relationship between wages and profits. The corn-wage, w, is, we assume, 'advanced' by the farmer to the labourer at the beginning of the agricultural year, along with the seed with which the labourer works. This total advance – the seed corn and the wage – is reckoned as the farmer's *capital*. Capital, it will be noted, need not consist entirely of tools and machinery. Anything which is 'tied-up' for a period of time in the production process may be regarded as capital. Through the advanced payment of wages the farmer is investing a quantity of food over a period of a year in the hope of a return to that investment. Thus the total capital used in the production of the output C is the amount $(wL + c)$. Naturally, the farmer would continue in production only so long as the amount of corn produced exceeded the amount used up,[8] the difference $C - (wL + c)$ being the farmer's profit. The rate of profit,[9] or the proportion of profit to capital advanced is given by

$$r = \frac{C-(wL+c)}{(wL+c)} = \frac{C}{(wL+c)} - 1. \tag{1.1}$$

The farmer's rate of profit therefore depends on the technical conditions of production (the ratios $L:C$ and $c:C$) and the annual wage rate, w. Assuming that the same technique of production is used by all other farmers and assuming also that competition amongst labourers equalises wage rates throughout the economy, then r is also the rate of profits for the whole economy.

The technical conditions of production in this simple economy refer to the methods of sowing, tending and reaping. This means that equality of the individual rates of profit depends on each farmer having equal access to knowledge on such matters. Each farmer, striving to maximise the profit on each unit of capital invested, would adopt the best-practice technique. But equality also means that production is not locally upset by accidental factors such as bad weather and disease. Such random, accidental variations of individual rates are not capable of being accommodated in this analysis and so we shall ignore them. There is, however, another way in which knowledge can become uneven: through innovation. Suppose that someone discovers a new method of cultivation (sowing in drills, rather than scattering, say). The reduced wastage of seed corn and the improved crop yield increase output relative to input and so have the immediate effect of raising that farmer's rate of profit above that of fellow farmers who, for some time yet, remain ignorant of the development. But if we assume that new knowledge is gradually diffused throughout the entire economy as other farmers get to hear of the improvement then, after some time, their rates of profit will also increase to the level enjoyed by the innovator. There is thus a transitional period when the uniformity of profit rates breaks down, but the general advance in productivity eventually succeeds in restoring uniformity at a higher rate. For every possible wage rate and for every set of fully diffused techniques there is an economy-wide rate of profits implied by equation (1.1). This we shall refer to as the *long-period* or *natural* rate of profits, as distinct from the transitional, *short-period* rates that may result from undiffused technical knowledge. During a period of continuous technological change it may be that a natural rate is never actually established. But the continuous adoption of improved techniques by farmers wishing to maximise the return to their capital means that actual rates are always chasing after, even if never catching, the succession of natural rates. We have said that, for every uniform wage rate, equation (1.1) implies a particular natural rate of profits. Conversely, for every natural r (1.1) implies a particular w (which we may also call 'natural'). We need to fix the value of one of these 'distributive variables' before we can determine the value of the other. In algebraic terms, (1.1) is a single equation in two unknowns and is, therefore, incapable of a solution. This 'degree of freedom'

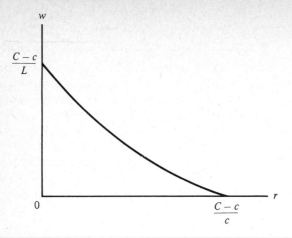

Figure 1.1

in the system can be exploited to show how r changes as w varies (or *vice versa*). In other words we can solve (1.1) for all possible levels of w and plot the resulting relation between w and r. This we shall call the wage–rate-of-profits, or w–r relation. Begin with the (purely hypothetical) case of $w = 0$. Here the only capital advanced would be the seed-corn, and the rate of profits would be given by

$$r = (C-c)/c.$$

Ruling out negative wages this is the highest possible rate of profits. As the wage is notionally raised from zero, profits decline at the same time as capital used increases. Thus as w increases r falls. The limit to the fall occurs where wages account for the entire net product, the maximum wage rate being given by

$$w = (C-c)/L.$$

The w–r relation for this simple economy is illustrated in fig. 1.1. The effect of technical improvements is to increase r for a given w, or w for a given r. If, for example, an improvement in the method of sowing reduced the wastage of seed-corn then, as can be seen from equation (1.1), the smaller amount of corn needed as capital occasions an increase in profits. In fig. 1.1, this would be reflected in an outward shift of the w–r relation.

For the most part, in this book we shall be concerned with investigating the w–r *relation*. But in applications of the basic theory (as, for example, in chapter 9) it is generally necessary to 'close' the system; that is, to make it determinate. To do this a separate theory is needed to account for one of the distributive variables. The other can then be read off the w–r relation. The choice of closure, or separate theory, may depend on the historical, geographical or other circumstances of the economy under consideration. Merely as an example, let us consider Ricardo's method of closure. As well as to his theory of rent, Ricardo also subscribed to Malthus' views on population. Malthus believed that an increase in workers' income, above current subsistence requirements, could result from, say, a spurt of economic growth at a rate greater than the growth of the workforce. But this improvement in the wellbeing of the working family would encourage an increase in the birth (or survival) rate which, over time, would increase the labour force. Thus an increase in the demand for labour raises wages above subsistence level and this in turn stimulates an additional increase in the supply of labour. The result is that wages will tend to return to the subsistence level. With continuously favourable conditions for economic growth, however, the improvement in demand may persistently keep ahead of the additions to supply so that wages remain high for a long period of time. Such a sustained increase in wages might be partially consolidated as such additions become socially accepted as part of the 'necessaries' of life. Thus the subsistence wage is not determined in a purely physiological way but contains possible 'moral' or social elements which vary with time and place. But the rate of permanent increase due to the consolidation of these moral and social elements is assumed to be sufficiently slow that at any one time the subsistence wage can be regarded as a datum. Thus the pressure of population growth would ensure that workers do not permanently share in the net product of society. With w as a datum, the corn-ratio theory becomes a theory of the determination of the rate of profits.

3 A two-sector model

Nowhere in the preceding section did we need to talk about prices. In a one-commodity world price is not a meaningful concept. All dealings are done in corn and the bushel, or some other measure, serves as the unit of account. But as soon as additional commodities are introduced we have to consider the nature of prices. Prices allow us to value one commodity in terms of another; that is, they tell us how much of one commodity will swap for some amount of another. It is common in modern economies to think of prices in money terms. That is because money is the generally accepted unit of account. Because a yard of silk exchanges for so many pounds or dollars the latter is considered the 'price' of silk. But for our purposes, money, as generally understood, is not an essential part of the analysis. Any commodity can serve as a unit of account and, having chosen such a commodity, all we need to know is the number of units that will exchange for, say, a yard of silk.

The unit of account is also known as the 'standard of value' or the *numéraire* of the price system. The price of the chosen commodity is, by definition, equal to unity.

Let us now introduce a second commodity, to be called 'silk'. Taking corn as the standard of value, the price of a yard of silk is the number of bushels of corn (the number of accounting units) for which it exchanges. Denote this by p_s. We shall worry later about how p_s is determined. First let us fill in the details of the silk production process. Suppose that to produce silk requires inputs of labour and corn (to feed the silk worms); schematically:

Inputs			Outputs
Labour	Corn		Silk
L_s	$+ c_s$	$\longrightarrow$	S

where S is the quantity of silk produced each year, L_s and c_s the amounts of labour and corn which together are used to produce S. Silk, being a luxury commodity, does not form part of the wage payments. The workers receive a corn-wage w which, by competition, is of the same quantity as that paid in corn production. (The skill and intensity of the work is assumed to be the same in the two sectors.) The total amount of corn used as inputs into silk production is, therefore, $(wL_s + c_s)$. When it comes to finding an expression for the rate of profits in the silk sector the problem that arises is that inputs and outputs are not the same homogeneous commodity: output consists of silk, inputs of corn. But quantities of silk can be converted into their corn-equivalents by multiplying them by their price in terms of corn, p_s. The corn-value of profits in the silk sector is then

$$p_s S - (wL_s + c_s)$$

and the sector rate of profits is given by

$$r_s = \frac{p_s S}{(wL_s + c_s)} - 1. \tag{1.2}$$

If competition prevails between the two sectors then the natural rates of profits are the same for both. Starting from a position of equality, any permanent improvement in the conditions of production of silk would raise the rate of profits in that sector above that of corn. But this could only be a short-period phenomenon. For the prospect of a higher rate of profits would attract capital out of corn production and into silk. With a given wage, the rate of profits in corn production cannot change since it is fully determined as a ratio of homogeneous quantities. The process of equalisation therefore

From $$p_s = (1+r)(wL_s + c_s)$$
$$1 = (1+r)(wL_c + c_c)$$

where $p_s = p_s^* / p_c^*$ we get

$$\frac{1}{wL_c + c_c} - 1 = r$$

The uniform rate of profits is dependent on corn sector so

$$p_s = (1+r)(wL_s + c_s) \qquad (1)$$

$$r = \frac{1}{wL_c + c_c} - 1 \qquad (2)$$

or 2 equations & 3 unknowns (p_s, r, w).

Note that we may have

$$r = \frac{p_s}{wL_s + c_s} - 1 \quad \text{which gives}$$

the illusion that p_s ~~can~~ (or silk sector) can determine r. Not so. So long as corn sector profit rate is as in (2), a _short-run_ change in p_s will change the ~~short-run silk~~ _short-run silk_ sector profit rate until capacity adjusts causing a return to the original r.

rests entirely on the variability of p_s in equation (1.2). With the movement of capital, the supply of corn decreases and the supply of silk increases. The increased abundance of silk relative to corn has the effect of lowering the corn-price of silk. This in turn would entail a reduction in the silk rate of profits which would continue until a uniform rate had been re-established throughout the economy (provided, of course, that no further disturbances occurred in the meantime). Since this rate is determined by the technical conditions in corn production, for a given wage rate the 'natural price' of silk follows from equation (1.2). This can be seen more directly by rearranging (1.2) and replacing r_s with r:

$$p_s = (1 + r)(wL_s + c_s). \tag{1.3}$$

Equation (1.3) says that the natural corn-price of silk is composed of the corn inputs plus profits on those inputs at the natural rate, r. It should be clear that the process by which the natural price is attained is the same process by which sector rates of profits are equalised. They are two sides of the same coin. The price of silk which corresponds to a particular short-period rate of profits in silk is known as the short-period or *market* price.

In the case just discussed supply changes respond to differences in short-period profits rates in such a way as to erode those differences. The differences themselves were the result of a permanent change in technical conditions of production. But a similar process would ensue in response to an enduring change in demand. Suppose, for example, that demand shifts away from corn in favour of silk. The result would be an increase in the market price of silk and an increase in the silk rate of profits. But so long as this demand shift were thought to be enduring this higher rate of profits could not be sustained. Capitalists would direct their investments away from corn production and towards silk production and supplies would change in such a way that market price would be restored to the natural level p_s. The *natural* price does not, therefore, respond to changes in supply and demand. It depends solely on the technical conditions of production and the distribution of income.

In extending the model by one sector we added one more equation, (1.2) or (1.3), whose sole function is to determine the corn-price of silk. The additional equation does not contribute in any way to the derivation of the w–r relation which is given entirely by equation (1.1). Figure 1.1, therefore, applies not only to the corn economy but also to the two-sector economy. Each point on the w–r relation corresponds to a different value for p_s, but since the effect of an increase in r is offset by a decrease in w there is no *a priori* way of telling which way p_s will vary. It depends entirely on the conditions of production of both silk and corn. Since p_s varies with distribution it is determined only when the system is closed from outside. But whereas solving p_s depends on solving distribution, the converse is not true: the problem of distribution is settled prior to (and is a prerequisite for) the determination of p_s.

This characteristic of the model is the result of an assumption to which we should now draw explicit attention, namely that silk is a 'luxury' good. That is to say, it is used neither as a means of production nor as an essential part of the wage (whose payment is fixed in corn). If silk were part of the means of production of corn then it would no longer be true that inputs and outputs of corn were the same commodity and the rate of profits could not be determined prior to p_s. The same, if only a little less obviously, is true if silk formed part of the wage payment: wL could no longer refer simply to a quantity of corn. Dropping the luxury assumption would mean that r and p_s would have to be determined simultaneously. We would no longer be able to talk about distribution without worrying about prices.

Now that we have introduced a second commodity the extension to an economy with many luxuries is straightforward. For each commodity we simply add equations of the type (1.3), each one allowing the determination of the natural price of that commodity in terms of corn. The relative price of two such commodities is determined directly from their corn prices. Thus the price of silk in terms of brandy is p_s/p_b. (The price of corn in terms of brandy is l/p_b).

4 Competition and natural values

It is important to emphasise that throughout this book we shall be concerned with the natural values of prices, the wage rate and the rate of profits. As should already be clear these are values which need not actually prevail – indeed, may never prevail – but to which there is a constant tendency. Adam Smith described them as 'centres of gravity'.[10] The concentration on natural values is a consequence of the nature of theoretical abstraction. For natural values are those which are believed to be the outcome of the major, persistent forces acting on distribution and prices. This does not deny the existence of minor, transitory forces which cause deviations from or fluctuations about the natural levels, but these deviations are taken to be of a secondary order of importance and to contain the mechanism of their own undoing. This abstraction is not as restrictive as might at first appear. To quote Garegnani (1976, p.28):

> The persistent, or non-temporary nature of the causes of long-period values, which was [thus] stressed by both Ricardo and Marshall, explains why the relevance of these values was not thought to be confined to the analysis of economies which are stationary or in steady growth. That persistence was thought to ensure that changes in the causes, if continuous, would be sufficiently slow as not to

endanger the gravitation towards the (slowly moving) long-period values. That same persistence would ensure that, should the changes be rapid, they would be once-for-all changes, and that, after a period of transition, gravitation to the new long-period values would again assert itself.

If natural values are regarded as 'centres of gravity' then it is important to be able to identify the gravitational force which generates a continuous tendency towards the centres. The force, we have seen, is that of competition. If a commodity's market price deviates from its natural price so also does its short-period rate of profits deviate from the natural rate. A positive deviation which is thought to be the result of an enduring change will induce capitalists from outside the industry to direct their capital into it; a negative deviation will encourage or force capitalists out. In this way, relative supplies of commodities are changed and market prices returned to their natural levels.

It is in this context that we should understand the concept of competition in classical theory. Competition implies only that the 'barriers to entry' of new capital into industries are sufficiently weak not to prevent the equilibrating tendencies. Of course, particular organisational structures may tend to promote or discourage entry barriers. But nothing we have said so far rules out the compatibility of competition with small numbers of firms in particular industries. Indeed, it may even be that oligopolistic structures are highly competitive in the classical sense. At any rate we should be clear that classical competitive firms are not necessarily the atomistic price takers of modern neoclassical theory.

5 Summary

A significant social division exists in capitalist countries between workers, who obtain their incomes mainly from their own labour, and capitalists, whose principal source of income comes from the ownership and employment of capital and land. A simple model was developed to explain the relationship between class incomes. In an economy which produces and uses only one commodity (corn) the rate of profits depends on the level of the wage (as a quantity of corn) and the technical conditions of production. For a given technique an increase in the wage implies a decrease in the rate of profits. The same $w-r$ relation also holds in a many-commodity economy, provided that only the corn process has the property that its inputs and outputs consist of the same commodity. The prices of the other commodities (in terms of corn) depend on the $w-r$ combination and their own conditions of production. The system is fully determined only when one of the distributive variables is given from outside. Here and throughout the book, the analysis is concerned with the long-period or natural values of the rate of profits, wages and prices, appropriate to the prevailing set of technical conditions. As a result of competition, short-period or market values of these variables gravitate continuously towards the natural values.

FURTHER READING

On the nature of class in modern capitalist countries see Miliband (1969) who also presents a critique of the 'pluralist' view that class is unimportant.

Though this chapter is not intended as a survey of early economic thought on value and distribution it does touch on some issues of current debate among historians. An insight into the development of Sraffa's own ideas can be gained from the editor's Introduction to the ten volumes of *The Works and Correspondence of David Ricardo*. The 'corn-ratio' interpretation of Ricardo's *Essay* is found in Vol. I (Sraffa and Dobb 1951, pp. xxx–xxxii). A critique of this interpretation is given in Hollander (1973) and a defence by Eatwell (1975*a*) and Garegnani (1982). Hollander's wider views on Ricardo, placing him within the neoclassical (more specifically, within the 'general equilibrium') tradition, are presented in Hollander (1979), and critically reviewed by O'Brien (1981) and Milgate (1982). For analyses of Ricardo's contribution to the theories of value and distribution more in keeping with Sraffa's, see Dobb (1973) and Napoleoni (1975). Pasinetti (1959) is an extremely useful and rigorous reconstruction of the Ricardian system, in the Sraffian tradition. A more abbreviated version is given in Pasinetti (1977).

Malthus' views on rent were expounded in a pamphlet published in 1815, entitled *Inquiry into the Nature and Progress of Rent*. They are also explained in chapter 3 of his *Principles of Political Economy* of 1820. (See Sraffa and Dobb (1951), Vol. II, which contains Ricardo's 'Notes on Malthus'.) The theory of population is explained in *An Essay on the Principle of Population* of 1798 (Malthus, 1970). Ricardo's views on wage determination are found in chapter V of his *Principles* (Sraffa and Dobb, 1951, Vol. I).

The distinction between market and natural values originated with Adam Smith's *The Wealth of Nations* of 1776 (Smith 1961), and was taken on board by Ricardo (see chapter IV of the *Principles*). Garegnani (1976) uses it to develop a methodological critique of the concept of equilibrium in neo-classical theories of value and distribution.

The term 'barriers to entry' is due to Bain (1956). The relationship between entry barriers and the classical conception of competition was, however, suggested by Sylos-Labini (1962). See also Roncaglia (1978), pp. 22–3. The connection between classical competition and natural values is discussed by Eatwell (1982). In a review of Eatwell, Vaggi (1982) suggests that natural values involve too restrictive an abstraction from reality.

2

The labour theory of value

1 The pure labour theory

The attractiveness of the corn-ratio theory was that it made possible the derivation of the w–r relation without entering into the problem of valuing commodities in terms of one another; that is, of determining relative prices. Considerations of value which did arise came after the problem of distribution had been settled. This theory is subject to the obvious criticism that we would be unlikely to find in reality a process whose entire inputs consisted of exactly the same commodity as its output. Whether or not the corn-ratio theory can be regarded as a valid interpretation of the *Essay*, Ricardo was attacked by Malthus on precisely these grounds.[1] In writing his *Principles*, Ricardo was thus aware of the need to generalise his theory of profits, but to do so required a different approach to the determination of prices. This approach consisted of a development of Adam Smith's labour theory of value.

Smith had supposed the labour theory of value to be relevant only to 'that early and rude state of society' (Smith 1961, p. 53) in which individuals laboured for their own subsistence. The absence of capitalists and hence the absence of capital as an advance implies the non-existence of profits in such a society. In these circumstances, Smith argued, the rate at which commodities would exchange for one another would be in proportion to the total amount of labour used up in procuring them; that is, to the quantities of labour 'embodied' in them. If p_i is the price of commodity i in terms of some arbitrary unit of account, and l_i the amount of homogeneous labour embodied in one unit of i, then the labour theory of value asserts that

$$p_i/p_j = l_i/l_j.$$

It is, of course, possible for temporary fluctuations of these exchange values, or relative prices, to occur in the short period due to changes in scarcity and demand, but the price ratios would always tend to equality with the 'labour values'. If, on the contrary, $p_i/p_j < l_i/l_j$ then, for the same amount of effort, a larger quantity of commodities could be obtained through exchange by expending the effort in producing commodity j rather than commodity i.

This would induce individuals to transfer from activity i to activity j, so altering relative supplies until the price ratio had returned to equality with the labour ratio.

But what happens when we leave this primitive subsistence economy and enter a capitalist one which, of its nature, implies a positive rate of profits? To keep things simple, consider a capitalist agricultural economy in which the production of a number of different crops takes place on an annual basis. As in the corn economy capital is advanced to the worker at the beginning of the year in the form of wage commodities. Unlike the corn economy, however, it is assumed that the seed needed for planting is sufficiently small that it can be neglected. All commodities are thus produced by homogeneous labour unaccompanied by any direct means of production. Naturally, farmers would continue in production only so long as their capital produced a quantity of output whose exchange value (command over other commodities) was greater than that of the capital itself. In other words they would produce only so long as their profits were positive. Moreover, competition between capitalists would ensure that there was just enough capital in each activity to allow a uniform rate of profits.

The determination of prices for this economy can be expressed in terms of the equation system formulated by V. K. Dmitriev (1974). Suppose there are k commodities. For the time being also suppose that the wage is given and paid as a basket containing each one of the commodities in the quantities $m_1, m_2, \ldots, m_k$. Now let us choose commodity 1 (call it corn) as the unit of account or standard of value. Then the wage, although not consisting solely of corn, can be expressed *in terms of corn*, as follows:

$$w = m_1 + p_2 m_2 + p_3 m_3 + \ldots + p_k m_k \tag{2.1}$$

where the relative price p_i $(i = 2, \ldots, k)$ converts a quantity of commodity i into its corn 'equivalent-in-exchange'. Since the wage is advanced and earns each farmer profit at the general rate r, the price equations for the k commodities may be written as follows:

$$1 = w l_1 (1 + r)$$
$$p_2 = w l_2 (1 + r)$$
$$\vdots \qquad \vdots$$
$$p_k = w l_k (1 + r). \tag{2.2}$$

Because the m_i are physically specified quantities, (2.1) and (2.2) provide $k + 1$ equations to determine $k - 1$ relative prices (all in terms of corn), w

and r.[2] The immediate conclusion that we can draw from equations (2.2) is that relative prices still maintain equality with the ratios of labours embodied:

$$p_i/p_j = wl_i(1+r)/wl_j(1+r) = l_i/l_j \quad (i,j = 1,\ldots,k)$$

The labour theory of value is therefore valid not only for a subsistence economy but also for this simple capitalist agricultural economy.

2 Income distribution and the pure labour theory

We are free to define units of quantity as we like. Let us then define a unit of corn as that amount embodying a unit of labour. It follows that the price of a unit of commodity i, p_i, is equal to the amount of labour embodied in that unit. If that is so, equation (2.1) tells us the total amount of labour embodied in the wage basket. In a similar fashion we can look at any other aggregate product, such as gross output, and calculate the labour embodied in that. Profits are equal to gross output minus wages and can also be measured in terms of labour embodied. Finally, since the rate of profits is the ratio of profits to capital (= wages), it too is a ratio of labour quantities.

Now, if the technical methods of production are fixed, the magnitudes $l_1, \ldots, l_k$ are specified prior to the determination of prices and the rate of profits and, indeed, can be used to determine them, as we have done above. But what is important to realise is that the rate of profits may be determined without any conscious consideration of prices simply by adding up the quantities of labour embodied in the gross product and in wages. Suppose that the total labour force employed during the year is L worker-hours. It follows, without need of knowing its composition, that the gross product embodies L worker-hours. If L' is the labour employed in making the commodities used to pay wages (that is, the labour embodied in the capital stock), then the rate of profits is given by

$$r = (L - L')/L' \tag{2.3}$$

which is the ratio of profits to capital. Given the technical conditions of production in the shape of the l_i, and given the form and quantity of the wage basket (the m_i), the rate of profits may thus be determined without any direct reference to prices. The solution of relative prices is purely incidental. Being, by assumption, homogeneous, labour has taken over the rôle played by corn in the corn-ratio theory.

From (2.1), the labour embodied in the unit wage basket (the annual payment to a unit of labour) is w. Thus the labour embodied in the economy's total wage bill is w multiplied by the total number of labour units employed,

L. Thus

$$L' = wL$$

Inserting this in (2.3) gives

$$r = (L - wL)/wL$$

or

$$r = (1 - w)/w. \qquad (2.4)$$

It follows that if r is to be positive we must have $w < 1$. This is a fairly obvious condition meaning that if a unit of labour is to be productive it must be paid a quantity of commodities which, themselves, require less than a unit of labour to produce.

Since we have assumed that the wage is given, (2.4) determines the rate of profits. If, however, the wage is allowed to vary (2.4) becomes an expression of the w–r relation for this economy. A variation in the wage may take the form of proportionate changes in each of the commodities entering the wage basket, but this is not necessary. An increase in w follows if the total labour embodied in the wage basket increases, irrespective of the commodity pro- portions. As w rises r becomes smaller, reaching zero when labour consumes all of its production. Conversely a fall in w leads to a proportionate increase in the share of profits while the rate of profits tends to infinity (profits becoming larger as capital gets smaller). This relation between w and r is shown in figure 2.1.

There is a further point worth noting. In section 1 we assumed that all k commodities enter the wage basket. This is because only those commodities which do enter are relevant to our problem. Consider another commodity, called n, which does not enter the wage; its price is given by

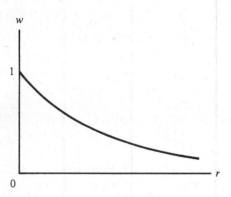

Figure 2.1

$$p_n = wl_n (1 + r).$$

This adds to system (2.2) one equation and one unknown, p_n. It does not affect in any way the existing equations which are already quite capable of solving for r. If we took this equation away we would not lose anything except the ability to determine p_n. If, on the other hand, we took away, say, the equation for k we would have a problem. Not only would we be unable to determine p_k itself, but we would also be unable to determine w (because p_k enters (2.1)) and, hence r and every other price. Only those commodities whose prices enter into equation (2.1) are relevant to the derivation of the w–r relation. This distinction between commodities like k and those like n corresponds to that between corn and silk in the last chapter. They are commodities which, respectively, do and do not enter the wage basket.

Of course, what has just been said of prices is true of the labour values l_k, l_n, etc. In defining the magnitudes L and L' it is only necessary to refer to the labour employed in the activities $1, \ldots, k$. The rates of profits in the other sectors will fall in line as a consequence of competition.

3 Different time structures of production

The conclusion that price ratios are equal to ratios of labours embodied is valid only on the assumption that all commodities take the same time to produce. This assumption ensures that prices are not affected by the rate of profits. In each activity wage-capital is advanced at the beginning of the year and, at the end of the year, the capital is returned with a profit in the proportion r. Since this proportion is the same for all commodities it affects all to the same degree. Relative prices are, therefore, independent of the existence or size of the rate of profits and are uniquely determined by the ratios of labours embodied.

Consider now a two-commodity economy in which the production processes require different times for their completion. As before, commodity 1 requires l_1 labour expended in one year. If it is taken as the standard of value its price equation is

$$1 = wl_1(1 + r). \tag{2.5}$$

Commodity 2, however, takes *two* years to produce and we shall suppose, for simplicity, that in each year of its production it requires the same amount of labour, l_2. In this activity one portion of the capital, an amount wl_2, is advanced two years before the completion of production. At the end of the first year the partly completed product will be work in progress of value wl_2 $(1 + r)$. This work in progress is still part of the producer's capital and at the beginning of the following year it is 're-advanced' along with that year's wages ($= wl_2$). (Thus in the second year, labourers work with the tools, and so on, produced in the previous year.) The total value of capital advanced in the second year then, is $wl_2 + wl_2 (1 + r)$, on which profit is earned at the rate r. So the price of commodity 2 is

$$p_2 = wl_2 (1 + r) + wl_2 (1 + r)^2. \tag{2.6}$$

The total quantity of labour used in producing a unit of 2 is, of course, $2l_2$. If the price is to remain equal to the ratio of labours embodied it should therefore be equal to $2l_2/l_1$, but it is clear that this cannot be so. Because profits are compounded over time different commodities are affected to different degrees depending, not only on the length of their production processes, but also on the time profiles of labour use. The simple 'law of labour value' requires modification whenever these 'time structures' of production differ between commodities.

In the case where all commodities were produced annually, capital could be directly identified with wage payments. The wage was all that was advanced and tied up in production over the year. In the present case, where production of some commodities may take more than a year, this identity breaks down. In the case of commodity 2, the value of the advance over the two years included an element for profits on the work of the first year, so that the total value of capital employed exceeded the value of the wage payments. It is therefore possible to draw a distinction in this case between the value of capital employed and the value of wages advanced. Since the latter always remains in proportion to the labour employed we may equally talk of differences in the proportions of capital : labour in the production of different commodities. Differences in time structures imply differences in capital : labour ratios.

4 The 'modified' law of value

With the appearance of different time structures of production price ratios are no longer equal to ratios of labours embodied. This is so as long as the rate of profits is positive. Any change in the time structures will change relative prices, even if the labours embodied are not affected. That is to say, a redistribution of labour over time will affect a commodity's price even if the total labour employed is unchanged. More important for our present purpose is to examine the relationship between distribution and prices with given differences in time structures.

The price equations of our previous example were

$$1 = wl_1 (1 + r) \tag{2.5}$$

$$p_2 = wl_2 [(1 + r) + (1 + r)^2]. \tag{2.6}$$

The relationship between r and w (expressed in terms of commodity 1) may be inferred directly from equation (2.5) and, defining $l_1 = 1$, has exactly the same appearance as in fig. 2.1. This is not, however, a relationship between r and the 'real' wage, as expressed in the purely physical sense of a commodity basket. Suppose, momentarily, that the real wage is given as a combination of the two commodities (m_1, m_2). The w–r relation inferred from (2.5) cannot tell us what the corresponding rate of profits will be because the connection between w and (m_1, m_2) cannot be known until prices are known. For that we also need the equation

$$w = m_1 + p_2 m_2.$$

The three equations can then be solved simultaneously to give r and p_2. (If we change the standard of value (putting $p_2 = 1$, instead) a w–r relation can also be inferred from equation (2.6). Although it will be downward sloping it will have a different appearance from the first relation, simply because wages are expressed in terms of a different unit of account.) Thus to know the rate of profits corresponding to any real wage the system of price equations must be solved simultaneously.

Consider now the consequences of a decline in r or, what comes to the same thing, an increase in w (expressed in terms of commodity 1). Commodity 1, being the standard of value, cannot by definition change in price. The increase in wage payments is exactly offset by the decrease in profits payments in this industry. The consequence for p_2 is less clear-cut. Although the wage rate is the same as in activity 1, the profits earned on the advances are greater, since the additional time needed for production involves compounding the rate. This means that the fall in r has a greater weight than the increase in w (compared to activity 1) and so p_2 must fall.[3] Thus each point on the w–r relation corresponds to a different price ratio. (It would appear from this example that, in relation to one another, commodities using less capital and more labour rise in price with a rise in wages; those using more capital and less labour fall in price. Any temptation to conclude that what is true in simple cases must always be true should, however, be resisted.)

We have now identified three causes of variation of relative prices. These are: (*i*) variations in the quantities of labours embodied; (*ii*) changes in the relative proportions of capital to labour, at a given wage; and (*iii*) changes in the wage with given capital : labour ratios. The first of these, on its own, conforms to the law of labour value. The other two involve modifications to this law. Although these modifications were set out clearly in the chapter 'On Value' in the *Principles*, Ricardo was of the belief that they were of a relatively small order of magnitude. If that were so – if the law of value could be regarded as very nearly correct – then the conclusion of our section

2 could be taken as a sufficiently close approximation to the truth. The question of distribution could be regarded as being settled prior to and independently of the determination of relative prices. Unfortunately, Ricardo's belief in the insignificance of the modifications stemmed from an undue reliance on numerical examples (see *Principles* pp. 35–6). In these examples the commodities compared are produced in one and two years, respectively. But the effect of a change in the rate of profits is compounded rapidly as the difference in the production periods increases. More general examples would tend to show considerable variations in relative prices even with quite modest variations in the rate of profits.

5 Summary

The labour theory of value retains the principle of homogeneity of inputs and outputs by measuring both in terms of labour embodied. Provided the theory holds, it is possible, as in the corn-ratio theory, to talk about distribution independently of prices. It holds, however, only on the restrictive assumption that all production processes are completed in one period. When time structures of production differ, relative prices are no longer the same as relative labours embodied and distribution cannot be determined independently of prices.

In the following chapter we shall investigate the relationship between distribution and prices in more sophisticated production models.

FURTHER READING

The starting point for this chapter is chapter 1 of Ricardo's *Principles* (Sraffa and Dobb, 1951, Vol. I). The editors' introduction to this volume provides invaluable background to Ricardo's approach and particularly to the transition from the *Essay*. For Adam Smith's use of the labour theory of value, see Smith (1961) chapter VI. For an excellent historical account of the development of the theory, see Meek (1973). The algebraic formulation of the labour theory of value in section 2 is due to Dmitriev in a paper first published in 1898. He and L. von Bortkiewicz (1952; first published in 1906) were responsible for the development of classical value theory along directions which closely parallel Sraffa's. See D. M. Nuti's introduction to Dmitriev (1974).

Readings listed in chapter 1 are also relevant to this chapter.

PART II

Single-product Sraffa–Leontief systems

3

A subsistence economy

1 Production by means of commodities

In the production schemes considered in chapter 2, each process could be considered as a one-way flow from labour to final commodity. This however would be an oversimplified view since it overlooks the fact that labour is itself a 'produced' input. Since particular commodities are required for the maintenance of labour, a part of the final output returns to production as inputs, *via* labour. Considered in this light, the production process is not a 'one-way' but a 'circular' flow: outputs returning to production as inputs. This is, perhaps, clearer in the corn-ratio theory where, in the corn sector, a part of the output is required in the following period as seed and means of subsistence. The simplicity of the corn-ratio theory arises from the fact that corn is the only commodity for which this circularity operates. For while corn is allowed to enter the production of other commodities, *via* the wage, the reverse is not true. These other commodities (such as silk) are pure luxury goods. It is true that in chapter 2 the wage consisted of many commodities but the characterisation of the production system as one in which commodities are produced by means of commodities was not well developed.

In the rest of this book we consider production systems in which any number of commodities may be used as means of production. Commodities may enter production *via* the wage basket, in which case we shall refer to them as 'means of subsistence', or they may enter directly as raw materials, tools and machinery. All production processes take place in the same uniform time period (say a year). This is not as restrictive as it may at first appear since an industry employing durable or *fixed* capital, such as a machine, can be considered as consisting of a number of annual processes, each using machinery of different ages. Since these annual processes produce not only finished commodities but also partly-used machines they are properly regarded as *joint-production* processes; that is, processes which produce more than one commodity. In Part II we consider the relatively simple case of production with single-products processes only. These, by implication, employ only *circulating capital* – capital which is fully used up in one period. Analysis of joint-production systems is left until Part III. Apart from fixed capital, these systems may include processes of the familiar mutton/lamb type, which we call 'pure' joint production, and, less obviously, processes employing land and natural resources.

Although we are already familiar with economies which produce a positive net product, we start Part II with a discussion of a subsistence economy. Since we are now investigating a new production scheme it seems advisable to start with the simplest case. In this chapter we shall formulate an explicit 'circular' production system which is a simple two-commodity generalisation of the production scheme involved in the corn-ratio theory. This is done by allowing the output of the second sector to enter the means of subsistence though, to begin with, neither commodity enters the means of production independently of its rôle as a subsistence commodity (a complication which is postponed until section 6). The model developed in this chapter is the basis of all subsequent analysis and so we shall investigate its properties in some depth and from a number of perspectives.

2 A simple production scheme

To dispel the image of the second commodity as a luxury good we now refer to the output of sector two as 'cloth'. Both corn and cloth are necessary components of the wage and since labour is necessary to produce both commodities, they enter (*via* labour) their own production and each other's. Representing corn and cloth by the subscripts 1 and 2 respectively, the wage is taken as a basket of fixed quantities, m_1 and m_2, of the two commodities. A unit of labour is defined as equal to the occupied workforce and this is distributed between the two processes in the proportions L_1 and L_2; thus

$$L_1 + L_2 = 1.$$

Since we are neglecting the seed-corn needed in the agricultural sector the amount of corn required as means of production in agriculture, denoted by c_{11}, is simply the corn component of the wage times the amount of labour employed in this sector:

$$c_{11} = m_1 L_1.$$

Likewise cloth is not used as a direct means of production, so we may write, in general

$$c_{ij} = m_i L_j \tag{3.1}$$

where c_{ij} is the amount of commodity i required by process j.

The production process may be represented in two ways. First, consider the following scheme:

	Inputs				Gross outputs
	Corn (1)	Cloth (2)	Labour		
Process 1	0	+ 0	+ L_1	$\longrightarrow$	C_1
Process 2	0	+ 0	+ L_2	$\longrightarrow$	C_2
L	m_1	+ m_2	+ 0	$\longrightarrow$	1(L)

The first row indicates that L_1 labour hours are required, each year, to produce a gross output C_1 of corn; similarly, in the second row L_2 labour results in C_2 cloth. The third row tells us that to sustain the total labour over the year requires 'inputs' m_1 and m_2. But this third, labour-sustaining, 'process' is only an intermediate stage between commodity inputs and commodity outputs. By using the c_{ij} coefficients defined in equation (3.1) this process can be incorporated into the other two. The resulting production scheme is as follows:

	Inputs			Gross	Net
	Corn (1)	Cloth (2)		outputs	outputs
Process 1	c_{11}	+ c_{21}	$\longrightarrow$	C_1	$C_1 - \Sigma c_{1j}$
Process 2	c_{12}	+ c_{22}	$\longrightarrow$	C_2	$C_2 - \Sigma c_{2j}$
	Σc_{1j}	Σc_{2j}			

Again, each row represents a production process. Row 1, for example, reads as follows: c_{11} units of corn plus c_{21} units of cloth are together necessary (through the sustenance of labour) to produce, each year, C_1 units of corn. The merit of this presentation is that it gives a much clearer picture of the circularity of production. The consequence of circularity is that, in general, each industry or process is dependent on the other process. Thus it is not possible, in general, for a closed economy to operate, say, process 1 in isolation, since this process requires supporting inputs of commodity 2.

This model is a straightforward generalisation of the production framework of the corn-ratio theory and it is the starting point of PC. Chapters I and II of Sraffa's book distinguish between 'Production for Subsistence' and 'Production with a Surplus' and we must now consider the meaning of these terms. In the production scheme above, the column sum Σc_{ij} tells us the amount of commodity i used up by both processes. If the economy is to continue, year after year, without running down, it is necessary that this sum should not exceed the gross output C_i. In other words, the net output of each commodity must be non-negative. It may be that the net output of one or both commodities is positive, so that production creates a physical surplus: commodities are produced in excess of the subsistence requirements of the workers. If this is so the surplus will have to be disposed of in some fashion. The analysis of a surplus economy will occupy us in the remaining chapters. To avoid introducing too many complexities at once we shall be concerned in this chapter entirely with a subsistence economy, reminiscent of Adam Smith's 'early and rude state of society'. Since nothing is produced over and above the provisions of the labourer (who works only for himself), net output is zero in each process:

$$C_i - \Sigma c_{ij} = 0. \tag{3.2}$$

For this economy, then, since all output is consumed as wages by the one unit of labour, $C_i = m_i$.

3 The determination of relative prices

In this subsistence economy we shall suppose that the division of labour has proceeded sufficiently to encourage a degree of specialisation in production: a part of the workforce concentrates on growing corn, another in making cloth. Since labourers will wish to make up the required proportions of their means of subsistence, there will be established an exchange ratio between corn and cloth. Our immediate concern is to determine what this ratio will be.

Given that the economy has one unit of labour the necessary output of corn is m_1 (the corn component of one labourer's wage), of which $m_1 L_1$ is used to feed labour producing corn. Consequently, $m_1(1 - L_1)$ or $m_1 L_2$ remains to exchange with cloth producers. Similarly, the amount of cloth available for corn growers is $m_2 L_1$. Thus the exchange ratio between corn and cloth is

$$m_2 L_1 / m_1 L_2 \ (= c_{21}/c_{12}) \ = \ (L_1/m_1)/(L_2/m_2).$$

Now, L_i/m_i (or, equivalently, L_i/C_i) is the amount of labour required to produce a unit of commodity i, denoted by l_i, so that, for this subsistence economy, commodities exchange in proportion to the quantities of labour embodied in them:

$$p_1/p_2 \ = \ l_1/l_2. \tag{3.3}$$

This may have been expected from our considerations in the previous chapters.

The rôle of prices in this economy is to allow labour of a given duration to obtain for the labourer the same wage basket, even though that labour may be highly specialised. Particular commodity surpluses are exchanged for particular commodity shortages in just that ratio which enables the same overall wage basket to be received for one hour's labour, irrespective of its occupation. If that were not so, labourers would move to those occupations in which least effort was required to obtain the wage basket, say from corn to cloth. The result would be a scarcity of corn and an excess of cloth. Relative prices would change so as to make cloth production less favourable and restore the balance between the two occupations.

4 Prices and quantities: an alternative presentation

The relations between inputs, outputs and prices for our two commodity economy are analysed graphically in fig. 3.1. The horizontal axis measures quantities of corn (1), outputs being indicated by points to the right of the origin, inputs by points to the left. Similarly, the vertical axis shows cloth outputs (above 0) and inputs (below 0). By convention, inputs are represented by negative quantities.

Consider process 1: the output of this process is represented by the point,

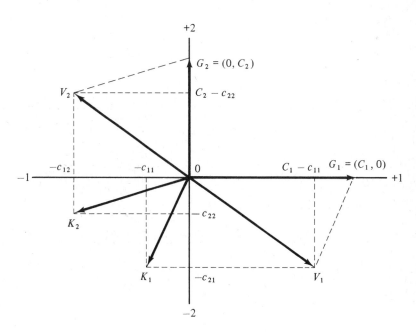

Figure 3.1

or *vector, G_1* on the horizontal axis. In an alternative notation the vector can be written in terms of its co-ordinates $(C_1, 0)$, the first element signifying that C_1 corn is produced, and the second that no cloth is produced. In order to produce this output corn inputs $-c_{11}$ and cloth inputs $-c_{21}$ are required and, together, these define the input vector $K_1 = (-c_{11}, -c_{21})$. The net outputs of process 1, on its own, are obtained by adding[1] the vectors G_1 and K_1 to give a new vector $V_1 = (C_1 - c_{11}, -c_{21})$. In a like manner we may define the corresponding vectors for process 2: G_2, K_2 and V_2. Now, this being a subsistence economy, the output of corn, say, is just sufficient to provide for the input requirements of corn of the two processes. Hence the net output of corn from process 1 $(C_1 - c_{11})$ should be of the same magnitude as the input of 1 into process 2 (c_{12}). Thus we could just as well write the co-ordinates of V_1 as $(c_{12}, -c_{21})$. Similarly the co-ordinates of V_2 may be written as $(-c_{12}, c_{21})$. It follows from this that V_1 and V_2 lie on the same straight line passing through the origin of slope $(-) c_{21}/c_{12}$. And this slope, which merely represents the rate at which each process's surpluses are exchanged, is the ratio of prices, p_1/p_2.[2]

5 A more general formulation

The analysis so far has been conducted in terms of an *actual* arrangement of inputs and outputs with the C_j and c_{ij} terms corresponding to particular amounts of commodities. This may help to give our hypothetical economy a more 'concrete' appearance, but we do not wish to be analytically confined to a given set of inputs and outputs. We could prefer to consider all sets of inputs and outputs which are technically feasible. This is most conveniently done by recasting the discussion in terms of the 'unit' input : output coefficients, u_{ij}, defined by

$$u_{ij} = c_{ij}/C_j,$$

that is, u_{ij} is the amount of commodity i required to produce *one unit* of commodity j. Corresponding to equation (3.1) we now have

$$u_{ij} = m_i l_j. \tag{3.1'}$$

We may also write unit price equations for each commodity:

$$p_1 = p_1 u_{11} + p_2 u_{21} \tag{3.4}$$

$$p_2 = p_1 u_{12} + p_2 u_{22}.$$

The first of these equations says that a unit of corn output must be of equivalent value (since there is no profit) to the combined value of the inputs into corn production. The second equation may be similarly interpreted.

Note, however, that the two equations are not independent of each other. Since there is only one unknown – the price ratio p_1/p_2 – one of these equations is sufficient to determine it. Solving each equation in turn gives

$$\frac{p_1}{p_2} = \frac{1-u_{11}}{u_{21}} = \frac{u_{12}}{1-u_{22}} = \frac{u_{21}}{1-u_{11}} = \frac{1-u_{22}}{u_{12}} \qquad (3.5)$$

again, a reflection of the fact that one process's surplus is the other process's inputs. Using (3.1′) the price equations can also be written

$$p_1 = (p_1 m_1 + p_2 m_2) l_1 = w l_1 \qquad (3.6)$$

$$p_2 = (p_1 m_1 + p_2 m_2) l_2 = w l_2$$

where w is the exchange value of the wage commodities. From (3.6) we can immediately confirm equation (3.3) which says that the price ratio is equal to the ratio of labours embodied.

The graphical analysis of fig. 3.1 can also be recast into 'unit' terms, as in fig. 3.2. The vector Q_1 shows the amount of 1 that could be produced if the entire labour force (one unit) were engaged in process 1. It is written $Q_1 = (1/l_1, 0)$ to signify that this output consists of an amount, $1/l_1$ of commodity 1, and nothing of commodity 2. In order to produce the quantity $1/l_1$ the necessary inputs are $-u_{11} \cdot (1/l_1)$ and $-u_{21} \cdot (1/l_1)$. These are

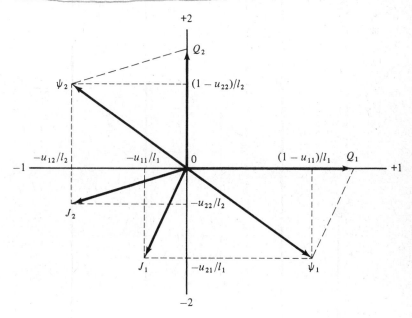

Figure 3.2

shown by the vector J_1. The corresponding net outputs of process 1 are indicated by the vector $\psi_1 = Q_1 + J_1$. The points Q_2, J_2 and ψ_2 can be described in a similar fashion. The slope of the line $\psi_1 \psi_2$ is described by either of the ratios on the right-hand side of equation (3.5) and, therefore, equals the price ratio.

Since we have assumed that the wage basket contains both commodities then, as we know, it is not actually possible to devote the entire labour force exclusively to one or other of the processes. A part of the workforce will have to be employed in making each commodity. The fixed requirements of production mean, however, that we do not have any freedom to choose the proportions of the outputs nor, therefore, the distribution of employment between the two processes (L_1 and L_2). In a subsistence economy net output is zero by definition: gross outputs must equal inputs. This is illustrated in fig. 3.3 as follows. With the fraction L_1 of the labour force devoted to producing commodity 1, the actual input vector for process 1 is $L_1 J_1$; similarly $L_2 J_2$ is the actual vector of inputs into process 2. The total input vector for the economy is $J = L_1 J_1 + L_2 J_2$. In the same manner we can write the actual gross output vector for the economy as the sum of the gross

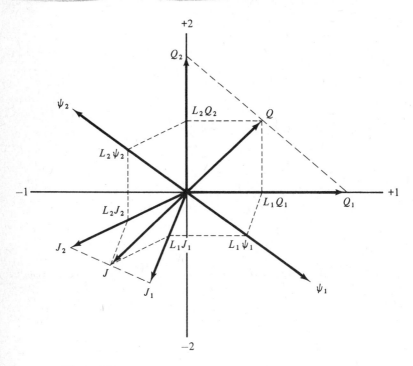

Figure 3.3

output vectors for the two processes: $Q = L_1 Q_1 + L_2 Q_2$. Zero net outputs means that J and Q sum to zero, which implies that they are of the same slope and magnitude, but of opposite sign. More directly we may write the net output vector as $\psi = L_1 \psi_1 + L_2 \psi_2 = 0$. There is one, and only one, set of labour allocations consistent with zero net output. If more labour were allocated to process 1 the Q vector would move clockwise, the J vector, anticlockwise. Their sum would be a point lying on the line $\psi_1 \psi_2$, south-east of the origin, implying a negative net output of commodity 2. Similarly, more labour allocated to process 2 would imply a negative net output of commodity 1.

Changing the nature of the analysis to 'unit' terms is merely a matter of convenience. It may be argued that in the subsistence economy there is little gain since, as it turns out, there is only one viable arrangement of inputs and outputs. This is so, but our discussions in this section will form a useful basis for the application of this approach in more complex cases where it will prove to be much more useful.

6 Means of production other than wage commodities

Up to now it has been supposed that commodities enter production only *via* the wage (seed-corn is negligible). What happens if corn and cloth enter production independently of the wage, as direct means of production? In that event the u_{ij} have to be modified to allow not only for commodities consumed by labour, the $m_i l_j$, but also the commodities *used* by labour. These are denoted by the coefficients a_{ij}, the amount of commodity i used as means of production in the unit of commodity j. While equations (3.4) are still valid once the u_{ij} are appropriately redefined, equations (3.6) are not: the value of the means of production must be accounted for in addition to the wage costs:

$$p_1 = (p_1 a_{11} + p_2 a_{21}) + w l_1 \qquad (3.7)$$

$$p_2 = (p_1 a_{12} + p_2 a_{22}) + w l_2.$$

Remembering that w can be expanded as in equations (3.6) we have, as before, two equations either one of which is sufficient to solve for the ratio of prices.

The conclusion that exchange values are proportional to quantities of labour embodied would, on the face of it, now require modification. Certainly, so long as the conclusion is that prices are proportional to 'direct' labours embodied (that is, the living labour employed during the year), this is so. But the means of production do, themselves, embody labour expended in previous years. Referring to such labour, already embodied, as 'indirect labour', we could ask whether prices are proportional to the sum of direct and indirect labour involved in production. Let the total amount of labour, direct and indirect, embodied in one unit of commodity j be λ_j. This is made up of the labour which is embodied directly, l_j, and that which is 'passed on' *via* the means of production. The amount of labour embodied in a unit of j *via* the input of commodity i is $\lambda_i a_{ij}$. So we may write

$$\lambda_1 = \lambda_1 a_{11} + \lambda_2 a_{21} + l_1 \tag{3.8}$$

$$\lambda_2 = \lambda_1 a_{12} + \lambda_2 a_{22} + l_2.$$

Now if we multiply both sides of equations (3.8) by w we obtain a pair of equations which is identical to those in (3.7) except that the p_i are replaced by $w\lambda_i$. This implies that prices are proportional to total labours embodied, the factor of proportionality being w. Alternatively the ratio of prices p_1/p_2 is equal to the ratio of labours embodied λ_1/λ_2.

7 More than two commodities

The simplicity of a two-commodity economy has allowed us to explore its properties quite thoroughly. In generalising the analysis to many commodities the geometry of figs. 3.1 and 3.2 is no longer adequate but the extension of the system of price equations is straightforward. If there are k commodities then, corresponding to (3.4), (3.7) and (3.8) we have

$$p_j = \Sigma_{i=1}^{k} p_i u_{ij} \tag{3.4'}$$

$$p_j = \Sigma_{i=1}^{k} p_i a_{ij} + w l_j \tag{3.7'}$$

and

$$\lambda_j = \Sigma_{i=1}^{k} \lambda_i a_{ij} + l_j. \tag{3.8'}$$

Each of these systems contains $k-1$ independent equations; (3.4') and (3.7') may be solved for $k-1$ relative prices, (3.8') for $k-1$ ratios of labours embodied. The price ratios are equal to these labour ratios.

These solution prices are the natural prices appropriate to a subsistence economy. No doubt period to period fluctuations in supply and demand due to unforeseen circumstances might make actual prices diverge from their natural levels. In this particular economy the competitive pressure takes the form of each labourer entering those production processes that minimise the amount of effort required to obtain the means of subsistence.

8 Summary

We started by analysing a system in which the only means of production are also means of subsistence. For such an economy the labour theory of value holds. It also holds when the means of production include raw materials, etc., so long as 'labour embodied' is understood to include the labour which is 'passed on' *via* the materials. With subsistence requirements fixed, there is only one viable pattern of inputs and outputs and, therefore, only one viable distribution of the labour force.

FURTHER READING

Begin with *PC*, chapter 1. Sraffa notes in the Preface to *PC* that 'others have from time to time independently taken up points of view which are similar to one or other of those adopted in this paper and have developed them further or in different directions from those pursued here'. This is possibly a reference to the works of J. von Neumann (1945), to be discussed in chapter 10, and W. Leontief (1951). The production structure of Leontief's 'input–output' model is essentially the same as that of Sraffa's single-products system. Leontief's model was intended primarily for empirical work, though its theoretical properties have since been thoroughly explored. The present chapter can be regarded as an account of some aspects of the 'static' Leontief model. See, for example, Dorfman *et al.*, (1958) and, for a more up-to-date account, Pasinetti (1977), chapters 2–4. A simple introduction to the Leontief model is given by Wolfson (1978).

The 'vector diagrams' introduced in this chapter and used throughout the rest of this book, also come from Dorfman *et al.* They were used to good effect by Hahn and Matthews (1964) Part III, and extensively developed by Goodwin (1970). These last two references are well worth consulting.

4

Production with a surplus

1 Introduction

Our analysis of the subsistence economy was really intended to lay the groundwork for the more interesting case in which production creates a physical surplus. In terms of the physical arrangements of inputs and outputs, the production schemes drawn up in section 2 of the previous chapter also apply to a surplus economy, but equation (3.2) must now be replaced by the inequality

$$C_i - \Sigma_{i=1}^{k} c_{ij} \geqslant 0$$

or, in unit terms,

$$1 - \Sigma_{i=1}^{k} u_{ij} \geqslant 0 \tag{4.1}$$

with $>$ holding for at least one i. At least one commodity is produced in excess of current input requirements or, alternatively, at least one commodity has a positive net output. (Of course, it is still essential to rule out negative net outputs if the economy is to be viable.)

Under capitalism, this physical surplus has a value counterpart, 'profits'.[1] Although economies other than capitalist ones may be capable of producing a surplus we are specifically interested in the capitalist mode of production and, therefore, in the formation and distribution of profits. On classical assumptions, the capitalist advances his capital, in the form of wage commodities and other means of production, to labour at the beginning of each year. The exchange value of a unit of output of industry j is p_j and the exchange value of the capital required to produce that output is $\Sigma_i p_i u_{ij}$. The difference between these two magnitudes represents profits received by capitalists in this industry. If the economy is competitive then the free movement of capital between industries ensures that industry rates of profits tend to equality with one another while simultaneously drawing prices to their natural levels. Thus the ratio of the value of profits to the value of capital tends to be the same in each industry, equal to the general rate of profits, r:

$$p_j = (1+r)\, \Sigma_i p_i u_{ij} \quad (i,j = 1, \ldots, k). \tag{4.2}$$

Because equation (3.2) has been replaced by inequality (4.1) it is no longer true that the net output of *i* from process *i* must exactly match the input requirement of *i* in all other processes. As a result the independence of the price equations is lost: the *k* equations (4.2) are just sufficient to determine $k - 1$ prices and the general rate of profits, r.[2]

2 Post-factum wages

Up to now we have retained the essentially classical assumption that the wage is advanced to the worker in the proportions necessary for subsistence, 'thus entering the system on the same footing as the fuel for the engines or the feed for the cattle' (*PC* p. 9). The assumption that the wage is advanced is rejected by Sraffa who wishes to include, in addition to the elements of subsistence, the possibility of workers sharing the net product or surplus of the system. This is most conveniently done if, instead, it is assumed that wages are paid at the *end* of the year, although this, in effect, means that the *entire* wage is variable. This procedure does raise some rather theoretical questions which are discussed in chapter 6. For the moment we may note that the notion of a subsistence minimum can be maintained 'by setting a limit below which the wage cannot fall' (*PC* p. 10).

Since the wage is no longer advanced the commodities consumed by workers cannot now be considered as capital. The u_{ij} coefficients no longer include the $m_i l_j$ elements, only the a_{ij}: capital now consists only of the direct means of production. Nevertheless, profits per unit of output in industry *j* are what remains after deducting from the price p_j the value of the means of production $\Sigma_i p_i a_{ij}$ *and* the wage costs, but the *rate* of profits is reckoned as the proportion of profits to means of production only. Wage costs may be written as $w l_j$ where w refers to the value (in terms of some standard) of the annual wage payment. It would still be correct to write

$$w = \Sigma_i p_i m_i$$

but the m_i are no longer fixed quantities but are free to vary provided that their combined value is equal to the wage.

The price of a commodity is thus made up of the price of its means of production plus a 'value added' or surplus. This surplus is somehow divided between wages and the profit of the producer, the latter being some proportion, r, of the price of the means of production. The price equations may therefore be written:

$$p_j = (1 + r) \Sigma_i p_i a_{ij} + w l_j \quad (i, j = 1, \dots, k). \tag{4.3}$$

The difference between this and equation (4.2) is that we have separated out the $w l_j$ term and, because of our assumption that wages are paid at the end of the period, changed its nature from 'capital' to 'surplus'. (Equation (4.3) may also be compared with the corresponding equation for the subsistence economy (3.7').)

The separation of the wage introduces a further problem which has both an economic and an algebraic manifestation. Because there are now two items of surplus, the k equations in (4.3) are no longer sufficient to determine all the unknowns (the $k-1$ relative prices, r and w). The implications of this 'degree of freedom' are considered in section 6.

3 Inputs and outputs: the two-commodity case

In this and the next two sections we develop the geometry of the two-commodity case. To be clear about the nature of the production process we begin by writing out the production scheme:

| | Inputs | | | Gross outputs | |
	Labour	1	2	1	2
Process 1	l_1 +	a_{11} +	a_{21} ⟶	1	0
Process 2	l_2 +	a_{12} +	a_{22} ⟶	0	1

Now since labour is paid out of the product at the *end* of the production period, wage commodities do not figure as part of the inputs. To emphasise this, in fig. 4.1 the input vectors corresponding to one unit of labour have been relabelled I_1 and I_2. The co-ordinates of I_1, for example, are $-a_{11}/l_1$ and $-a_{21}/l_1$. The associated gross output vectors are Q_i and the net output vectors are $\alpha_i = Q_i + I_i$. As before, these vectors are purely notional since labour has to be allocated to both processes, but, as compared to a subsistence economy, we now have rather more flexibility. Figure 4.2 shows a situation in which 2/3 of the unit labour force is allocated to process 1 and 1/3 to process 2. The net output vector α for this allocation is the sum of $2/3\alpha_1$ and $1/3\alpha_2$ and lies on the straight line joining α_1 and α_2. In fact, the line $\alpha_1\alpha_2$ shows all algebraically possible combinations of net outputs that can be obtained by varying the proportions of labour used in the two processes. (A reallocation of labour from 1 to 2 would move α in the direction of α_2.) It is known as the *net output frontier*. Some of these algebraic possibilities do, however, have to be ruled out since negative outputs are not possible. Thus only that segment of the frontier which lies in the non-negative quadrant is economically relevant.

Returning now to fig. 4.1 we can see that the line joining Q_1 and Q_2 shows all algebraically possible combinations of gross outputs. Q_1Q_2 is,

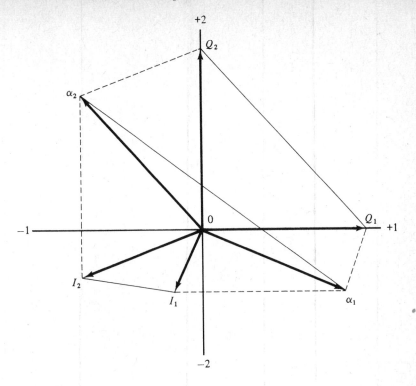

Figure 4.1.

accordingly, known as the *gross output frontier*. Similarly, the line I_1I_2 showing all possible combinations of inputs is known as the *input frontier*. In each case, of course, the economically relevant ranges are much narrower than the algebraic ranges.

4 The price vector

We are already familiar with the idea of representing the price ratio by the slope of a straight line, such as the line *KOM* in fig. 4.3. Here $p_1/p_2 = \tan\theta = KL/OL$; in other words *KL* of commodity 2 exchanges for *OL* of commodity 1. The line *K'M'* gives the same information since it is the slope, not the position, of the line that is relevant. An alternative (and often more convenient) way of representing prices is as the angle between the axis and a line *OP* drawn normal to *KM*. The choice of which axis depends on whether we wish to express that ratio as p_2/p_1 or, as in this case, p_1/p_2. Indeed, the vector $P = (p_1, 1)$ may be regarded as a vector of prices when commodity 2

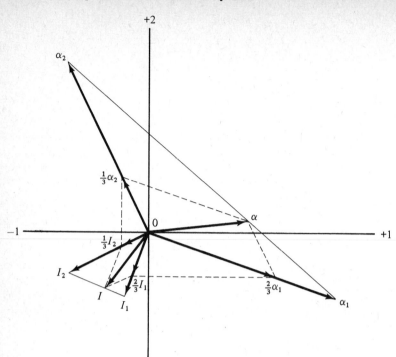

Figure 4.2

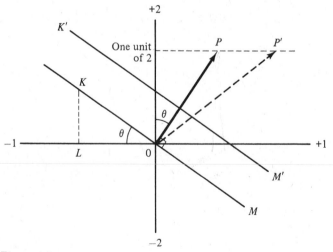

Figure 4.3

is used as a standard of value. Thus a rightward movement of the price
vector to P' would indicate an increase in the relative price of commodity 1.

The next task is to explain the operation of vector multiplication. Multiplication of two vectors, say a vector of prices $P = (p_1, p_2)$ and a vector of
quantities $X = (x_1, x_2)$ yields the sum $p_1 x_1 + p_2 x_2$, which is a scalar ($P \cdot X$ is
referred to as the *scalar product* of the vectors.) Geometrically, the scalar
product is obtained as follows (fig. 4.4). Along the vector OP mark off the
point N, such that XN is normal to OP. (ON is the 'vertical projection' of
X on P.) Then $P \cdot X = ON \cdot OP$. Since our main concern with vector multiplication is to value quantities, that is find products such as $P \cdot X$, this geometrical representation suggests a useful method of 'normalising' prices.
Rather than choose some arbitrary standard of value we could simply make
the length of $OP = 1$. The scalar product $P \cdot X$ is then the distance ON.

In the subsistence economy where profits, by definition, are zero, we
found that the price ratio was given by the slope of the net output frontier.
In a surplus economy profits may be positive or (notionally, at least) zero.
If all the surplus is used for wage payments then profits, and the rate of profits, are zero. It can now be shown that when $r = 0$ the slope of the net
output frontier still measures the price ratio. Competition ensures that the
wage per unit of labour is the same in each process. When profits are zero
the value of net output per worker must be equal to the wage rate. It follows
that the values of the net outputs per worker in each process are equal:
$P\alpha_1 = P\alpha_2$. A price vector which is normal to $\alpha_1\alpha_2$ is clearly the only one
which is consistent with this result (fig. 4.5).[3]

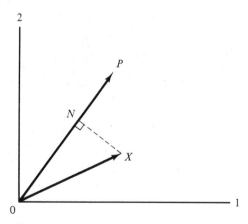

Figure 4.4

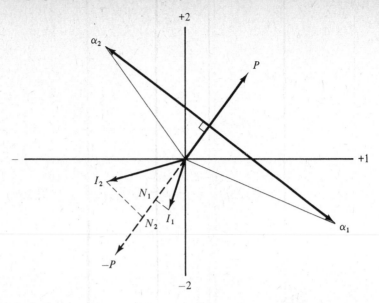

Figure 4.5

5 The wage frontier

Consider now a positive uniform rate of profits, r. When process i employs a unit of labour, the value of inputs used is PI_i. (Geometrically, the vertical projection of P on $-I_i$ is obtained by extending P into the negative quadrant, as in fig. 4.5. The scalar product of two negative vectors is, of course, positive.) The value of net output per worker is now used to pay both the wage and profits, the latter being an amount rPI_i:

$$P\alpha_1 = w + rPI_1$$
$$P\alpha_2 = w + rPI_2$$

from which it follows that

$$P(\alpha_1 - rI_1) = P(\alpha_2 - rI_2)$$

or, writing

$$\beta_i = (\alpha_i - rI_i),$$
$$P\beta_1 = P\beta_2.$$

The β_i are obtained by adding the α_i and $-rI_i$ vectors (see fig. 4.6; alternatively we may add Q_i and $-(1+r)I_i$). The condition $P\beta_i = P\beta_2$ requires that P is now normal to the line joining β_1 and β_2. The slope of the line $\beta_1\beta_2$ is thus equal to the price ratio.

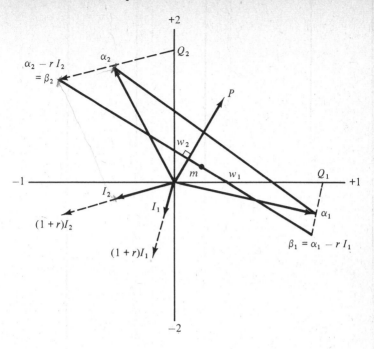

Figure 4.6

It is important to note that the lines $\alpha_1\alpha_2$ and $\beta_1\beta_2$ are not, in general, parallel to one another. The reason for this is not difficult to see. Suppose, for example, that process 2 uses up more (of both) means of production than process 1. Then the addition of a uniform proportion r of the $-I_i$ vectors to the α_i has the effect of pushing β_2 away from α_2 to a greater extent than β_1 is pushed from α_1. Indeed, as we shall confirm later, this uneven shift will occur in all cases in which $PI_1 \neq PI_2$. This can be given a straightforward economic interpretation. In fig. 4.5 the price vector is the one appropriate to $r = 0$. At these prices the value of capital per worker in process 1 is less than the value of capital per worker in process 2. With the emergence of a uniform positive rate of profits it is necessary for the price of the commodity using a relatively higher value of capital per worker to rise relative to the other commodity's price.[4] It should be emphasised, however, that this observation applies only to the two-commodity case; with more than two commodities we can make no such definite statement.

We can also find an economic interpretation of the line $\beta_1\beta_2$. If all labour were used in process 1, β_1 would be the vector of wage commodities (what is left of net output after payment of profits); and similarly for β_2 when all workers are employed in process 2. When the processes are operated together the vector of wage commodities will be somewhere on the line $\beta_1\beta_2$, which is accordingly referred to as the *wage frontier*. In any actual system the processes must operate at intensities which allow the attainment of a point on the wage frontier within the non-negative quadrant. (If α is the net output vector and m the vector of wage commodities then $\alpha-m$ is the vector of commodities which make up profits.)

Imagine now the consequences of a notional increase in r. With each increase there would be an inward shift of the wage frontier. In general, the slope of the frontier would continue to change, becoming flatter and flatter, or steeper and steeper, indicating a monotonic change in the price ratio. The amount of commodities available for wages would get smaller and smaller. At some point – when the wage frontier passes through the origin – nothing at all is left for the wage basket (fig. 4.7). Once this has been reached further increases in the rate of profits are ruled out: profits now fully exhaust the net output of the system.

6 The $w-r$ relation

The relationship between the wage and the rate of profits which

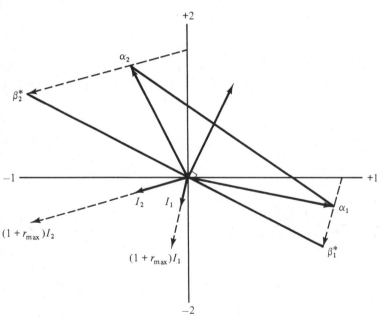

Figure 4.7

is implicit in the vector diagrams used in this chapter can be made more explicit. As we noted in section 2, the two-commodity system has three unknowns: r, w and p_1/p_2 and, as a result it is not possible to solve the equations as they are. If, however, a particular value is specified for one of the unknowns there will be a corresponding solution for the remaining two. If the value of the first is allowed to vary the solution values of the other two will also vary (in general). This means that any one variable can be described as a function of any other. In particular, it is possible to describe the wage (in terms of some standard) as a function of the general rate of profits. Similarly, the price ratio can be written as a function of either r or w.

Consider the net output and wage frontiers that are drawn in fig. 4.6. We have seen that, with a rise in the rate of profits, the wage frontier $\beta_1\beta_2$ shifts towards the origin. The fall in the wage can be quantified once a standard of value is specified. In the diagram, for example, the chosen wage basket on the frontier $\beta_1\beta_2$ is $m = (m_1, m_2)$. The value of this basket in terms of commodity 2 is

$$w_2 = m_2 + m_1 (p_1/p_2).$$

Recalling that p_1/p_2 is equal to the slope of the wage frontier, it follows that w_2 is the point where the wage frontier cuts the vertical axis. (Similarly, w_1 is the intersection of the wage frontier and the horizontal axis.) The wage, in terms of, say, commodity 2, which is associated with each rate of profits can thus be read off the vertical axis as the $\beta_1\beta_2$ line shifts inwards. The wage falls from its maximum, when $r = 0$, to zero when r has reached its maximum, corresponding to a wage frontier $\beta_1{}^*\beta_2{}^*$. The relation is plotted in fig. 4.8 (a).

Let us summarise the properties of the w–r relation that have now been established.

(1) The w–r relation is downward sloping;

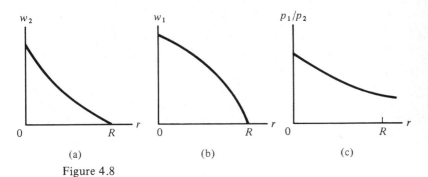

(a)   (b)   (c)

Figure 4.8

(2) There is a maximum rate of profits, which Sraffa calls R, which obtains at a zero wage. This occurs when the wage frontier is pushed back to $\beta_1^*\beta_2^*$, passing through the origin (fig. 4.7). It will be clear that, in this case, R is finite.

(3) Similarly, there is a finite maximum wage (in any standard) that corresponds to $r = 0$.

Note that property (1) only applies within these limits. Properties (2) and (3) are really reflections of the technological limitations of the economy. This is one aspect in which Sraffa's w–r relation differs from that implicit in Ricardo's *Principles* (see fig. 2.1). In Ricardo r approaches infinity as w approaches zero because wages form the only capital. If the productivity of labour is maintained with zero wages then the system becomes infinitely productive. There is an obvious biological qualification to this possibility.

(4) For r, $0 < r < R$, the price ratio, while in general varying with r, nevertheless remains positive and finite (fig. 4.8 (c)). By construction and the limitations of technology the slope $\alpha_1\alpha_2$ is negative. Also by the nature of its construction, the slope of the wage frontier $\beta_1\beta_2$ must remain negative. It follows that the price vector (which is normal to the appropriate frontier) is always positive.

The above properties do not, of course, depend on which commodity is chosen as the standard of value.

(5) The *precise* shape of the w–r relation does depend on which commodity is chosen as standard. Because, in general, the wage frontier changes its slope as it shifts, the trace of its intersection with the vertical axis will have a different appearance to the trace of its intersection with the horizontal axis. Thus figs. 4.8(a) and 4.8(b) are w–r curves for the same system with different standards.

Finally:

(6) With a given standard, the shape of the w–r relation is not affected by the size of the output of any process. The precise position of the α vector or indeed, the m vector in fig. 4.6 is irrelevant to the derivation of the w–r relation.

7. The conflict over income shares

The creation of a physical surplus from production is a common feature of non-primitive forms of society and, for capitalism, a surplus is an essential characteristic. Without it there can be no reason for capital. Under the classical assumption that the wage is advanced as a well-defined bundle of commodities, profits, or the return to capital, are clearly defined. They are the exchange value of the surplus: the excess of net output over wage goods.

All societies are subject to evolution and capitalism is no exception. Over the last century the living standards of workers in capitalist countries have improved enormously. Changes in worker organisation and in social institutions have allowed workers to share part of the surplus they create. This changed position is reflected in Sraffa's assumption that wages are paid in terms of some standard of value, at the end of the period. Even so, nothing of real substance is involved in this change of assumption. In the classical case an increase in the wage bundle would imply a reduction in the total surplus and hence in profits. On Sraffa's assumption, the surplus is a more or less fixed magnitude but the share of profits rises as the share of wages falls. The essentially antagonistic nature of the class claims on income is retained. It may be that this conflict is resolved by the relative strengths of capitalists and workers, with or without the intervention of the state; or it may be that there exist other economic forces by which the division of income is determined independently of the actions of individuals or classes.

8 Summary

The picture which has emerged so far is of a set of relationships between wages, profits and relative prices. The relations involved appear deceptively simple: an inverse relation between w and r accompanied by a one-directional change in the price ratio. The two-commodity analysis is useful in that it allows us to derive these basic propositions in a relatively simple and transparent fashion. But it does involve the danger of overlooking many subtle and important complications of more general models, and we must be careful to try and avoid this. In chapter 7 we shall derive these relations for the k-commodity case and analyse their properties in rather more detail.

FURTHER READING

See chapter 7.

5

Consumption versus growth

1 Introduction

So far we have considered the division of the net product between the two classes. We have not considered the uses to which it may be put. If we eliminate the possibilities of storage and waste, the net product can either be consumed or used to enlarge the means of production. In the absence of technical progress, net investment requires an increase in the level of employment. We shall assume that the workforce is always sufficient to provide for the needs of the growing economy.

2 The consumption frontier

The analysis of the division of net output between consumption and investment bears a striking resemblance to the analysis of its division between worker and capitalist. Allowing for the absence of a price vector, fig. 5.1 is, in all but notation, identical to fig. 4.6. Suppose, to begin, that process 1 is operated in (purely algebraic) isolation. *One worker*[1] produces the net outputs indicated by the vector α_1, having used the inputs I_1. If g is the rate of growth of the process, then *net* investment equal to gI_1, is provided from the *net* product. What is left, $\alpha_1 - gI_1$, is the vector of consumption goods γ_1, per worker (henceforth, p.w.), which would obtain from this process in isolation.

If instead process 2 were operated alone, and subject to growth *at the same rate g*, we could derive a p.w. consumption vector $\gamma_2 = \alpha_2 - gI_2$. In reality, as we know by now, both processes must be operated together to avoid the impossibility of negative outputs and, in this case, negative consumption. In particular, they need to be operated at relative intensities which allow consumption to take place at some non-negative point on the line $\gamma_1\gamma_2$, the *consumption frontier*. The interesting thing about the consumption frontier is that it is derived in exactly the same way as the wage frontier $\beta_1\beta_2$; that is, by subtracting from each α_i a uniform proportion of the corresponding I_i – in the first case a proportion g and, in the second, a proportion r. This means that the behaviour of the consumption frontier is identical to that

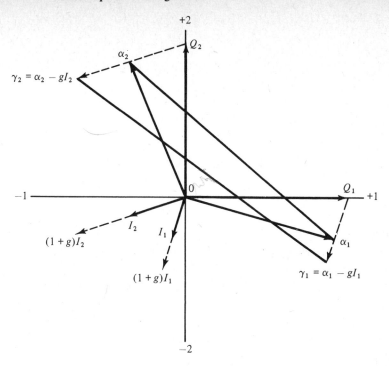

Figure 5.1

of the wage frontier. Thus, at zero growth the consumption frontier is identical to $\alpha_1\alpha_2$. Then, as we notionally increase the uniform growth rate, the frontier moves towards the origin. In general, this shift is accompanied by a monotonic change in slope. When all the net product is devoted to investment the frontier passes through the origin.

Although processes can grow at different rates over short periods of time, it is not possible to maintain these differences over longer periods. The faster growing process will eventually run out of inputs of the other commodity. If, for example, process 1 is growing faster than process 2, the vector of net outputs, per worker, α, would gradually shift towards α_1. The imbalance in growth rates would have to be corrected before α reached the horizontal axis for, beyond that, outputs of commodity 2 are negative. In all our discussions of growing economies we shall be concerned with the case of uniform growth.

3 The c–g relation

The similarity of the analyses of wage and consumption behaviour suggests that it might be possible to derive a function relating the rate of

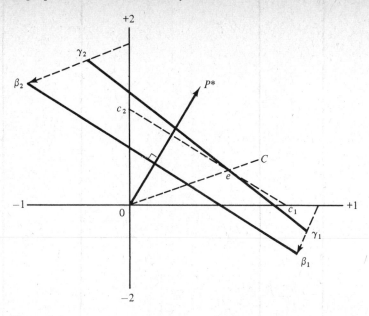

Figure 5.2

growth to the level of consumption p.w. That is indeed the case, but first we have to decide what is meant by the 'level' of consumption. Since consumption consists of heterogeneous commodities the only sensible measure of its level is its value at the *ruling* price ratio, given by the slope of the wage frontier. Thus, in fig. 5.2, a p.w. consumption basket $e = (e_1, e_2)$ has a value c_1, if commodity 1 is the standard of value, and c_2 if commodity 2 is the standard. If we take the consumption proportions $e_1:e_2$ as given (as represented by the line OC) then, *for a given price ratio*, it is clear that as the consumption frontier moves inwards the value of consumption p.w., in either standard, falls. There is, therefore, an inverse relationship between the rate of growth and the value of consumption p.w. This c–g relation, as we may call it, has two other properties worth noting immediately. The first is that there is a finite maximum value of consumption p.w. corresponding to $g = 0$ (that is, when $\gamma_1\gamma_2$ coincides with $\alpha_1\alpha_2$). The second is that there is a finite maximum rate of growth, which we call G, which obtains at zero consumption p.w. (that is, when $\gamma_1\gamma_2$ passes through the origin). Moreover, since the properties of variation of $\gamma_1\gamma_2$ are identical to those of the wage frontier (though, of course, the two frontiers will not generally coincide) the maximum rate of growth, G, is equal to the maximum rate of profits, R.

These three properties, it may be noted, are identical to the first three properties of the w–r relation listed in chapter 4, section 6. Both functions are downward sloping and the rates of growth and profits both vary from zero to the same maxima. One might be tempted from this to postulate further that, given the standard of value, the functions are identical in appearance. Unfortunately, this is not generally the case, though it is worth seeing why not.

The c–g relation just derived was for given consumption proportions and a given price ratio. Thus, in terms of commodity 1, the basket e in fig. 5.2 has a value c_1 at the price P^*. If the price were to change (as a result of a shift in $\beta_1\beta_2$), then so would c_1 – even though e and g were constant. There are thus an infinite number of c_1–g frontiers, corresponding to the infinite number of price ratios. The same would be true if the position of e on the consumption frontier were to vary when the price ratio remained constant. Compare this behaviour with that of the w_1–r relation in figs. 4.6 and 4.8(b). For any $\beta_1\beta_2$ frontier there is only one price ratio and only one possible valuation (in terms of commodity 1) of a given wage basket. Even if the wage basket were to vary along $\beta_1\beta_2$, w_1 would still be the same. Thus, for a given rate of profits there is one and only one w_1. But for a given rate of growth there may be any number of c_1s. It is therefore unlikely, except by coincidence, that the c_1–g relation should be the same as the w_1–r relation. Can we perhaps identify a coincidence?

One way is to rule out variations in consumption proportions, as we did above, and at the same time remove the possibility of revaluation due to a price change. The second task can be accomplished if we take as the standard of value a composite commodity made up of the two actual commodities in the same proportions as they appear in the consumption basket. Then, not only can the level of consumption be measured independently of prices, it can also be compared in purely quantitative terms with the wage. In fig. 5.2, the easiest way to see this is to suppose that consumption consists of a single, actual commodity, say commodity 1. Then e_1 coincides with c_1, no matter how much prices change, and c_1 can always be compared directly with w_1. Moreover, as $\gamma_1\gamma_2$ and $\beta_1\beta_2$ shift towards the origin they trace out exactly the same functions along the horizontal axis.

We can, at last, state the following proposition. If the consumption basket is of fixed proportions, and if the standard of value is an actual or composite commodity of the same proportions, then the w–r and c–g relations are identical (fig. 5.3). In mathematical terms they are called *dual* functions. When, but only when, duality holds, the variation in consumption p.w. and the growth rate is totally independent of the variation in the wage and the rate of profits. Although duality only occurs in very special circumstances it is such a useful property, analytically, that it is often worth our while to assume these circumstances exist. The slight restriction in the realism of the model is a price well worth paying for the analytical rewards that come from duality. An example of its use is given in chapter 9.

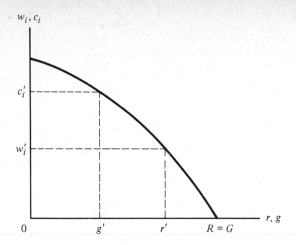

Figure 5.3

4 The algebra of consumption and growth[2]

The c–g relation can be formulated algebraically using what are referred to as 'quantity' equations. Let q_i be the gross output p.w. of commodity i, e_i the consumption p.w. of commodity i. Then the quantity equations are:

$$q_1 = (1+g)(a_{11}q_1 + a_{12}q_2) + e_1 \tag{5.1}$$

$$q_2 = (1+g)(a_{21}q_1 + a_{22}q_2) + e_2. \tag{5.2}$$

Equation (5.i) says that the gross output p.w. of commodity i is used to provide for the replacement of the means of production necessary to occupy one worker, equal to $(a_{i1}q_1 + a_{i2}q_2)$; plus net investment equal to a multiple, g, of these means of production; plus consumption of an amount e_i p.w.

In addition to the quantity equations we need a third equation restricting the range of variation of the q_i. In any period, the total amount of labour employed in process i, L_i, is equal to the number of workers required to produce one unit (l_i) times the number of units produced (q_iL = output p.w. times total workforce). The total workforce is, therefore, equal to

$$L = L_1 + L_2 = q_1Ll_1 + q_2Ll_2.$$

Dividing though by L,

$$1 = q_1l_1 + q_2l_2 \tag{5.3}$$

(Equation (5.3) is a statement of the gross output frontier Q_1Q_2.)

The derivation of the dual c–g relation from (5.1)–(5.3) is a somewhat messy affair so we merely go through the steps involved. First it is necessary to restrict consumption possibilities to a single commodity, say commodity 1; then e_1 becomes identical to c_1. Next we solve (5.1) and (5.2) simultaneously to obtain p.w. gross outputs as functions of g and c_1:

$$q_1 = f_1(g, c_1) \tag{5.4}$$

$$q_2 = f_2(g, c_1). \tag{5.5}$$

Multiplying both sides of (5.4) by l_1 and of (5.5) by l_2, the resulting equations can be added to give, from (5.3),

$$l_1 \cdot f_1(g, c_1) + l_2 \cdot f_2(g, c_1) = 1 \tag{5.6}$$

(5.6) is an implicit statement of the c_1–g relation.

The argument can be generalised in an obvious way to allow for any number of commodities.

5 Savings behaviour

In the previous sections we have allowed for the possibility that both workers and capitalists may retain part of their incomes for investment. The c–g relation is, in fact, completely independent of any assumption relating to the class-composition of savings, as is the duality between the c–g and w–r relations. It is nevertheless instructive to consider a particular form of savings behaviour merely to see one way in which the four variables involved, w, c, r and g, may relate to one another. The particular case we shall consider is sometimes referred to as 'classical' savings behaviour, in which workers do not save at all while capitalists may save any fraction s, between zero and unity, of their profits.

A familiar condition for macroeconomic equilibrium is that total intended savings must equal total intended investment. In a model in which savings and investment both take place in physical terms it is difficult to see how this condition should fail to be satisfied, but it is still useful to consider its implications. Since, in our analysis the replacement investment has been allowed to look after itself, equilibrium requires equality between savings out of net product and net investment – that part of investment which contributes to the *growth* of the capital stock. Denoting the value of the capital stock in any one period as K, then net investment in that period is gK. Profits on that capital, at the rate r, equals rK and, if a proportion s is saved, total savings are srK. The equilibrium condition may, therefore, be written

$$gK = srK$$

or,

$$g = sr. \tag{5.7}$$

If s is fixed, (5.7) gives a direct relation between g and r. The relation between c and w can be obtained directly from the dual w–r and c–g relations, as in fig. 5.3. Since $s \leqslant 1$, g can never exceed r and w can never exceed c. Put another way, the wage frontier $\beta_1\beta_2$ can never lie above the consumption frontier $\gamma_1\gamma_2$.

To the extent that workers also save (and invest) they, too, receive profits. Somewhat paradoxically, (5.7) also holds in this case (within very wide limits), the proportion saved out of workers' incomes having no bearing on the equilibrium condition.[3]

It must be emphasised that equation (5.7) does not provide us with a theory of how any of the four variables in fig. 5.3 are determined, though it may provide an important part of such a theory. If, for example, we have a theory about how g is determined outside of our model, and if we assume classical savings behaviour with some particular value of s, then there will be one, and only one, equilibrium value of r which is consistent with that theory; c and w will follow automatically from the dual functions. In fact, a separate theory about the determination of any one of these variables, together with a value for s, is sufficient to determine the equilibrium values of the other three variables. A number of such theories exist usually beginning with g, r or w.

6 Simple national income accounts

Net product, or net national income, can be considered as the sum of all expenditures – consumption plus investment – or as the sum of all incomes – wages plus profits. This double perspective is illustrated in fig. 5.4 where, for simplicity, it is supposed that consumption consists entirely of commodity 2. Net product p.w. in terms of 2 is Oy_2. Its division between wages and profits is indicated by point w_2 on the wage frontier, and between consumption and investment by point c_2 on the consumption frontier. The difference $c_2 - w_2$ indicates that part of consumption p.w. undertaken by capitalists.

The same division of national income can also be illustrated in terms of the dual c–g and w–r relations once we have found a way of representing net output. This can be done by drawing a straight line through the particular c_i–g and w_i–r combinations, as in fig. 5.5. This line has a slope k_i equal to the value of capital p.w. Net product p.w. can then be accounted as the sum of consumption p.w. plus investment p.w.

$$y_i = c_i + gk_i$$

or, as the sum of the wage rate plus profits p.w.

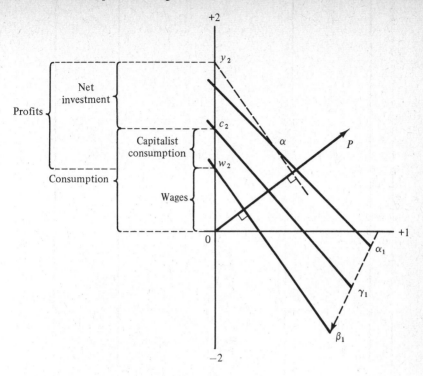

Figure 5.4

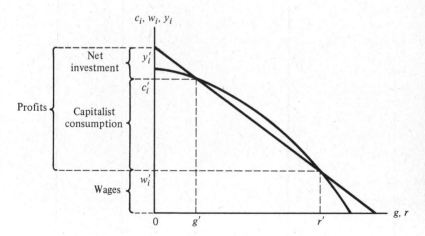

Figure 5.5

$$y_i = w_i + rk_i.$$

It is worth remembering that the simplicity of fig. 5.5 is due entirely to the assumption of duality.

7 Summary

Analysis of the division of net outputs between consumption and investment proceeds in the same way as the analysis of the division between wages and profits. In fact, the wage and consumption frontiers behave in an identical fashion, and the maximum rate of growth, G, is equal to the maximum rate of profits, R. If consumption proportions are fixed then a standard of value with the same proportions will yield c–g and w–r relations which are complete duals. Specification of savings behaviour allows us to connect the 'expenditure' and 'incomes' sides of the model.

FURTHER READING

The input–output model with a positive growth rate is sometimes referred to as the 'dynamic Leontief model'; see Hahn and Matthews (1964). For a comprehensive and rigorous discussion of the c–g relation, see Pasinetti (1977), chapter 7. The duality between the 'quantity' and 'price' aspects of the economy has been demonstrated in a wide variety of models; see, for example, Spaventa (1970), Nuti (1970a) and, for the Sraffa–Leontief model, von Weizsäcker (1971). There is now an extensive, and generally quite mathematical, literature on this subject; for further references see Morishima (1976).

Equation (5.7) is known as the 'Cambridge equation' and is due to Kaldor (1955), whose work was generalised by Pasinetti (1962) to include the possibility of workers' savings. This, too, has spawned an enormous literature; see Pasinetti (1974) for further discussion.

In the literature, the possibilities for closing the price/quantity systems include:

(*i*) taking w as fixed in real terms, either for Malthusian reasons, as in Ricardo, or through the continuous replenishing of a 'reserve army of labour' through the adoption of capital-intensive techniques, as in Marx; see, for example, Sweezy (1942), chapter V;

(*ii*) taking the growth rate as exogenous, given by the growth rate of the workforce and a tendency to full employment; this approach is implicit in Kaldor's work;

(*iii*) following Kalecki (1971), taking the general rate of profits as determined by the 'degree of monopoly' in the economy; see, for example, Mainwaring (1977). None of these approaches is particularly satisfactory; for a critical discussion see Nuti (1970b) and Dobb (1973), pp. 267–71.

6

The Standard system and basic commodities

1 A maximum-growth economy

We begin this chapter by examining in more detail the properties of a system growing at the maximum rate G. The consumption frontier appropriate to this case, $\gamma_1^*\gamma_2^*$, passes through the origin (fig. 6.1). The only feasible consumption vector is zero. All net outputs are used to add to the means of production a fraction G of their stock in the previous period. It follows that the proportions in which the commodities enter net outputs are exactly the same as the proportions in which they enter the means of production. If these proportions were unequal then the two processes could not grow at the same rate without one commodity being made available for consumption or else wasted. Diagrammatically, this equality of proportions is indicated by the output vector, $O\alpha^*$, and the input vector, OI^*, lying on the same straight line through the origin. (Mathematically, these vectors are said to be linearly dependent.)

A simple numerical example of a system growing at the maximum rate is given in the following table:

Table 1

| | | Inputs | | | Outputs | |
	Labour	1	2		Gross	Net
Process 1	0.4	24	24	⟶	48	12
Process 2	0.6	12	18	⟶	56	14
	1	36	42			

As may be seen, the net output of this system consists of commodities 1 and 2 in the proportions $6:7$. The same is true of the aggregate means of production (and gross outputs). The maximum rate of growth is equal to the ratio of the net output of any one commodity to the quantity of that

57

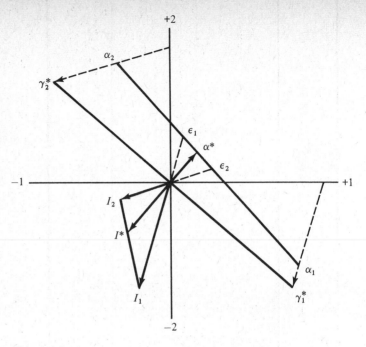

Figure 6.1

commodity used as means of production for the entire system; that is,

$$G = 12/36 = 14/42 = 1/3.$$

Since net outputs and inputs are made up of commodities in exactly the same proportions (and the only use of net output is as an input), then it is effectively as though we have a one-commodity economy. We may think of it as a commodity such as an axe: the axe itself is a composite commodity made from wood and steel (commodities 1 and 2) and always in the same proportions. Although wood and steel can, in principle, be used and produced in different proportions, the properties of the system are such that they never are. The rate of growth of the entire system can be measured as the proportionate net addition of axes each period.

2 The Standard system

The discussion so far has concerned a particular, and perhaps unlikely, configuration of the actual processes of an economy. It would seem to have little relevance to an economy in which, because consumption out of surplus is positive, the composition of net output differs from the composition of aggregate inputs. What it does show however, is that any system of production is, in principle, capable of a re-arrangement which transforms it into a one-commodity system. In other words, it is possible to find levels of operation of each process such that the output vector and the input vector have the same proportions, as in fig. 6.1. In the previous section this was taken to be an actual physical arrangement of the processes in the system. But our interest in the properties of a one-composite-commodity system are analytical rather than descriptive and there is no need for us to be constrained to actual systems. In the rest of this chapter we shall be concerned, firstly, to analyse the properties of purely imaginary reconstructions of actual systems and, secondly, to consider the implications of that analysis for the actual systems themselves.

Let us begin with the following *actual* system:

Table 2

	Inputs Labour	1	2		Outputs Gross	Net
Process 1	0.3	18	18	$\longrightarrow$	46	4
Process 2	0.7	14	21	$\longrightarrow$	$65\frac{1}{3}$	$26\frac{1}{3}$
	1	32	39			

This certainly does not have the properties of a composite-commodity system: the proportion in which commodities enter net outputs are quite different from those in the aggregate means of production. We shall not even enquire how much of the net output is invested and how much consumed. Yet, comparing this actual system with the one in the previous section, we see that they involve exactly the same processes. The only difference is the relative intensity with which they are operated. Since table 2 represents our actual economy, table 1 now refers to the purely imaginary reconstruction. Such a reconstruction is known as the *Standard system*, and the associated composite commodity as the *Standard commodity*.

An important finding of the last chapter was that the maximum rate of growth of an economy is equal to the maximum rate of profits, R. In the numerical example, therefore, we could just as well have written $R = 1/3$. This means that, in the system of table 1, R, as well as G, can be measured in purely physical terms, as the ratio of the net output of Standard commodity to the input of Standard commodity – the *Standard ratio*. But since R is independent of the intensities at which processes are operated, it is also the maximum rate of profits for the actual system. Thus for the system in table 2 we can write $R =$ Standard ratio $= 1/3$.

How do we transform an actual system into its corresponding Standard system? In the numerical example above the transformation can be affected by multiplying process 1 in the actual system by 4/3 and process 2 by 6/7. But how are these multipliers obtained? Denote them by ϕ_1 and ϕ_2 respectively. These, when applied to the processes of the actual system, must transform them in such a way that the new, imaginary system has the property that the amount of commodity i ($i = 1, 2$) in gross output is $(1 + R)$ times the amount of i in its aggregate means of production. Thus, in the example,

$$\phi_1 36 = (1 + R)(\phi_1 18 + \phi_2 14) \tag{6.1}$$

$$\phi_2 65\tfrac{1}{3} = (1 + R)(\phi_1 18 + \phi_2 21). \tag{6.2}$$

Now these two equations contain three unknowns, ϕ_1, ϕ_2 and R. On their own they are sufficient to give us R and the ratio $\phi_1 : \phi_2$, the Standard proportions. The ϕs may, however, be fixed in absolute terms by the restriction that the Standard system employs the same amount of labour as the actual system. The transformed labour inputs, therefore, add up to unity:

$$\phi_1 0.3 + \phi_2 0.7 = 1. \tag{6.3}$$

A solution to (6.1)–(6.3) is, as we know, $\phi_1 = 4/3$, $\phi_2 = 6/7$ and $R = 1/3$.

Unfortunately, (6.1)–(6.3) reduce to a quadratic equation and thus allow for two possible solutions for the unknowns. It is, however, quite easy to show (at least in the two-commodity case) that the solution set with non-negative values is unique. Depending on the amount of labour that is allocated to each process, the net output vector may be at any point on the line $\alpha_1 \alpha_2$ in fig. 6.1, while the input vector may be anywhere along $I_1 I_2$. A set of non-negative ϕ-multipliers is capable of re-arranging the respective inputs and outputs only within these ranges. It is easy to see that the range of input variation is wholly encompassed within the range of output variation. In the diagram, the input vectors I_1 and I_2 are projected into the positive quadrant until they cut the net output frontier at ϵ_1 and ϵ_2. As we change the intensities of the processes, subject to equation (6.3), the input vector moves, let us say away from I_1 towards I_2. The projection of this vector on the net output frontier moves in the direction: ϵ_2 to ϵ_1. At the same time we know that the net output vector moves in the opposite direction: α_1 to α_2. Since $\alpha_1 \alpha_2$ completely overlaps $\epsilon_1 \epsilon_2$ there must always be a unique point at which the positive projection of the input vector coincides with the net output vector, which is, therefore, a unique Standard vector obtained by non-negative multipliers.[1]

In the k-commodity case, the Standard system is obtained by a straight-forward generalisation of the procedure described above. If actual gross outputs are A_i $(i = 1, \ldots, k)$ then the ϕ-multipliers are determined as the solution to

$$\phi_i A_i = (1 + R) \sum_j \phi_j a_{ij} A_j \quad (i, j = 1, \ldots, k) \tag{6.4}$$

and,

$$\sum_i q_i L_i = 1. \tag{6.5}$$

These $k + 1$ equations can be solved for the k multipliers and R. Of the k solution sets only one involves non-negative multipliers.[2]

3 The *w–r* relation reconsidered

We saw in chapter 4 that as the wage decreases the rate of profits gets bigger, reaching its maximum R when wages are zero. The precise shape of this relation depends on the standard in which wages are measured, but it does not depend on the intensities at which processes are operated. Here we consider the nature of the *w–r* relation when the Standard commodity, corresponding to some actual system, is used as the measure of wages in that actual system.

Naturally, the value of R will be the same as for all other measures, though we know now that R can be determined in purely physical terms, as a ratio of quantities of Standard commodity. To see how the wage varies when r falls from its maximum value suppose, to begin, that the actual and Standard systems are identical and that the wage is actually paid in Standard proportions. Then, with net output and the wage both as quantities of Standard commodity, their difference, profits, must also be of the same composition. Since everything comes in lumps of Standard commodity we are well and truly in a one-commodity world. To make things even simpler we shall take as a unit of Standard commodity, the net output of the Standard system. The wage (of the one unit of labour) can therefore be thought of as w units of Standard commodity or as a fraction, w, of the Standard net output. The rate of profits is the share of profits in Standard net output divided by Standard inputs

$$r = (1 - w) \times \text{Standard net output/Standard inputs}$$

or

$$r = (1 - w) R. \tag{6.6}$$

Thus, with everything paid as quantities of Standard commodity, the *w–r* relation is a straight line (fig. 6.2). The wage varies from its maximum, unity, when it accounts for all the Standard net output, to zero, when all the Standard net output goes to profits. In between, as one rate rises the other falls, in strict proportion. But if (6.6) applies when the actual and Standard systems are the same it also applies when they are different, for the *w–r* relation is, as we have already noted, independent of process intensities.

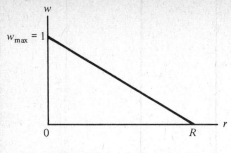

Figure 6.2

Nor does this depend on wages being paid as a quantity of Standard commodity, any more than the w_i–r relation depends on wages being paid as a quantity of commodity i. This can be confirmed with the help of fig. 6.3. Standard proportions are indicated by the ray $O\alpha^*$. If the wage were paid in these proportions then the wage basket would lie somewhere on $O\alpha^*$, contracting towards the origin as r rises, the variation being one of strict proportionality. But suppose, instead, the wage (at some rate of profits) were given by the basket m. Remembering that the slope of $\beta_1\beta_2$ is the price

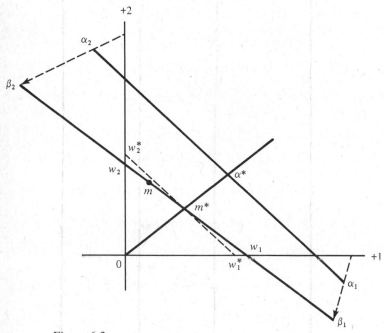

Figure 6.3

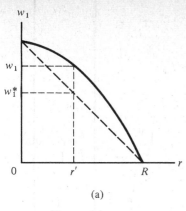 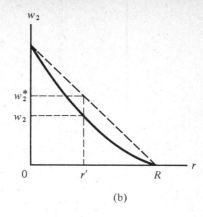

(a)   (b)

Figure 6.4

ratio, m is equivalent in value to a basket m^* made up in Standard proportions. Thus, provided that it is measured in terms of Standard commodity,
the wage, whatever its actual composition, will still vary in inverse proportion to the rate of profits. Equation (6.6) continues to apply.

This discussion should enable us to see why it is that a w–r relation using
some other standard of value is not, in general, a straight line. As r rises,
then, no matter what the composition of the wage, its equivalent in terms
of Standard commodity moves down the ray $O\alpha^*$ at a rate proportionate
to the increase in r. If the same were to be true of wages in terms of commodity 1, then corresponding to m^*, the wage would be w_1^*; and, in terms
of commodity 2, it would be w_2^*. It would be as though the wage frontier
moved in a parallel fashion. But the wage frontier does not move in this
way. In general, as r rises, prices change and so, therefore, does the slope of
the wage frontier. Because, in fig. 6.3, p_1/p_2 is falling as r rises, the actual
w_1 does not fall as far as w_1^*. By dragging its heels it gives rise to a w_1–r
relation which is concave to the origin (fig. 6.4(a)). Commodity 2, though,
becomes relatively more expensive so that the actual w_2 rushes ahead of
w_2^*, and the w_2–r relation is convex to the origin. Clearly, the shape of the
w–r relation is intimately connected to the variation in relative prices. A
more detailed analysis of this connection will have to wait until chapter 7.

4 Basic and non-basic commodities

In the Standard system the proportions in which commodities enter
output is the same as those in which they enter the means of production.
In that case, in constructing the Standard system, what do we do with those
actual processes which produce only final consumption goods, if such exist?

Such goods cannot be part of the Standard commodity and the processes which create them cannot be part of the Standard system. Their ϕ-multipliers must be zero. Thus in table 2 if we were to add a third process, producing commodity 3 which was not itself used as an input, then, to obtain the corresponding Standard system, that process would first have to be eliminated (multiplied by zero). The Standard system appropriate to this augmented actual system would be the same as the one appropriate to the original actual system. (Similarly, in a system growing at the maximum rate, there would simply be no room for a process producing consumption goods.) Commodities which are capable of entering the Standard system are known as *basics*; those which are not are called *non-basics*.

Non-basics may include commodities other than final consumption goods. Suppose that to our actual system we now add a fourth process. Commodity 4 is used as an input, but only in its own production and that of commodity 3. The fully augmented actual system is presented, in unit terms, in table 3.

Table 3

Labour	Inputs 1	2	4		Gross outputs 1	2	3	4
l_1	$+$	$a_{11} +$	a_{21}		$\longrightarrow$	1			
l_2	$+$	$a_{12} +$	a_{22}		$\longrightarrow$		1		
l_3	$+$	$a_{13} +$		a_{43}	$\longrightarrow$			1	
l_4	$+$		$a_{24} +$	a_{44}	$\longrightarrow$				1

If process 3 can find no part in the Standard system, then process 4, which is wholly subsidiary to process 3 (one stage in an integrated consumer goods industry, as it were), can find no part either.

This distinction between basic and non-basic commodities corresponds to two types of sectoral interdependence. Basic commodities use and are used by all other basic commodities as means of production. In our example, commodity 1 uses commodity 2 and commodity 2 uses commodity 1. The linkages need not, however, be as direct as this. In more general systems the product 'pig iron' may need to be traced through several industries before its contribution to the production of tractor tyres becomes apparent. Similarly, tractor tyres may exercise only a very roundabout influence on the production of pig iron. In the case of non-basics, the linkages with the rest of the system are all one-way. Perhaps pig iron is used, directly or indirectly, to produce garden gnomes but garden gnomes are not used to produce pig iron. In our example, commodities 3 and 4 do not enter the production of 1 and 2 in any way. There is simply no feed-back from non-basics to basics. The elimination of a non-basic process might affect other non-basics, but that would be the extent of its impact. The elimination of a basic process, however, would lead to a breakdown in the entire system of production. For a system to be capable of self-replacement all its basic processes must be active.

The importance of the pattern of inter-industry linkages may be seen more clearly by writing out the price equations corresponding to table 3:

$$p_1 = (1+r)(p_1 a_{11} + p_2 a_{21}) + wl_1 \tag{6.7}$$

$$p_2 = (1+r)(p_1 a_{12} + p_2 a_{22}) + wl_2 \tag{6.8}$$

$$p_3 = (1+r)(p_1 a_{13} + p_4 a_{43}) + wl_3 \tag{6.9}$$

$$p_4 = (1+r)(p_2 a_{24} + p_4 a_{44}) + wl_4. \tag{6.10}$$

We shall suppose – and this is important – that wages are accounted in terms of one or more basic commodities. Then if either w (so measured) or r is taken as fixed from outside, equations (6.7) and (6.8) are fully determinate: they may be solved for p_1/p_2 and r or w. Given the solution to basics prices and distribution, (6.9) and (6.10) may then be used to solve for p_3 and p_4. But these equations make no contribution to the determination of w or r, or of the relation between them.

To emphasise these points, suppose that, due to a technical improvement, fewer means of production and less labour are required in the production of commodity 1. As a result, the ratio p_1/p_2 would fall and the possible combinations of r and w would be enlarged. (If, say, w were given r would increase.) But that is not all. The change also affects the prices of non-basics. An improvement in the production of pig iron will affect the price of garden gnomes. On the other hand, an improvement in the production of garden gnomes has no effect on the price of pig iron. A fall in p_3 simply has no way of making itself felt on p_1 and p_2: it does not affect r and w which are already determined in the basic system, and commodity 3 itself does not enter into the basic processes. Process 4 is slightly different in that an improvement there does affect itself and commodity 3, but that is the limit of its influence.[3]

5 The problem of non-basic wage goods

In chapter 1 we saw that luxury commodities such as silk had no part to play in the determination of distribution. The silk price equation served the sole purpose of determining the price of silk in terms of corn. A similar distinction occurred in chapter 2 between commodities which did and did not enter the wage basket. In each case the distinction seemed to hinge on whether or not a commodity was a luxury good. But Sraffa's definition of a basic concerns its rôle as a means of production and there is no reason why wage commodities should not also be non-basic.

Suppose that, instead of being such luxury items as garden gnomes or silk, the group of non-basics includes essential goods like bread and clothing. It is, after all, quite likely that such goods should be in this category. It may even be that all, or a large proportion of wage commodities are non-basic. In that case, there would be little significance in a wage denominated in terms of basic commodities which had few representatives in the actual wage basket. But if, instead, we were to take the more sensible course of denominating the wage in terms of the actual wage basket, then it would no longer be true that the w–r relation is independent of the conditions of production of non-basics. If, for example, the wage were fixed as a quantity m_3 of commodity 3, the effect of an improvement in process 3 would be to reduce p_3 and also w $(= p_3 m_3)$. Although p_3 does not appear explicitly in the basic equations (6.7) and (6.8), w does. Thus r will rise (and basics prices will change) even though no changes have taken place in the basic sector. We may conclude from this example that the w–r relation in terms of the actual wage basket depends on the conditions of production of all commodities which enter, directly or indirectly, into the wage basket. This includes all basics (commodities 1 and 2 in the example) and it may also include some non-basics (commodity 3).

This problem is a direct result of Sraffa's decision to regard the entire wage as paid out of the surplus which, as he puts it 'involves relegating the necessaries of consumption to the limbo of non-basic products' (*PC*, p. 10). There is, as Sraffa notes, a 'more appropriate' method of dealing with the wage which avoids the difficulty of essential wage commodities being included among the set of non-basics. This involves splitting the wage into two: a 'necessary' part, consisting of the means of subsistence and which is advanced along with the means of production, and a 'surplus' part which represents the workers' share in the social surplus. But Sraffa prefers to avoid 'tampering with the traditional wage concept' (in which the entire wage is potentially variable), justifying his decision by the claim that his analysis 'can easily be adapted to the more appropriate, if unconventional, interpretation' (*PC*, p. 10). We shall follow Sraffa's procedure in subsequent chapters. However it will simplify matters greatly if we assume that all wage commodities are basic. This allows us to avoid explicit consideration of the price equations of non-basics.

6   A rehabilitation of classical distribution theory?

In the corn-ratio theory of chapter 1, given the wage as some amount of corn, the rate of profits is defined in purely physical terms as a ratio of quantities of corn. The conditions of production in other sectors do not matter for distribution, and the determination of relative prices comes after the question of distribution is settled. In order for the theory to hold corn must be a basic commodity and, indeed, it must be the *only* basic, for 'it is obvious that only one trade can be in the special position of not employing the products of other trades while all the others must employ *its* product as capital'.[4] The criticism of the theory was that it would be impossible to find such a process in which input and output consisted of the same commodity. (In Ricardo's *Principles*, the attempt to resolve distribution before prices hinged instead on the measurement of commodities in terms of quantities of embodied labour. But since the labour theory of value holds only under extremely restrictive conditions, that attempt was also unsuccessful.)

In Sraffa's own model, we have seen that the prices of non-basics also follow once the basic equations have been solved. This represents a partial restoration of classical theory. Many people have gone much further, arguing that Sraffa has overcome the fundamental objections to the corn-ratio theory by providing a single (composite) commodity, concocted from bits of the actual basic system, whose process has just those properties required of the corn process, namely, that inputs and outputs are homogeneous. Distribution can be settled in the Standard system without the need to know prices. But the rate of profits which in the Standard system corresponds to some wage (expressed in terms of Standard commodity) is the rate of profits which also obtains in the actual system at the same wage (similarly expressed). As Sraffa puts it: 'the actual system consists of the same basic equations as the Standard system, only in different proportions; so that, once the wage is given, the rate of profits is determined for both systems regardless of the proportions of the equations in either of them. Particular proportions, such as the Standard ones, may give transparency to a system and render visible what was hidden, but they cannot alter its mathematical properties' (*PC*, p. 23). The *w–r* relation, in terms of Standard commodity, is a particularly simple one: a straight line. Its use is not affected by the expression of wages in terms of some abstract and generally unknowable substance. So long as the *w–r* relation is drawn as a straight line it follows that the wage must be expressed in terms of Standard commodity. As Sraffa says 'it is curious that we should thus be enabled to use a standard without knowing what it consists of' (*PC*, p. 32).

These considerations have led a number of commentators to argue that Sraffa's construction completely vindicates the classical approach to distribution and value. Thus, according to Pasinetti, 'The most remarkable theoretical implication of this construction is to be found in the demonstration that it is possible to treat the distribution of income independently of prices and in the demonstration, moreover, that this possibility is not tied to the pure labour theory of value. It is at last possible to state rigorously that the short-comings of the classical pure labour theory of value or, indeed, even the abandonment of such a theory, leave quite unscathed the possibility of treating the distribution of income independently of prices' (1977, p. 120). This unqualified claim does, however, appear to be an overstatement, for two reasons. First, whatever their similarities, Sraffa's Standard system and the corn-model are not logically identical. In the latter, corn is both Standard commodity and the wage commodity, so that measuring the wage in terms of corn makes absolute sense. In Sraffa's own model, however, there is absolutely no reason why wages should be paid as Standard commodity. There is nothing to stop us measuring them in terms of Standard commodity, but it is not clear why a wage relation with wages measured in terms which may be quite unrelated to the wage basket is of especial interest. If the wage is consumed entirely as a quantity of commodity i then the w_i–r relation would seem to be of far greater interest. Secondly, insofar as a Standard wage is relevant, the independence of distribution and price determination is valid only in a very special and quite unrealistic circumstance, namely, where there is available only one process for producing each commodity. We shall see in chapter 8 that when there is available a choice of methods of production this independence breaks down. These considerations lead us to ask whether this independence, so clearly prized by Pasinetti and others, is such an important loss to modern theory. It is difficult to see why it should be. After all, Sraffa's own equations provide us with the means to solve the distributional and price problems simultaneously. The w–r relation in terms of the actual wage basket may not be as simple and elegant as the linear one in terms of Standard commodity, but it is not clear why simplicity and elegance should be of such overwhelming consideration. An analysis of relative prices and distribution can be made without the Standard commodity. Perhaps that is why Sraffa himself regarded it as a 'particular point' rather than a 'central proposition' of his work (PC, p. vi).

In that case, why spend so much time on the Standard commodity? In the first place, the issues just discussed occupy an important part of the literature and it is worth being clear about them. In the second, even if the Standard commodity is not essential it is still very helpful in understanding the properties of actual systems. Determining the conditions necessary for the simple and regular behaviour of the distributive variables helps us to see how the absence of those conditions leads to the more complex and irregular behaviour of variables in the actual system. For that reason, the Standard commodity crops up again in chapter 7, where it gives us a little extra insight into the nature of price changes resulting from a change in distribution.

7 Summary

If a system is capable of self-replacement without need of some commodities, those commodities are called non-basic. Basic commodities, on the other hand, are essential means of production in a self-replacing system. Basic processes are necessary under all circumstances to the determination of distribution and to the prices of both basics and non-basics. But when the wage is measured in terms of basic commodities, non-basics have no rôle to play in the determination of distribution nor in the price of basics. A particular self-replacing basic system is the Standard system in which aggregate inputs and aggregate outputs consist of the same composite commodity, the Standard commodity. Any actual basic system can be transformed into a Standard system by appropriately changing the intensities of operation of its processes. If wages are accounted in terms of Standard commodity the w–r relation of both the Standard and actual systems is a straight line. It is possible to settle distribution in these terms without reference to the price system.

FURTHER READING

Basics and non-basics are distinguished in chapter 2 of *PC*, and the Standard system discussed in chapters 4 and 5.

The Standard commodity has been used by many writers to help provide a rigorous reformulation of certain aspects of classical theory. For a general discussion, see Roncaglia (1978), chapter 4. In relation to certain aspects of Ricardo's work, including the search for an 'invariable measure of value', see also Bharadwaj (1963), Dobb (1973), chapter 9, Pasinetti (1977), chapter 5, and Sraffa himself, *PC*, p. 32 and p. 94. In relation to Marx's theory of value and exploitation, see Meek (1961), Medio (1972) and Eatwell (1975*b*).

The significance of Ricardo's distinction between necessities and luxuries was first rigorously established by Bortkiewicz (1952). Sraffa's own definition of basic commodities has been the subject of correspondence between him and P. Newman, published as an appendix to Bharadwaj (1970). Of particular importance in this correspondence is the question of 'self-reproducing' non-basics. Sraffa's original treatment of this subject is given in Appendix B to *PC*; theoretically more satisfactory is Pasinetti (1977), pp. 109–11.

See also readings listed in chapter 7.

7

Relative prices and the rate of profits

1 Introduction

In this chapter we examine in greater depth the relationships between the wage, the rate of profits and relative prices. First, the properties so far uncovered for the two-commodity system are generalised to the many-commodity case. We then try to see why it is that prices change with distribution and whether it is possible to say anything about the direction of these price changes. It is assumed throughout that the wage is measured in terms of a basic commodity, or a basket of such commodities. Since the basic system then has logical priority over the determination of distribution, only cursory consideration is given to the prices of non-basics.

2 The w–r relation with many commodities

Let us briefly remind ourselves of the price-distribution properties of the two-commodity system, listed in chapter 4, section 6:
(1) There is a negative relationship between w and r (for $w > 0$, and $r > 0$).
(2) r reaches a finite maximum, R, when $w = 0$.
(3) w reaches a finite maximum when $r = 0$.
(4) For r, $0 < r < R$, the price ratio varies with r, in general, but remains positive and finite.
(5) The shape of the w–r relation varies with the chosen standard of value.
(6) For a given standard the w–r relation is independent of the size of the outputs of the various processes.
We now see whether these properties remain valid for a k-commodity basic system, represented by the price equations

$$p_j = (1+r) \sum_i p_i a_{ij} + w l_j \qquad (i, j = 1, \ldots, k). \qquad (7.1)$$

It is most convenient to begin with property (4), concerning the behaviour of prices. It was shown in chapter 4, section 4 that when $r = 0$ the system of prices is logically equivalent to that of a subsistence economy: equations (7.1) above become equivalent to equations (3.7$'$). In chapter 3 we found that the subsistence economy prices are proportional to the ratios of labour directly and indirectly embodied in the commodities. Now, so long as labour is employed somewhere in the basic system, all basic commodities will embody some labour. It follows that when $r = 0$ all prices, being proportional to the positive quantities of labour embodied in them, are themselves positive. (In passing, we may note that the entire physical surplus goes to labour when $r = 0$. This surplus valued at positive prices yields a positive wage at $r = 0$. This is property (3), above.) Starting at this point Sraffa uses a simple and elegant argument to show that all prices must remain positive as r increases from zero, provided that w remains positive. As r is varied, relative prices change continuously,

> so that any p to become negative must go through zero. However, while wages and profits are positive, the price of no commodity can become zero until the price of at least one of the other commodities entering its means of production has become negative. Thus, since no p can become negative before any other, none can become negative at all (*PC*, pp. 27–8).

The possibility of a price becoming infinite is ruled out by similar reasoning. For if the price of any *basic* commodity were to become infinite relative to the other prices then, taking that same commodity as the standard of value, all other prices must become zero. But this cannot happen so long as w and r are positive, for the price of one component of the means of production of all commodities (namely the newly chosen standard) is positive. Hence the prices of all basics must be positive so long as w and r are also positive.

We have now established property (4) and, in the process, property (3). Property (2) follows directly: when $w = 0$ all of the physical surplus goes to profits. These, like the means of production, are valued at positive finite prices and so it follows that there is a maximum finite rate of profits, R, corresponding to a zero wage.

We now turn our attention to property (1) and, again, we can rely on Sraffa to provide the demonstration (*PC*, pp. 38–40). When the rate of profits rises prices change. (The nature and purpose of these changes is analysed in greater depth in the following sections.) Relative to some standard some prices may rise and some may fall. What Sraffa shows is that at no time will a price fall at a greater rate than the wage (expressed in terms of the same standard). In other words, the wage always falls at a faster rate than that of the fastest falling price. Consider the ith commodity: its price is made up of wage costs, profits and the prices of its means of production. To begin, suppose that the third element is constant. Then since profits are rising the wage must be falling more rapidly than p_i to maintain the balance of the price equation. The argument is equally valid if the third element, the value of the means of production, is rising in aggregate. But what happens if, in aggregate, the value of the means of production is falling? Well, then,

> it is sufficient to turn our attention to the product whose rate of fall exceeds that of all the others: this product, since it cannot have means of production which are capable of falling at a greater rate than it does, must itself fall less than the wage (*PC*, p. 39).

Thus the wage must fall more rapidly than any price. This means that, as *r* rises, the wage is capable of purchasing less of every commodity, so that it does not matter in which commodity we choose to express the wage: it falls in terms of them all. This is property (1).

On the other hand, the rate of fall will vary from commodity to commodity because prices change at different rates. Thus the shape of the *w–r* relation is dependent on the chosen standard: property (5). (When wages are measured in terms of Standard commodity, the *w–r* relation is, of course, a straight line.) Since relative prices can no longer be relied upon to behave monotonically, as in the two-commodity case, the resulting relation may take on a more complex appearance, as in fig. 7.3 below.

Only property (6) remains to be established and fortunately this is straightforward. The *w–r* relation can be regarded as a continuous set of solutions to equations (7.1), corresponding to the continuous variation of *r* between 0 and *R*. But equations (7.1) are 'unit' price equations which are completely independent of the size of the outputs of each industry. Multiplying each side of equations 7.1 by the corresponding output would leave the solution unaffected.

There does exist one further important property that has not yet been mentioned: the set of positive prices which is associated with any point on the *w–r* relation is unique. Of the more rigorous proofs of this proposition, Sraffa's (*PC*, chapter V) is probably the easiest. On an intuitive level, uniqueness is implied by the continuity of price variation starting from the unique set of positive prices at $r = 0$.

If there exists a set of unique positive prices for all basic commodities then, in most cases, there will also be unique positive prices for non-basics. Sraffa's argument, quoted above, concerning the possibility of a price becoming negative by passing through zero is just as applicable to non-basics. But it does leave open the possibility of a price becoming negative by passing through infinity. For non-basics which use only basic inputs this can be ruled out since the various components of price are themselves finite. But where non-basics are used in their own production this argument no longer holds and the uniqueness of the prices of these non-basics is not assured.[1]

3 Why prices change

The purpose of this section is to try to uncover the economic logic which underlies the solution to the system of equations (7.1). In particular, we wish to discover the economic significance of the changes in relative prices which occur as r and w change. Taken together, equations (7.1) define the w–r relation for the entire system of basic industries. If the rate of profits is given, at say r', the solution to (7.1) represents a point on the relation and to which corresponds a unique set of positive prices. Denote these by $p'_1, \dots, p'_k$. Now we know that as r changes from the given value r' the mathematical solution to (7.1) will not be consistent (in general) with these prices. But what we are going to do here is to try to hold these prices constant while leaving r potentially variable in order to see how the inconsistency works itself out.

We begin by inserting the prices $p'_1, \dots, p'_k$ into equations (7.1) and rearranging as follows:

$$w = \frac{p'_j}{l_j} - \frac{\sum_i a_{ij} p'_i}{l_j} - \frac{r \sum_i a_{ij} p'_i}{l_j} \qquad (i,j = 1, \dots, k). \qquad (7.2)$$

At the given solution-prices each of these equations describes a straight-line relationship between w and r for a particular industry. We refer to them as w–r *trade-offs*, each set of k trade-offs being specific to a particular set of solution prices. The most important property of each trade-off is its slope, $(-)\sum_i a_{ij} p_i / l_j$, which is the ratio of the value of means of production to labour in industry j or, for short, the capital:labour ratio in that industry. System (7.2) is a set of k linear equations. A solution to a set of simultaneous linear equations is depicted graphically by the common intersection of all the straight lines representing the individual equations. Although there are only two unknowns in (7.2), w and r, it is nevertheless the case that the lines have a common intersection – and hence a unique solution – at r', for that is where we began (see fig. 7.1).

Consider now two distinct possibilities concerning the set of w–r trade-offs. The first is that *all* industries have the same capital:labour ratios. Then, at the set of prices $p'_1, \dots, p'_k$ the individual w–r trade-offs in (7.2) have the same slopes and, since they must pass through the same point on the w–r relation, they coincide (fig. 7.2). This means that they have an infinite number of intersections and they therefore provide solution prices $p'_1, \dots, p'_k$ to an infinite set of values for r, including r'. Since for any rate of profits the associated prices are unique, the w–r relation must be a straight line and relative prices must be constant. This rather special possibility will be considered further in section 6.

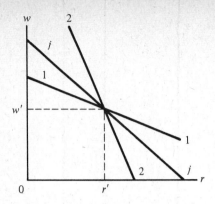

Figure 7.1

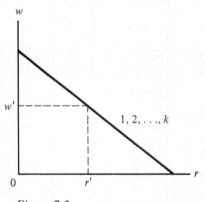

Figure 7.2

This is the only case in which prices remain unchanged at different points on the w–r relation, for now consider the second possibility: that at least one process has a capital:labour ratio different from the other processes. Then for the given set of prices the slopes and intercepts of at least two trade-offs are different which means that their intersection is unique. These prices are, therefore, uniquely associated with a single point on the w–r relation, and at any other point on the relation there prevails a different set of prices.

Our discussion has now brought us to Sraffa's distinction between 'deficit' and 'surplus' industries (*PC*, p. 13). The former are those industries or processes having relatively high capital:labour ratios at a given level of r and w, and the latter those industries having relatively low ratios. (The ratios are defined to be high or low relative to an imaginary 'watershed' industry to be discussed in section 5.) In other words, deficit industries are those whose

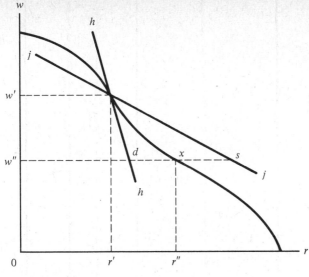

Figure 7.3

straight-line trade-offs have a relatively large (absolute) slope, surplus industries those having a relatively small slope, at the set of prices prevailing at a
given rate of profits.

   In fig. 7.3, the trade-offs are drawn for a deficit industry h and a surplus
industry j. Consider a move along the w–r relation from the initial point
$w'r'$ to $w''r''$, and suppose, to begin, that this move could be completed without any change in relative prices. It follows that the trade-offs for h and j are
fixed. With a reduction in the wage from w' to w'' at a constant set of prices,
after payment of the wage at the *new* rate, deficit industries do not have
sufficient value of net output to make profits payments at the new general
rate r''. That is, they have a deficit on their profits payments. Thus industry h
is able to pay profit at the rate of only $w''d$ and is in deficit by the amount
dx. (Alternatively, if such industries pay the full rate of profits they have a
deficit on their wages payment.) On the other hand, surplus industries have
more than sufficient value of net output to pay both the wage and profits
at the new general rate. Thus, after payment of the wage at a rate w'' and
profits at the rate r'' industry j is left with a surplus sx.

   The point which Sraffa makes is that, in order to remove the deficits and
surpluses the fixity of prices cannot be maintained. The positions and slopes
of the w–r trade-offs must be altered so that they now intersect at the point
x with all industries receiving profits at the uniform rate r'' while paying a
common wage rate w''. To accomplish this relative prices must change. The

entire rationale of such changes is, therefore, to sustain the uniformity of w and r dictated by the competitive tendencies of the system.

4 The nature of price changes

We have seen that the purpose of changes in relative prices is to remove the potential deficits and surpluses which would arise as a consequence of changes in w and r. But what form do these changes take? Intuitively it might be supposed that with a rise in r it would be necessary for the prices of deficit commodities to rise relative to the aggregate value of their means of production. On the face of it this would increase the profitability of these industries thus removing the deficit. Similarly, it might be expected that the prices of surplus commodities should fall relative to their means of production. It turns out, however, that this intuition is misleading.

Consider, for example, the group of potential deficit commodities. Many of these may have prices which, following our intuition, do indeed rise with r. But it does not follow that they must all do so. Single out one commodity, call it h, from this group and compare the price of h with those of its means of production (prices being measured in terms of an arbitrary standard). Now the price of h *may* rise in terms of the standard but, if its means of production are made up predominantly of other deficit commodities, the value of the latter may rise even more. Thus the price of h relative to its means of production will have fallen. Where then do the increased profits come from if industry h is to pay the general rate? The answer is that it must come from the increase in p_h relative to the wage.

Consider now a second deficit commodity, g, which has a higher capital:labour ratio than that of h (and, therefore, a higher potential deficit). Can we say that p_g must rise relative to p_h? The answer, again, is 'no', for it depends on the composition of the respective means of production. If process g is dominated by surplus commodities while process h is dominated by deficit commodities it is possible that p_g/p_h will fall. Even if g and h were respectively deficit and surplus commodities again we could not be sure how their relative prices would vary. It depends, as before, on the composition of the means of production. But we cannot even stop there, for the behaviour of the prices of the means of production depends on their means of production, and so on.

We see then that not only may a deficit commodity fall in price relative to its means of production but it may also fall in price relative to other deficit commodities or even relative to surplus commodities. But,

> However complex the pattern of the price-variations arising from a change in distribution, their net result, and their complete justification, remains the simple one of redressing the balance in each industry (*PC*, p.15).

There is one case in which the adjustment which conforms to intuition is correct: namely where there are just two basic commodities. In this case we must have one deficit and one surplus commodity, so that the deficit commodity cannot have in its means of production other commodities with greater potential deficits. Thus a rise in the price of the deficit relative to that of the surplus commodity is the only way a uniform rate of profits can be restored. It follows that in a two-commodity system the price ratio is monotonically related to the rate of profits.[2]

5 The 'watershed' industry

Consider a commodity, f, having the property that its price relative to the value of its aggregate means of production does not change with changes in r, while ruling out the possibility that the prices of *all* commodities are the same at different rates of profits (requiring equal capital:labour ratios in all processes). Taking the unit net output of process f as the standard of value,

$$p_f - \sum_i a_{if} p_i = 1 \qquad (7.3)$$

then p_f is invariant with respect to a change in r if the value of its means of production is also unchanging. By the same token, if the composite commodity consisting of the a_{if} is to remain constant in value, then so must the value of *its* means of production, and so on, for each successive layer of means of production without limit.

Of course, if the value of the means of production of a commodity does not vary then neither does the capital:labour ratio of its process. A process having such a property possesses what Sraffa calls a 'critical' or 'balancing' proportion of means of production to labour (*PC*, p.16) representing a watershed between deficit and surplus industries. If the quantity of labour in the system is defined such that one unit is employed in producing a unit of commodity f (that is, $l_f = 1$), then the trade-off for that 'watershed process' is

$$w = p_f - \sum_i a_{if} p_i - r \sum_i a_{if} p_i$$

or, from (7.3),

$$w = 1 - r \sum_i a_{if} p_i. \qquad (7.4)$$

Since $\sum_i a_{if} p_i$ does not vary with variations in w and r, the trade-off (7.4) is a straight line having constant slope and constant intercept ($= 1$) on the w-axis, no matter how much the prices of other commodities may change. Moreover since the $w-r$ relation, for the entire system, is defined as the locus of the intersections of the trade-offs for all processes at continuously varying prices, the *w–r relation is also a straight line* whenever the standard of value is taken to be the watershed commodity or its net product. Dividing (7.4) by $\Sigma_i\, a_{if} p_i$ and re-arranging gives the equation of the *w–r* relation as

$$r = (1/\sum_i a_{if} p_i)(1-w) = R(1-w)$$

where R, the maximum rate of profits is equal to the ratio of net output to means of production in process f.

It may be emphasised that a straight-line *w–r* relation only arises if the watershed commodity is taken as the standard of value. If some other commodity, j say, is taken as the standard then variations in w and r would give rise to variations in p_f and $\Sigma_i\, a_{if} p_i$ relative to the price of j, and the position of the trade-off for process f would not be invariant with respect to such changes.

In any actual system it would be difficult to conceive of any one commodity having the properties required of a watershed commodity. But what about the possibility of constructing a composite commodity with these properties from bits of actual commodities? The crucial requirement is that the ratio of the value of its net product to means of production is invariant with respect to movements in w and r. That, of course, is precisely the property of the Standard commodity. The Standard system is simply a grand, fictional watershed industry.

6 The special case of equal capital : labour ratios

Only in the case illustrated in fig. 7.2, in which all industries have the same capital : labour ratios, are the deficits and surpluses of all processes necessarily zero. This is because, for any decrease in the wage, each industry, having the same ratio of capital to labour, saves just a sufficient amount on wage payments to pay the additional profits, and maintain a common rate of profits, without need of a change in relative prices (PC, pp.12–13).[3] It may be readily demonstrated that for this case prices are proportional to direct labour ratios: since all the *w–r* trade-offs coincide, the intercept terms in (7.2) must be equal:

$$\frac{p_j'}{l_j} - \frac{\sum\limits_i a_{ij} p_i'}{l_j} = \frac{p_h'}{l_h} - \frac{\sum\limits_i a_{ih} p_i'}{l_h} \qquad (i,j,h = 1,\ldots,k).$$

The second terms on each side of this equation are also equal to the slopes of the respective trade-offs which, being the same, may be cancelled to leave

$$p_j'/p_h' = l_j/l_h$$

This case has two characteristics. The first is that relative prices do not vary with the rate of profits and the second is that the $w-r$ relation is a straight line. The second property is shared with any system in which wages are measured in terms of a watershed commodity such as the Standard commodity. The first property, however, is unique. This is the only case in which the wage frontier, $\beta_1\beta_2$, in the 'vector diagrams', moves in a parallel fashion as r varies.

7 Summary

The Standard system is one in which inputs and outputs are effectively homogeneous. As a result the price of the Standard commodity cannot change relative to its own means of production; as the general rate of profits increases just enough is released from the payment of wages to pay the new higher rate without need of a price change. The prices of actual commodities, however, must vary if a uniform rate of profits is to be maintained throughout the system. This is their one and only justification. In general the pattern of price variation is a complex one and, except in very special cases, nothing *a priori* can be said about it.

FURTHER READING

The discussions of this chapter relate to what may be regarded as the core of Sraffa's analysis of single-products systems: chapter III of *PC*. The references cited in the preface are relevant here, but readings beyond this level almost inevitably take us into the realm of mathematics. An important early article is Newman (1962) which provided the first mathematically rigorous formulation of Sraffa's single-products system. Attention should also be drawn to the independent work of Schwartz (1961) which contains a mathematical presentation of an economic model which is, in all essentials, the same as Sraffa's. More recent texts include Abraham-Frois and Berrebi (1979), Walsh and Gram (1980), chapter 13, and Pasinetti (1977), chapter 5, of which the latter is most strongly recommended.

The 'complex pattern of price variations' resulting from a change in distribution is often referred to as the 'Wicksell effect' after Wicksell (1934); see Harcourt (1972), chapter 1.

(The analysis of section 3 of this chapter draws heavily on Mainwaring (1976).)

8

Many techniques

1 Introduction

So far in Part II, it has been assumed that there is available to the economy only one method of producing each commodity. Since a *technique* of production is defined as a combination of methods for producing the k commodities, it has, in other words, been assumed that there is just a single technique. It would, however, be unrealistic to suppose that the technical knowledge in a modern capitalist economy is so limited that only one feasible method is available to produce each commodity. To take one example, the conversion of iron into steel can be achieved using open hearth furnaces, electric furnaces, Bessemer converters or modern oxygen converters (and, no doubt, by many other methods). As soon as we admit the possibility of even a few commodities having available a small number of alternative processes, the number of process combinations, or techniques, becomes very large. We could go to the opposite extreme and suppose that the a_{ij} coefficients are continuously variable so that, in effect, there are an infinite number of techniques. This is the way in which production possibilities are often represented in neoclassical theory. Although this way of looking at production can be regarded as a special case of the following analysis we shall not pursue it in any positive fashion. Bessemer converters and open hearth furnaces are not points on a continuous multidimensional spectrum, incorporating more or less firebricks, more or less oxygen, etc. It is true that certain proportions can be varied: labour can put in overtime or work more intensively. But we regard such variations as akin to variations in market supply and market prices which take place in the short period. The a_{ij} coefficients, on the other hand, represent the design blueprints: the technically efficient proportions given current practices concerning the length of the working day, and so on. They may thus be considered as 'normal' coefficients, underlying the natural or long-period prices.

2 A two-commodity, two-technique economy

We begin with the relatively simple case in which one of the two (basic) commodities has two feasible methods of production. Conferring

80

this honour upon commodity 2, we denote the alternative sets of coefficients by (a_{12}, a_{22}, l_2^a) for method a and (b_{12}, b_{22}, l_2^b) for method b. The two commodities can now be produced by combining process 1 either with method a or with method b, which means that there are now two techniques, called α and β, respectively. To each of these techniques (taken on its own) there corresponds a w–r relation having all the properties described in chapter 7, section 2. Of course, the two relations will not have exactly the same properties because they are, after all, based on different sets of coefficients. But they will both be downward sloping and they will both have maximum finite values for the wage and rate of profits. In fig. 8.1 the two relations are superimposed. This requires that wages be expressed in terms of the same unit. We let commodity 2 perform this function and denote the wage by w_2, accordingly. It is assumed that the relations intersect one another in the positive quadrant.

Suppose now that the wage (in terms of 2) is the exogenously given distributive variable and consider the capitalists' reactions to exogenous

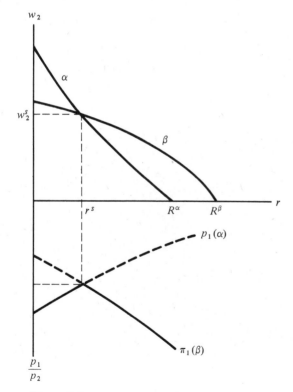

Figure 8.1

variations in w_2. Clearly, so long as $w_2 > w_2^s$, in fig. 8.1, capitalists will prefer to use technique α for this yields a higher return than β. Similarly, for $w_2 < w_2^s$, β is the preferred technique. That technique is chosen whose w–r relation happens to form the outer boundary of the relations at the given level of w_2. The same result would be obtained if, instead, r were given exogenously. At $r < r^s$, technique α is more 'profitable'. This will not manifest itself in a higher rate of profits since that, of course, is given. But capitalists using α will be able to offer higher wages than those using β and competition between workers will ensure that those capitalists who persist with β will go out of business. As r rises above r^s then β takes over as the most profitable technique. Indeed, if $r > R^\alpha$, α is no longer a feasible method of production, but β can continue to pay positive wages up to R^β. Once again we see that it is the outer boundary which tells us which technique is adopted. This boundary we refer to as the w–r *frontier*.

It would be natural now to ask: what happens when $w_2 = w_2^s$ (or $r = r^s$)? This combination of r and w_2 is referred to as a *switch-point*. At a switch-point the two techniques are equiprofitable and can co-exist. If this is so it is necessary that they pay not only the same wages and rate of profts, but also generate the same set of prices. For, if α produced (say) commodity 1 at a higher price than did β, then no-one would buy the product of α and α-capitalists would go out of business. This, in itself, implies that equiprofitable techniques generate the same prices, and this can easily be checked by inspecting the price equations of the two techniques. To avoid using too many superscripts, we denote β-prices by π_i. At the switch-point then, we have (remembering that commodity 2 is *numéraire*),

$$p_1^s = (1 + r^s)(p_1^s a_{11} + a_{21}) + w_2^s l_1 \left.\right\}_{\alpha} \tag{8.1}$$

$$1 = (1 + r^s)(p_1^s a_{12} + a_{22}) + w_2^s l_2^a \left.\right\} \tag{8.2}$$

$$\pi_1^s = (1 + r^s)(\pi_1^s a_{11} + a_{21}) + w_2^s l_1 \left.\right\}_{\beta} \tag{8.3}$$

$$1 = (1 + r^s)(\pi_1^s b_{12} + b_{22}) + w_2^s l_2^b \left.\right\} \tag{8.4}$$

Comparing (8.1) and (8.3) we see that they are identical except that p_1^s is replaced by π_1^s. These prices must, therefore, have the same switch-point solution values. The p_1–r and π_1–r relations are shown in the lower quadrant of fig. 8.1.

3 More than two techniques

There may, of course, be more than two methods for producing commodity 2, as well as alternatives for producing commodity 1. As additional methods are introduced the possible combinations rapidly increase. We must now see whether our previous conclusions apply when more than two techniques are available. This is not a straightforward matter of extending the pair-wise comparisons, for our previous analysis compared techniques which, by assumption, differed in only one method. Fortunately this assumption can be shown to be a necessary outcome of the competitive process.

This proposition can be understood as follows. We noted earlier that, at a switch-point, prices must be the same for both techniques, that is $p_i^s = \pi_i^s$. At a switch-point, then, there are three unknowns to be determined: w_2^s, r^s and p_1^s. If techniques differ in one method there will be three equations to determine these unknowns: that of the shared process and one for each of the alternative processes. But if techniques differ in both methods there are four equations and the system is over-determined.[1] This inconsistency will be removed by competitive forces, by making one of the four methods unprofitable.

Since it is the case that 'adjacent' techniques differ in only one method then our previous analysis can be applied to a pair at a time. Thus our conclusions hold even when a large number of techniques exist. Thus, in fig. 8.2, the four techniques may be made up as follows: $\alpha = (1a, 2a)$, $\beta = (1a, 2b)$, $\gamma = (1b, 2b)$, $\delta = (1b, 2a)$. Moving along the frontier, one process changes at a time. Of course, there is an intersection between the α and γ w–r relations, but this intersection lies below the frontier and does not represent a viable price system. It is sometimes referred to as a 'false' switch-point. Technique δ has w–r possibilities lying wholly within the frontier and it does not come into consideration at any rate of profits.

4 More than two commodities

The generalisation to many basic commodities is straightforward. The conditions of equal profitability again imply that, at a switch-point, relative prices are the same for both techniques. At a switch-point there will be $k + 1$ unknowns to be determined ($k - 1$ relative prices, r^s and w_i^s) which requires there to be $k + 1$ processes. This is only satisfied if there are $k - 1$ common processes and one process specific to each technique. It follows, therefore, that adjacent techniques differ in only one method. Once that is established then the previous arguments conducted for a two-commodity economy can be repeated for the k-commodity case.

Since only the k basic processes are relevant to the determination of the w–r relation for each technique, it follows that changes in the methods of producing non-basics do not affect the profitability ranking of techniques, the position of switch-points, or any other properties of the w–r frontier. Even if a commodity h is basic with one technique but non-basic with

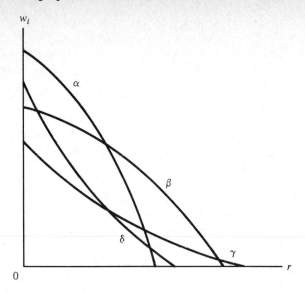

Figure 8.2

another, the change in its status must be due to a change in the method of producing a *basic* commodity which now no longer uses h. (There is, of course, no reason why $k^\alpha = k^\beta$.) This involves no significant changes to our arguments and we shall not pursue the matter any further.

5 The standard of value

The comparison between techniques has taken place on the basis that wages and prices are expressed in terms of some arbitrary standard of value. Choosing another commodity as standard would, of course, mean that there is now a different measure on the w-axis. The precise shape of the w–r relations would change but, as we know, the maximum rate of profits for each would be the same. It is possible to show that the ordering of profitability of techniques is independent of the chosen standard which, in turn, implies that the positions of switch-points along the r-axis are the same.

Consider a change of technique at some given value of r (not necessarily a switch-point). Call the (basic) process whose method has changed, process h. To see the effect on the wage in terms of any commodity, put $w = 1$ in the system of price equations; that is, do not choose a commodity standard of value but let a unit of labour act as the standard.[2] We shall suppose that as a result of the change in methods the price of *h* falls. It necessarily follows that the prices of all other commodities also fall. For *h*, being basic, enters directly or indirectly into all other processes; directly or indirectly the value of the means of production of each process falls, as, therefore, do their prices. This means that the purchasing power of the wage in terms of any commodity rises.

A similar argument holds where the price of *h* increases (the wage in terms of any commodity falling) or where, at a switch-point, the price of *h* remains the same. Thus no matter which commodity is used as a measure of wages, one technique is always unambiguously more profitable, except at a switch-point when two techniques are equiprofitable and may co-exist.

This discussion has important implications for the rôle of the Standard commodity. The Standard proportions of technique α depend on the coefficients of that technique and these coefficients must differ in some respect from those of β. A Standard commodity therefore exists for each technique. A linear *w–r* relation (with its associated *R*-value) corresponds to a given Standard commodity only so long as its associated technique is in operation. The Standard commodity of technique α is just another variable standard when used with any other technique. This means that the classical view that the entire problem of distribution can be settled prior to the determination of prices is no longer sustainable. While we can still specify either the real wage or the rate of profits exogenously, it is no longer true that they can both be known in advance of price determination. Once we admit a multiplicity of techniques then prices, distribution and the choice of technique have to be resolved simultaneously.

6 Technological progress

The fact that, switch-points apart, one technique is always the most profitable might be thought to imply that technical change only occurs at switch-points, the result of a change in an exogenous distributive variable. But changes away from switch-points can occur as a result of technological progress. Suppose that at an exogenously given natural rate of profits, and the corresponding natural prices, an invention reduces the cost of producing commodity *h*. The first capitalists to adopt the new method can earn a rate of profit higher than the natural rate by selling at a *market* price equal to the initial natural price. This attracts other capitalists to the new method until the market price falls to the new natural level, and the rate of profit for each producer is restored to its natural value. In the process wages, in terms of any commodity, will have risen. Similarly, if the wage is fixed, in terms of any commodity, a technological improvement will lead to an increase in the natural rate of profits. In either case it is the prospect of 'super-natural'

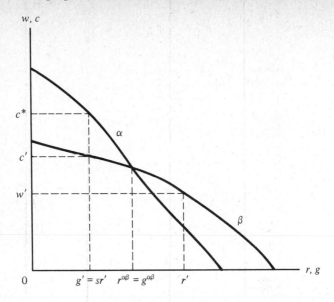

Figure 8.3

profits that induces producers to adopt new techniques. But under competitive conditions these profits exist only in the short period and are the cause of their own elimination.

7 The Golden Rule of Accumulation

For each technique there exists not only a w–r relation but also a relation between consumption p.w. and the rate of growth. If we let a fixed consumption basket act as standard of value then there is complete duality between the w–r and c–g relations. Thus a rate of profits which marks a switch-point between two w–r relations is equal to a rate of growth which marks a switch-point between two c–g relations. An example with two techniques is shown in fig. 8.3. The diagram needs careful interpretation. Consider a particular rate of profits, r'. The most profitable technique at this rate is β and that, therefore, is the technique that is chosen. If the Cambridge equation holds, the growth rate is given by $g' = sr'$. The highest consumption p.w. that can be attained at this growth rate is c^*, but this involves the use of technique α. Since, in fact, profitability considerations have already led to the choice of β, the actual level of consumption p.w. is somewhat lower, at c'. When looking at the c–g possibilities it is essential to check first which technique is in operation.

This discussion has yielded an interesting conclusion. If the rate of profits and the rate of growth are not equal then we cannot be sure that the level of consumption p.w. is the highest attainable at the prevailing growth rate. In the diagram, a switch to technique α, although less profitable, would give a higher level of consumption p.w. We can therefore state the following: in general, the choice of technique criterion, 'maximise c for given g', is not the same as the criterion, 'maximise w for given r'. In a competitive capitalist economy it is the latter criterion which prevails (though in planned economies the former may). There are, however, certain conditions in which the two criteria give the same result. A sufficient condition is that $r = g$ (which on our savings assumptions implies $s = 1$). This condition is known as the *Golden Rule of Accumulation*. It is not, however, a necessary condition, as can be seen by the fact that for any $g > g^{\alpha\beta}$ the two criteria will lead to the same choice of technique.

If it is deemed that the first of the two criteria is the more significant then there is a sense in which a competitive solution to the choice of technique may involve waste, specifically the loss of consumption equal to $c^* - c'$. The class, and therefore ideological, implications of this depend on the determinants of distribution. If, for example, w were fixed then the loss is borne entirely by capitalists. But if g were fixed then satisfaction of the Golden Rule would yield a higher wage ($w = c^*$). The policy implication of the Golden Rule is that the first criterion can be satisfied in a way which also satisfies competitive pricing if g and r can be bought into line by operating on their determinants. The consequences of implementing such a policy generally favour the working class. If, say, g is unalterable, bringing r into line gives the benefit of increased consumption entirely to the workers. If r is unalterable, raising g also means a loss of consumption to capitalists but in return they are able to accumulate at a faster rate. This faster growth may also benefit the working class.

8 The critique of naive neoclassical theory

In certain simple versions of neoclassical theory, capital is considered as a 'factor of production' on the same footing as the primary factors land and labour. If commodities are produced by these factors then their prices are determined by the relative intensities with which they employ the factors, the relative scarcities of the factors, and the relative demands for the commodities. But if capital scarcity is to be a determinant of relative prices then it is necessary that capital be quantifiable prior to the determination. It should already be clear that such an assumption would be very restrictive, being applicable only to cases in which capital consists of a single homogeneous commodity. Where capital consists of more than one commodity it can only be measured in value terms, that is, once prices are determined.

In these simple versions of neoclassical theory, the opportunity cost or scarcity price of capital is governed by the rate of interest, generally regarded as the 'reward' for saving, or the abstention from present consumption. Competition has the effect of ensuring that no firm earns 'super-normal' profits and this means that, in equilibrium, the rate of profits is the same as the rate of interest. If the prices are to be determined in terms of the supply of and (derived) demand for factors, it is important that there exists a 'well-behaved' (in neoclassical terms) demand curve for capital: as the scarcity price of capital increases there should be a continuous substitution to less capital-intensive techniques. This idea of continuous substitution in response to relative factor prices is captured in the notion of an 'aggregate production function'.

We have already noted that 'aggregate capital' is a meaningful concept only in a one-capital-good world. Despite this it was nevertheless thought that a fundamental proposition derived from this simple model was of general validity. Even in many-capital-goods models, as the r/w ratio increased there was thought to follow a monotonic variation in (value) capital intensity: successive techniques having lower capital : labour ratios. We shall now see whether this proposition really does carry over to the general case.

Suppose, for the sake of simplicity, that the duality conditions hold and, to make things simpler still, that $g = 0$. Recall, from chapter 5, section 5, that the value of capital p.w. in the economy may be measured by drawing a

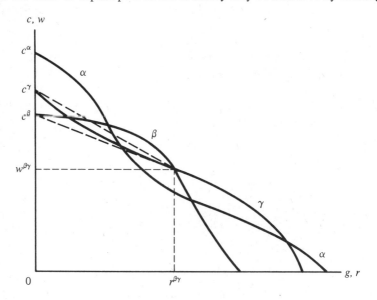

Figure 8.4

straight line through the r/w and c/g combinations on the dual relations. In fig. 8.4, by drawing a straight line from c^α to each point on α's w–r relation, the value of capital p.w. (or capital:labour ratio) corresponding to each rate of profits may be determined for that technique. The same may be done for each other technique. Thus, at the rate of profits $r^{\beta\gamma}$, the capital: labour ratio using technique γ is greater than the capital:labour ratio using technique β.

It can be seen that technique α makes two appearances on the w–r frontier, a phenomenon known as *reswitching*. That a technique may be profitable at low rates of profits, fall out of favour at intermediate rates, but return at high rates, seems contrary to any expectation based on the simple neoclassical proposition. Even if allowance is made for changes in the value of α's capital as we move along its w–r relation, it is still the case that α is more capital-intensive in either of its profitable ranges than either β or γ in theirs. While reswitching is sufficient to invalidate the simple neoclassical proposition it is by no means necessary. Even if α did not appear on the frontier a second time there would still be a clear case of *capital reversing* – an increase in the capital:labour ratio in response to an increase in the rate of profits – as capitalists switched from β to γ.

These findings undermine the simple neoclassical theories employing the notion of 'aggregate capital'. It is important, however, to stress that there is, in Sraffa, no *logical* basis for a critique of sophisticated neoclassical theory based on the work of Arrow, Debreu and McKenzie. The relationship between Sraffa and modern 'General Equilibrium' theory is discussed in chapter 13.

9 Summary

The fundamental properties of the general relationship between the wage and the rate of profits are not significantly affected by the existence of a choice of technique. The w–r frontier, although made up of segments of individual w–r relations, has properties very similar to its component parts. In particular, the inverse relationship is maintained. There is, however, one inescapable casualty. Since the Standard commodity is no longer unique, its use in determining distribution independently of prices is no longer possible.

The existence of many techniques may give rise to conflicting choice criteria. The competitive profitability criterion may lead to the adoption of a technique which, at the prevailing growth rate, fails to maximise the level of consumption p.w. The conflict can be resolved by pursuing the Golden Rule of equalising r and g. Finally, the belief, based on the naive neoclassical theory of capital, that an increase in the r/w ratio leads to a substitution in favour of more labour-intensive techniques may be shown to be inapplicable to a world of many capital goods.

FURTHER READING

Sraffa discusses choice of technique in Part II of *PC*. One of the best general accounts of the subject is Pasinetti (1977), chapter 6. This chapter is not as technical as the rest of the book. See also, Walsh and Gram (1980), chapter 15. A rigorous proof that adjacent techniques normally differ in only one method is given by Bruno *et al* (1966).

On technical change in this type of model see Rymes (1971). Useful insights are also contained in Schefold (1976), or (1980*a*) Part III. This is mainly concerned with fixed-capital systems but parts of it are also relevant to simpler cases.

The Golden Rule of Accumulation was discovered (in the context of the neoclassical model) by Phelps (1961). See also, Spaventa (1970) and Nuti (1970*a*). The latter article contains an excellent discussion of some of the ideological implications of the Golden Rule. Schefold (1980*a*) is also of interest on this; although generally a technically advanced article, the discussion on pp. 183–7 is reasonably accessible.

The simple neoclassical theory referred to in this chapter is associated with the names of Jevons (1871), Böhm-Bawerk (1891), J. B. Clark (1899) and Wicksell (1934). The critique of this theory has its roots in an article by Robinson (1953) and was given added impetus by the publication of *PC*; see, especially, chapter VI. The best account of its development is Harcourt (1972). Collections of articles relating to this debate are Harcourt and Laing (1971) and Hunt and Schwartz (1972). In the former, see especially Samuelson (1966), and in the latter, Garegnani (1970).

9

An application to international trade

1 Introduction

So far we have been concerned entirely with the distribution of net output between classes and between uses within a closed economy. This chapter is a digression from that theme and is intended to be illustrative of the possibilities of extending the Sraffa–Leontief analysis in various directions. We shall try to show how some of the concepts developed in the preceding chapters can be used to provide a theory of the causes and consequences of trade between countries. But first we shall give a brief account of Ricardo's theory of international trade and discuss some of its limitations. This should make understanding of the subsequent sections a little easier.

2 Ricardo's theory

It is in Ricardo that we find the first rigorous theory of international trade.[1] In chapter 7 of the *Principles*, titled 'On Foreign Trade', he explains the principle of 'comparative advantage' which subsequently became the centrepiece of modern neoclassical trade theory.

We saw in chapter 2 that Ricardo believed that relative prices depend primarily on the relative quantities of labour required in the production of commodities. Although he recognised that price ratios would depart from ratios of labours embodied, it is clear that he regarded any such modification to be of little significance. As a result, in those parts of the book where value theory is applied it is the pure labour theory that is used. In the pure labour theory of value it is not possible for one technique to generate diffcrent prices through differences in income distribution. Thus, ignoring the costs of land and other natural resources, and assuming that labour is everywhere of the same quality, the implication of Ricardo's approach is that between any two closed economies relative prices can differ only if their techniques of production differ; that is, only if different quantities of labour are required (as the result of, say, climatic differences) in the production of one or more commodities.

Thus, two economies A and B each capable of producing two commodities 1 and 2 will trade with each other only if their closed-economy or 'autarkic' price ratios differ. In the context of the model of chapter 2, suppose that in autarky

$$\frac{p_{1a}}{p_{2a}} \left(= \frac{l_{1a}}{l_{2a}} \right) < \frac{p_{1b}}{p_{2b}} \left(= \frac{l_{1b}}{l_{2b}} \right)$$

Relative to commodity 2, commodity 1 is cheaper in A than in B. Those who wish to dispose of commodity 2 in exchange for commodity 1 will, therefore, get a better deal by buying 1 from producers in A. By the same token, everyone will want to buy commodity 2 from B's producers. And so, in the absence of any intervention by governments, trade will occur. It is, of course, necessary that the difference in prices is not absorbed by the costs of transport and in the rest of this chapter we shall assume, for simplicity, that transport costs are zero. (The term 'comparative advantage' refers to the fact that only the ratios of labour coefficients need differ for trade to occur and not, as was earlier supposed, for the absolute coefficients to differ. That is, it is not necessary that $l_{1a} < l_{1b}$ and $l_{2b} < l_{2a}$. That this is so may seem obvious to anyone used to thinking in terms of relative prices, but in Ricardo's time it was a major insight.)

If constant returns prevail, so that the price ratio is not affected by the scale of the output, it will, potentially, be to the advantage of purchasers if country A concentrated all its labour in producing commodity 1, where it is more productive, and country B all its labour in producing 2. It is the relative price signals which indicate to capitalists that this pattern of specialisation is the most profitable. (Whether or not the two countries can specialise in this way may, however, depend on their relative sizes. If, say, B is relatively very small it may not be able to supply the two countries' requirements of commodity 2 on its own. But in what follows we shall assume that both countries can specialise fully.) Whether the potential advantage can be realised for *all* purchasers depends on the other assumptions of the model. Quite clearly, if, as Ricardo assumes, the real wage is fixed then there is no benefit to workers in employment. Potential gains to wages are lost through competition for employment and passed on to the capitalists in the form of a higher rate of profits. To see this consider what happens in country A as a result of a switch from a closed to a trading economy.

Under autarky, the country produces both commodities itself at the following prices (we shall drop the 'a' subscripts):

$$p_1 = wl_1(1 + r)$$

$$p_2 = wl_2(1 + r).$$

The wage, we suppose, is a fixed basket (m_1, m_2), so that

$$w = p_1 m_1 + p_2 m_2.$$

We could obtain an expression for the rate of profits by re-arranging either of the two price equations (having first substituted for w) – it would not matter which we choose. But in a trading economy specialised in the production of commodity 1 only the first price equation is relevant. When re-arranged it gives

$$r = \frac{p_1}{(p_1 m_1 + p_2 m_2)l_1} - 1,$$

an expression which applies to both the autarkic and trading regimes. The only difference is that the ratio p_1/p_2 is greater with trade than without it. (A unit of 1 can buy more of 2.) As a result the rate of profits will be greater with trade than without. An exactly symmetrical arguments holds for country B.

It is in this sense that we may say there is a 'gain from trade'. The workers are no worse off but capitalists realise a greater rate of profits.[2] Whether these gains are consumed or invested is another matter. Ricardo, it is probably fair to say, would have regarded an increase in the rate of profits as having a favourable and significant effect on the rate of accumulation. Indeed, his theory of international trade can be regarded as the intellectual underpinnings of his advocacy of the abolition of the British Corn Laws which imposed duties on the importation of cheaper foreign corn. His case against the Corn Laws was that cheaper corn would allow more profits and greater growth. Thus, although Ricardo overlooked the possibility that income distribution could be a causative factor in international trade he most certainly was aware that trade could have consequences for income distribution and, in turn, for the dynamic behaviour of the economy. The typical modern international economics textbook which reports Ricardo as having demonstrated that trade increases the general consumption possibilities of participating countries, and nothing more, does him a serious injustice.

What changes do we need to make to Ricardo's theory if we drop the labour theory of value? Most obviously, since prices may now vary with income distribution, it is no longer necessary for countries to have different techniques to engage in mutually profitable trade. But the consequences go much further than that. Since price ratios are no longer equal to the ratios of labours embodied it is possible that they no longer reflect the comparative labour costs of producing the commodities. The pattern of specialisation implied by relative labour ratios may be reversed as a result of the deviations of p_1/p_2 from l_1/l_2 in each country. Although purchasers still get one commodity relatively more cheaply from abroad and capitalists still get a higher rate of profits, the specialisation in the process in which labour is relatively *un*productive makes the economy in some broader sense worse off. This is a situation similar to that discussed in section 7 of chapter 8, on the Golden Rule of Accumulation. That is to say, the use of the profitability criterion may lead to the choice of an alternative which would be rejected on the basis of some other, perhaps more fundamental, criterion. We shall, in fact, see in the following sections that the choice of the pattern of specialisation is merely a particular case of the general choice of technique, and that a 'loss from trade' may arise through failure to comply with the Golden Rule.

Of course, it may be objected that labour is not the only cost of production and that the rate of profits represents payment for some sort of effort or sacrifice on the part of capitalists so that the concern with labour productivity alone is misplaced. If profits are a proper compensation for costs incurred by capitalists then the prices which dictate the pattern of trade do so in a way which reflects the comparative costs of all inputs into production. This is the position that would be taken by neoclassical economists; but it is one we reject. Our reasons for this are discussed in chapter 13. For now we proceed on the basis that profits are a deduction from net output and do not represent a reward for effort on the part of capitalists.

3 Trade in the Sraffa–Leontief model

Before we introduce the possibility of international trade into the analysis of the preceding chapters let us just remind ourselves of some points which will be basic to our analysis. In chapter 7 we showed that in the two-commodity case (but only in that case) it is possible to identify unambiguously one deficit and one surplus industry. That is, the deficit industry remains a deficit industry at all rates of profits and the surplus industry remains a surplus industry. Starting from a position of equilibrium, an increase in the uniform rate of profits requires the price of the surplus commodity to fall and that of the deficit commodity to rise. (Again this applies only to the two-commodity case.) Figures 9.1 illustrate three possibilities. In part (a), 1 is the deficit industry and 2 the surplus industry so that as the rate of profits increases so also does p_1/p_2. The w–r relation is concave to the origin because the standard of value is the commodity whose price is falling in relative terms (see chapter 6, section 3). In part (b), 1 is the surplus industry, 2 the deficit industry, which means that p_1/p_2 must fall as r rises. Keeping commodity 2 as the standard of value means that the w–r relation in this case is convex to the origin. Part (c) illustrates the case in which the commodities have the same capital : labour ratios. Both industries are permanently in balance, which means that p_1/p_2 is constant and the w–r relation a straight line.

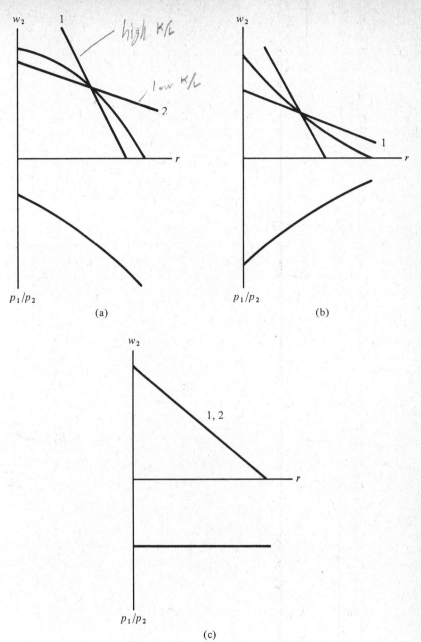

Figure 9.1

We are now in a position to introduce trade in two commodities between two countries, A and B. It is assumed that there exists no impediments to trade nor any reason why specialisation should not be realised in either country. Also, for illustration, the rates of profits are taken to be exogenous in each country and are assumed to be the same in the autarkic and trading regimes. Finally, each closed economy has available just one technique.

The technique used by a closed economy consists, of necessity, of the activities for producing both commodities – of necessity, because in a closed economy a single process cannot provide all its own inputs. But with trade it is possible to have a single activity supported by imported inputs of the other commodity. So the possibility of trade presents an economy with two additional techniques, each consisting of a single process. In the last chapter we presented the problem of technical choice by superimposing the w–r relations for each technique to obtain an outer frontier. Then, for a given r, that technique which is most profitable (and hence chosen under competitive conditions) is the one which allows the maximisation of the wage; that is, the one on the frontier. The choice of specialisation in international trade can be considered as a particular case of this analysis. The immediate task is to determine the nature of the w–r relation appropriate to specialised production. But this turns out to be no real problem for we have already implicitly derived single-process w–r relations in chapter 7. These are simply the w–r trade-offs of figs. 7.2, which were used to describe surplus and deficit industries, and which have been reproduced here in figs. 9.1. It is true that for any process there is (in general) a separate trade-off for each price ratio but we are interested in only one price ratio – the one at which countries trade. This international price ratio, or 'terms of trade', we shall denote p_I (taking commodity 2 as standard of value). The equations of the trade-offs are then:

and
$$w = [p_I - (1+r)(a_{11}p_I + a_{21})]/l_1 \qquad (9.1)$$
$$w = [1 - (1+r)(a_{12}p_I + a_{22})]/l_2. \qquad (9.2)$$

It is, of course, necessary that p_I lie between the closed-economy price ratios p_a and p_b or both countries will want to import the same commodity.

We already know from Ricardo that if A and B have different techniques trade is profitable. Let us then begin with the 'non-Ricardian' possibility of trade between countries with the same technique but different rates of profits (fig. 9.2). Because the two countries have the same no-trade techniques they also have the same w_2–r and p–r relations. Suppose that $r_a < r_b$ so that, with the technique represented in part (a), $p_a < p_b$. With trade at price p_I, the w–r relations are now given by the trade-offs appropriate to this price. (The intersection of the trade-offs occurs at a point on the closed

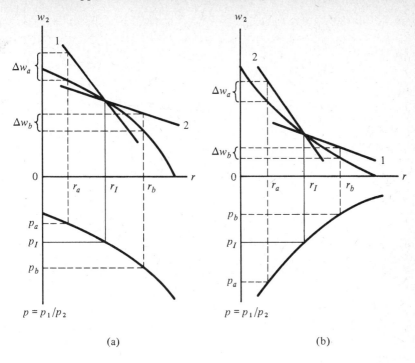

Figure 9.2

economy w–r relation associated with price p_I.) Since p_a is less than p_I, country A will specialise in the production and export of commodity 1. That this is the most profitable alternative is shown by the fact that this is the choice which maximises w_a at the given r_a. The increase in the wage relative to the closed-economy rate is shown by Δw_a. Similarly, B gets a higher wage through specialisation in commodity 2. (Obviously, if wages were held constant in the comparison each country would get a higher rate of profits.) If p_I were equal to either of the no-trade price ratios individuals in the country concerned would be indifferent to trade and would not be induced to specialise. The precise determination of p_I within the limits set by p_a and p_b requires a knowledge of demand in each country. But only when p_I coincides with one of the closed-economy price ratios does its position affect the qualitative nature of our conclusions.

Figure 9.2(b) shows the pattern of specialisation when the no-trade technique is such that p decreases with r. It is evident from fig. 9.1(c) that when the price ratio is invariant with respect to the rate of profits then, no matter how different the values of r, trade does not allow the attainment of a superior w–r combination. This is the one case where the labour theory of value holds and Ricardo's analysis of trade is appropriate.

4 The gains from trade

Suppose that commodity 2, apart from being the standard of value, is also the only consumption commodity. That being so then, for the no-trade economy, the w_2–r relation is the dual of the c_2–g relation. But do we still have this useful property when the countries trade with one another? Consider the country specialising in commodity 2. In *value terms*, consumption p.w. is equal to gross output p.w. minus the value of inputs required for the next period's production:

$$c_2 = q_2 - (1+g)(p_I a_{12} q_2 + a_{22} q_2). \tag{9.3}$$

In physical terms, everything is already in the form of commodity 2 except for $a_{12} q_2$ which must be obtained from imports. It can be converted into an amount of commodity 2 by exchange at the international price ratio p_I. Since, when process 2 is operated on its own, $q_2 = 1/l_2$ (that is, gross output p.w. is the reciprocal of the number of workers per unit of output), we can rewrite (9.3) as

$$c_2 = [1 - (1+g)(p_I a_{12} + a_{22})]/l_2. \tag{9.4}$$

We thus have an expression relating consumption p.w., as a quantity of commodity 2, and the rate of growth. This procedure is valid so long as one bundle of commodities can be transformed into another bundle by means of exchange at the ruling price ratio. Clearly it is not valid (in general) in the non-specialised or no-trade economy where net output and consumption combinations are transformed according to a technical relationship. Comparing (9.2) and (9.4) we see that the expressions are identical except that g has taken the place of r and c_2 of w_2.

In the case of process 1 the procedure is the same except that here we have two items to transform into commodity 2:

$$c_2 = p_I q_1 - (1+g)(p_I a_{11} q_1 + a_{21} q_1) \tag{9.5}$$

and, from $q_1 = 1/l_1$,

$$c_2 = [p_I - (1+g)(p_I a_{11} + a_{21})]/l_1. \tag{9.6}$$

Comparison of (9.1) and (9.6) again reveals the duality of these single-process w_2–r and c_2–g relations.

If we assume classical savings behaviour then $g < r$ in both A and B. Figure 9.3(a) reproduces Fig. 9.2(a) but adds information about consumption and growth rates. With trade both countries have higher real wages (the

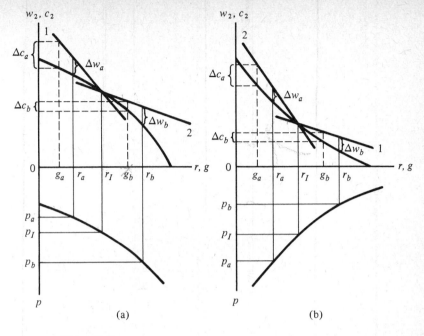

Figure 9.3

differences denoted by Δw_a and Δw_b). In A, the difference in consumption p.w. is larger than the difference in wages so that capitalist consumption p.w. must be greater with trade. In B, total consumption p.w. is greater with trade *if $g_b > r_I$* (where r_I is that profits rate associated with a price ratio p_I) *and less if $g_b < r_I$*. But even in the first case $\Delta w_b > \Delta c_b$ so that capitalist consumption p.w. is less.[3] The interpretation of fig. 9.3(*b*) is not quite so straightforward since, in this case, the consumption p.w. changes can, in principle, be greater or less than the wage changes in each country (depending on the slopes of the single-process trade-offs compared to the no-trade dual relation). Hence we cannot be certain whether capitalists gain or lose in p.w. consumption terms in either country.

5 Differences in no-trade techniques

Trade between countries with different no-trade techniques can be represented in the back-to-back diagram of fig. 9.4. On the left are the w_2-r, c_2-g and $p-r$ functions for A; on the right those for B. The analysis follows exactly the same principles as in the preceding sections and shows the possibility that positive rates of profits may offset or even reverse the pattern of relative prices implied by technical differences at zero rates of

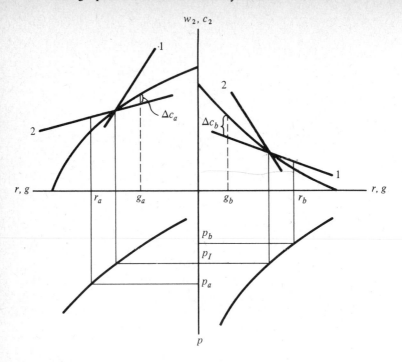

Figure 9.4

profits (prices which are proportional to the direct and indirect labours embodied). It follows, of course, that the pattern of specialisation may also be reversed. This would be the case if the rate of profits in A corresponds to a price ratio which is greater than that associated with r_b (as is the case in the diagram). In that event it can easily be seen that *both* countries may lose from trade in the sense of having lower consumption possibilities p.w. at their respective rates of growth (Δc_a, $\Delta c_b < 0$).[4]

6 Summary

In Ricardo, price ratios are equal to embodied labour ratios and trade takes place according to the principles of comparative advantage. Each country specialises in and exports that commodity which it produces most efficiently. But in Sraffa, price ratios do not, in general, equal embodied labour ratios and so may give the wrong signals about efficiency. Trade according to comparative advantage is still rational but it may not take place under competitive conditions. Profitable specialisation may then lead to a loss from trade in the sense that, for a given rate of growth, consumption p.w. is less. This is merely an example of the failure to comply with the Golden Rule of Accumulation. If r and g were the same in each country, as recommended by the Rule, then no trade losses would occur. It is worth repeating that it is implicit in our argument that the rate of profits does not represent a payment for a real cost incurred by capitalists. This issue is discussed further in chapter 13.

This chapter has been concerned with a very simple case of international economic relations – that of international *trade*. No account has been taken of capital movements or labour migration, both of which would complicate the analysis considerably.

FURTHER READING

For the typical textbook treatment of Ricardian theory, see Caves and Jones (1981), chapter 5. Sections 3–6 of this chapter are drawn from Mainwaring (1974). This and other papers of a similar nature are collected in Steedman (1979a); see, especially, Steedman and Metcalfe (1973a and b), and Parrinello (1973). For a discussion of the issue from a somewhat neoclassical perspective, see Samuelson (1975); and, on its relationship to neo-Marxian and other theories, Evans (1980). Steedman (1979b) develops a comprehensive trade model using Sraffian foundations.

For Ricardo, comparative costs meant comparative labour costs. In neoclassical theory trade takes place according to the same principle but both labour and capital costs are included (see Caves and Jones, chapter 7). The great bulk of the neoclassical literature on international trade is 'naïve' in the sense discussed in chapter 8, section 8 and is, therefore, subject to the criticisms raised there. These are made explicit in Metcalfe and Steedman (1972) and (1973), both reproduced in Steedman (1979a).

For an analysis of international investment in a Sraffa–Leontief model, see Mainwaring (1982).

PART III

Joint-production systems

10

Pure joint production

1 Introduction

In the systems so far discussed the gross output of each process has consisted of a single commodity. In Part II of *PC* Sraffa considers systems in which processes are capable of producing more than one commodity (commonly referred to as joint-production processes). Sraffa's treatment of the general case of joint production is intended as a preliminary to his analyses of fixed capital and land, both of which may be regarded as important particular cases. In this chapter we shall be concerned with what we call 'pure' joint production, of the mutton/wool or corn/straw variety, which need not involve either fixed capital or land. Pure joint production is, however, of much wider interest than these familiar examples might lead us to expect. In modern industrial economies many processes involve the production of important 'by-products' (basic slag and combustible gases from metal smelting, for example), while in some industries it is difficult to say which is the main product and which the by-products (examples would be the petrochemicals industry and the production of weapons-grade plutonium and electricity from nuclear power stations).

To focus on this particular aspect of joint production we shall consider only systems involving circulating capital as means of production. We therefore maintain the assumption of an annual cycle of production. Indeed, the only major change of assumption is the possibility of each process being able to produce many commodities. For the most part we confine ourselves to two-commodity systems, continuing to exploit the relative simplicity of the two-dimensional geometry developed in Part II. The extension of the analysis to the general k-commodity case does not involve any major new principles. One implication of joint-production systems is that only one process may be needed to provide both commodities. The question of whether, and in what circumstances, the number of processes will be equal to the number of commodities is discussed in sections 4–6. But to begin we suppose that this equality holds. One further complication is that with joint products the identification of basic commodities is a much trickier business.

105

This is discussed in section 7; until then we avoid the issue by considering systems which consist exclusively of basic commodities.

We have exhausted the Standard commodity of all its pedagogic powers. Given the tangential relevance of the concept to our analysis of joint-production systems, further consideration of the subject is relegated to an appendix.

2 A two-commodity system

A two-commodity, two-process joint-production system may be represented as follows:

	Labour	Inputs 1	2		Gross outputs 1	2
Process 1	L_1	$+\ c_{11}$	$+\ c_{21}$	$\longrightarrow$	C_{11}	$+\ C_{21}$
Process 2	L_2	$+\ c_{12}$	$+\ c_{22}$	$\longrightarrow$	C_{12}	$+\ C_{22}$
	$\Sigma L_i = 1$	Σc_{1j}	Σc_{2j}		ΣC_{1j}	ΣC_{2j}

where c_{ij} is the input of commodity i into process j and C_{ij} the output of commodity i from process j. Thus, process 1, operated with L_1 units of labour, produces a net output of commodity 2 of $C_{21} - c_{21}$. The net output of commodity 2 for the system as a whole is $\Sigma_j(C_{2j} - c_{2j})$. It is not strictly necessary that all the entries in the above table be positive and, clearly, if $C_{21} = C_{12} = 0$ the system reduces to a single-products one.

Previously we defined a unit of process j as that level of operation which produced a unit of commodity j. But when each process can produce many commodities it is more convenient to define a unit of some process as the level of operation at which one unit of labour is employed. (It is assumed throughout that no process is fully automated; that is, each requires a positive amount of direct labour.) Since the entire labour force of the economy is one unit it follows that this is the maximum level of operation of either process and that processes can only be operated together at less than unit intensity. In fact, if process 1 is operated at intensity L_1 then process 2 cannot operate at an intensity L_2 greater than $(1 - L_1)$. Even so, it is useful to define for both processes technical coefficients appropriate to operation at unit intensity. These coefficients are denoted by $A_{ij}(= C_{ij}/L_j)$ and $a_{ij}(= c_{ij}/L_j)$.

If process 1 were operated at unit intensity its gross outputs would be A_{11} and A_{21}, indicated in fig. 10.1 by the vector Q_1. The corresponding input

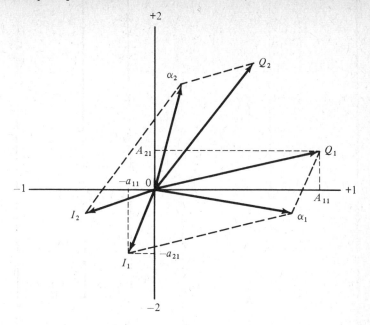

Figure 10.1

vector is $I_1 = (-a_{11}, -a_{21})$. The net outputs of this unit process are $(A_{11} - a_{11})$ and $(A_{21} - a_{21})$ and these are described by the vector $\alpha_1 = Q_1 + I_1$. Similarly the operation of process 2 at unit intensity would imply a gross output vector Q_2, an input vector I_2 and a net output vector α_2. The vectors Q_1 and Q_2 lie wholly within the positive quadrant reflecting the fact that both processes produce positive gross outputs of both commodities. If the *net* output of one of the commodities from some process is negative then that process's net output vector lies in a non-positive quadrant (as, for example, α_1 in the diagram). This may be compared with the single products system of fig. 4.1 in which the Q_i lie on the axes and the α_i necessarily lie within opposite non-positive quadrants.

3 Relative prices and the w–r relation

The price equations of the two-commodity, two-process system are:

$$p_1 A_{11} + p_2 A_{21} = (1+r)(p_1 a_{11} + p_2 a_{21}) + w$$
$$p_1 A_{12} + p_2 A_{22} = (1+r)(p_1 a_{12} + p_2 a_{22}) + w. \tag{10.1}$$

These may be compared with the 'labour-embodied' equations (*cf.* equations (3.8)):

$$\lambda_1 A_{11} + \lambda_2 A_{21} = \lambda_1 a_{11} + \lambda_2 a_{21} + 1$$

$$\lambda_1 A_{12} + \lambda_2 A_{22} = \lambda_1 a_{12} + \lambda_2 a_{22} + 1. \tag{10.2}$$

Multiplying both sides of (10.2) by w yields equations identical to (10.1), for $r = 0$, except that $w\lambda_i$ takes the place of p_i. Thus, as in the case of single products, prices are proportional to labours embodied when $r = 0$.

In single-product systems it was shown in chapter 4, section 5, that the slope of the wage frontier, $\beta_1\beta_2$, defines the price ratio. The same reasoning applies to joint-production systems without modification, but the properties of joint-product prices are considerably different. For single-product systems we know that the wage frontier is always downward sloping. Since the price vector may be represented as a line drawn normal to the frontier, this tells us that prices are necessarily positive in such systems. But with joint production this is no longer so. To see this, consider the example of fig. 10.2. Since α_1 and α_2 can, in principle, lie in any but the negative quadrant there appears to be nothing to ensure that the line joining them will always slope downwards. If not, the price ratio at $r = 0$, when $\alpha_1\alpha_2$ and $\beta_1\beta_2$ coincide, will be negative. We thus have the peculiar possibility of a commodity 'embodying' a negative amount of labour.

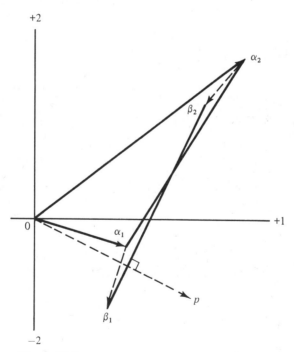

Figure 10.2

What happens as r rises? In single-product systems the wage frontier shifts in a south-westerly direction. Moreover, because α_1 and α_2 lie in opposite non-positive quadrants, it is necessarily the case that, in the positive quadrant, a frontier corresponding to a high r lies everywhere below a frontier corresponding to a low r. (See fig. 4.6, where $\beta_1\beta_2$ lies everywhere below $\alpha_1\alpha_2$.) But in joint-production systems the simplicity of this movement is lost. In fig. 10.2, for example, because the wage frontier is upward sloping, a south-westerly shift nevertheless increases the wage possibilities over a certain range. Figure 10.3 shows a case in which the $\alpha_1\alpha_2$ and $\beta_1\beta_2$ lines, although downward-sloping, intersect within the positive quadrant.

The behaviour of the wage frontier has obvious implications for the $w–r$ relation. If the price of some commodity is negative at some rate of profits, then the wage, expressed in terms of that commodity, will also be negative. In fig. 10.2 the line $\alpha_1\alpha_2$ intersects the 2-axis in its negative range, implying that $w_2 < 0$ when $r = 0$. On the other hand, the same wage (in physical terms), expressed in terms of commodity 1, would be positive. In fig. 10.3 both prices are positive but even this case has further implications for wage behaviour. As r increases from zero to some positive value the wage in terms of commodity 2 falls from w_2' to w_2''. But in terms of commodity 1 it increases from w_1' to w_1''. It is clear that joint-production systems admit $w–r$ relations of a much wider variety than single-product systems. Examples of

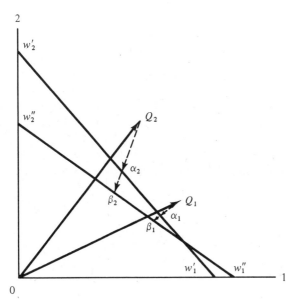

Figure 10.3

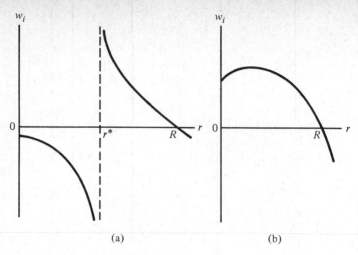

(a)   (b)

Figure 10.4

such relations are shown in figs. 10.4.[1] Part (*a*) is consistent with fig. 10.2 when commodity 2 is used as standard; part (*b*) is consistent with fig. 10.3 when commodity 1 is the standard.

We must, however, be very careful how we interpret these wage variations since their peculiarities may be the result of the arbitrary choice of the standard of value. The idea of a negative wage is obviously absurd. The possibility of wages rising with the rate of profits may be less so but the apparent rises suggested by some *w–r* relations may be quite deceptive. Consider fig. 10.3 again. In an actual economy the wage basket would be confined to that part of the wage frontier which lies to the south of α_2, and to the west of α_1. A wage basket represented by w_1'' would be a physical impossibility. In this case any actual wage basket must get smaller as *r* increases. In fig. 10.2 this does not appear to be the case. But even here we have to ask whether all the factors that need to be taken into consideration have been. These issues are bound up with the choice of technique with joint production which will be discussed in the following sections. Meanwhile, we should take care not to read too much into the mathematical properties so far uncovered.

4 The choice of technique

If one process is capable of producing both commodities why do we need a second process? The answer that Sraffa gives is that it is necessary for 'the number of processes . . . to be brought to equality with the number of commodities so that the prices may be determined' (*PC*, p. 43). This is

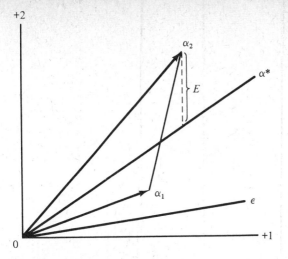

Figure 10.5

not altogether satisfactory since it is based on mathematical convenience rather than economic logic. Sraffa does, however, add a footnote: 'considering that the proportions in which the two commodities are produced by any one method will in general be different from those in which they are required for use, the existence of two methods of producing them in different proportions will be necessary for obtaining the required proportion of the two products through an appropriate combination of the two methods'. This argument is illustrated in fig. 10.5 where α_1 and α_2 are the net output vectors of two processes. If outputs are required in the proportions indicated by the line $O\alpha^*$ they can be obtained by a suitable combination of α_1 and α_2.

This, however, is not the end of the matter. What, for example, would be the outcome if requirements were indicated by $O\epsilon$ which does not intersect the segment $\alpha_1\alpha_2$? Even if requirements are given by $O\alpha^*$ there are other alternatives to be considered. One possibility would be to operate process 2 on its own, discarding an amount E of commodity 2, per unit of the process. In this case commodity 2, which is produced in excess of its requirements would, if it could be disposed of costlessly, become a 'free good': its price would be zero. Similarly, process 1 could be operated alone, the excess of the free good, 1, being disposed of. These problems become more acute as the number of commodities increases. If there are three processes available for jointly producing three commodities then there is a choice of up to seven combinations of processes or, as we have defined the term, of up to seven techniques of production. Which of the alternatives is chosen depends not on analytical convenience but on comparative profitability.

Since a choice of technique is inherent in joint-production systems, even where the number of processes available does not exceed the number of commodities, the question arises as to whether the mathematical necessity of equalising the number of processes *in operation* to the number of commodities represents a fundamental flaw in Sraffa's theoretical structure. Some economists have, in fact, argued precisely this point and have suggested that a superior method of dealing with joint products exists, based on the approach of J. von Neumann. Before considering Sraffa's analysis any further we shall give a brief outline of the von Neumann system.

5 The von Neumann model

In chapter 5 we developed, in the context of the single-products system, a model of maximum growth. The von Neumann model differs only in its generality. Not only does it include joint production, it also allows for the possibility that the number of processes in operation is different from the number of commodities. The technique, or combination of processes, is chosen by the criterion: maximise the uniform rate of growth subject to the fixed requirements of workers' subsistence. Like the classical economists, von Neumann assumes that the wage basket is advanced thus forming part of the capital. As in chapter 3 we may add the subsistence and other capital requirements to obtain for each process a set of inclusive input : process coefficients.

The essential analytical difference between the Sraffa–Leontief and von Neumann approaches is that the price and quantity relations in the latter are expressed as inequalities rather than as equations. Suppose there are two commodities and three available processes. The von Neumann quantity relations may be written as follows:

$$(1 + g)(a_{11}L_1 + a_{12}L_2 + a_{13}L_3) \leqslant A_{11}L_1 + A_{12}L_2 + A_{13}L_3 \qquad (10.3.1)$$

$$(1 + g)(a_{21}L_1 + a_{22}L_2 + a_{23}L_3) \leqslant A_{21}L_1 + A_{22}L_2 + A_{23}L_3 \qquad (10.3.2)$$

where, as before, $a_{ij}(A_{ij})$ is the input (output) of commodity i into (from) process j; and L_i is the intensity of operation of process i. The first of these relations says that the aggregate outputs of commodity 1 (shown on the right-hand side) must be at least as great as the input requirements of commodity 1, after allowing for growth at the rate g. The second relation may be given a similar interpretation with respect to commodity 2. Should the strict inequality hold for, say, relation (10.3.1) then outputs would exceed requirements in each period of steady growth, so that commodity 1 would be a free good. A strict equality must, however, hold for at least one commodity otherwise both commodities would be in surplus, and g could not be the largest possible growth rate. This means that the maximum rate of growth of the system is the rate of growth of the slowest-growing commodity. Commodities which grow faster than that rate must become free goods.

Whereas there is a quantity relation for each commodity, there is a price relation for each process:

$$(1 + r)(a_{11}p_1 + a_{21}p_2) \geqslant A_{11}p_1 + A_{21}p_2 \tag{10.4.1}$$

$$(1 + r)(a_{12}p_1 + a_{22}p_2) \geqslant A_{12}p_1 + A_{22}p_2 \tag{10.4.2}$$

$$(1 + r)(a_{13}p_1 + a_{23}p_2) \geqslant A_{13}p_1 + A_{23}p_2. \tag{10.4.3}$$

Relation (10.4.1) says that, in a competitive economy, the value of output cannot exceed the costs of production plus profits at the uniform rate. If it did, then superprofits would be earned in that industry, contrary to the assumption of free competition. Where the strict inequality holds the firms in that industry do not make a return on capital at the uniform rate and go out of business. That particular process therefore operates at zero intensity.

The duality between the Sraffa price system and the Leontief quantity system which we noted in chapter 5 also holds for the two parts of the von Neumann system. We can take advantage of this duality in the following way. Multiply (10.3.1) by p_1 and (10.3.2) by p_2. This converts the relations into equations, for if any one was previously a strict inequality the commodity involved is a free good and both sides are multiplied by zero. Adding the converted relations gives the following expression:

$$(1 + g)(\sum_j p_1 a_{1j} L_j + \sum_j p_2 a_{2j} L_j) = \sum_j p_1 A_{1j} L_j + \sum_j p_2 A_{2j} L_j \tag{10.5}$$

or $(1 + g)$(value of inputs) = value of outputs.

Next, perform a similar operation on relations (10.4), multiplying each by its associated L_j. Since a strict inequality is associated with zero intensity, this operation also converts the relations into equations. Adding the equations gives the following:

$$(1 + r)(\sum_j p_1 a_{1j} L_j + \sum_j p_2 a_{2j} L_j) = \sum_j p_1 A_{1j} L_j + \sum_j p_2 A_{2j} L_j \tag{10.6}$$

or $(1 + r)$(value of inputs) = value of outputs.

Equations (10.5) and (10.6) are clearly identical, apart from the g and r terms which are therefore equal. This is not surprising since capitalists' consumption has been assumed to be zero. In both expressions it must be remembered that one p_i and one or two L_j *may* be zero. Given the set of available processes the precise identification of the redundant processes and free goods is a matter for linear programming methods to determine, and the maximisation of the growth rate leads to precisely the same solution as the *minimisation* of the rate of profits.

The rather strict assumptions of the von Neumann model have been relaxed to some extent by subsequent writers. But for us the important point is that the choice of technique 'falls out' of the procedure of maximising the growth rate. There is no need to prescribe the number of operative processes; the process intensities are themselves part of the set of variables.

6 Sraffa reconsidered

Whereas the choice of technique is an integral part of the von Neumann 'inequalities' approach to joint production, Sraffa includes only a brief and rather opaque discussion of the matter, in relation to the possibility of negative or zero prices. Thus, referring to the sort of behaviour depicted in fig. 10.4(a) he asks what would happen to a system, viable at $r > r^*$, if the rate of profits were to fall below r^*. In that case, he says, 'those among the methods of production that gave rise to such a result would be discarded to make room for others which in the new situation were consistent with positive prices' (PC, p. 59). Sraffa's requirement that there should be as many active processes as there are commodities implies that the number of methods discarded is equal to the number newly adopted. This precondition seems unduly restrictive and suggests that, compared to von Neumann's, Sraffa's analysis is inferior.

Recently, however, Steedman (1976) has argued that, far from being contradictory, the two analyses *may* be compatible with one another, in the Golden Rule case in which $r = g$, provided we interpret the word 'commodity' to refer to *a product whose price is positive*. If so, then it can be shown that choice under competitive conditions generates techniques in which the number of processes is necessarily equal to the number of commodities, appropriately defined. A further and important implication is that the w–r frontier (the outer boundary of the w–r relations for each technique) is necessarily downward sloping when the wage is measured in terms of a real wage basket. A proper proof of these assertions requires mathematics beyond the level assumed in this book, but a graphical illustration of the principles involved is possible.

Consider an economy with two products and two available processes. Figure 10.6 shows the wage frontiers for four successive rates of profits, beginning with $r^0 = 0$, and increasing through r', ..., r'', ..., r''', ... etc. The associated wage frontiers are marked in a corresponding notation: $\beta_1^0 \beta_2^0$, ... etc. To avoid cluttering the diagram we assume that the wage basket consists of the two commodities in exactly the same proportions as the vector β_1^0. We shall call the line Ow the 'wage line'. Let δ denote the technique consisting of both processes together, ϵ the technique consisting solely of process 2, and η the technique consisting solely of process 1. In general, the operation

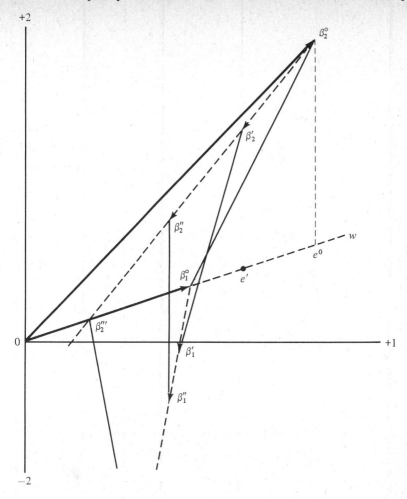

Figure 10.6

of either ϵ or η will require the disposal of one or other product in order to attain a point on the wage line. It is assumed that such disposals can take place at zero cost. With technique δ, however, it will, in general, be possible to attain a wage vector of the desired proportions without need of disposals.

From fig. 10.6 it is possible to derive the w–r relations appropriate to each of these techniques. Begin with ϵ. At r^0 the net output from this technique is β_2^0. If an amount $e^0\beta_2^0$ of product 2 were discarded we would be left with a wage basket e^0. As r rises the *potential* wage vector contracts along the line $\beta_2^0, \ldots, \beta_2', \ldots$ etc., and the actual wage vector (after allowing for the disposal

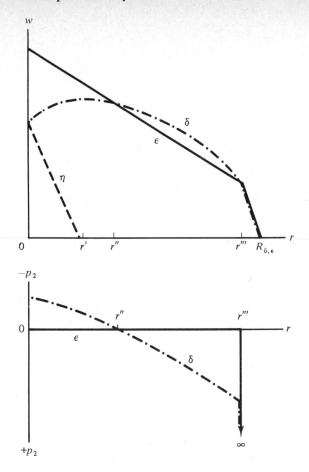

Figure 10.7

of some unwanted product 2) contracts along the line $e^0, \ldots, e', \ldots$ etc. This process continues until we reach r''' when the potential and actual wage vectors coincide at β_2'''. Further increases in r would require the disposal of un-wanted product 1. Over that range the wage basket would contract at a faster rate, quickly becoming zero. The $w-r$ relation for technique ϵ is thus made up of two linear segments joined at a point corresponding to r''' (fig. 10.7).

Now look at technique δ, which combines the two processes. At r^0 it is possible to produce a wage vector β_1^0. Strictly speaking, technique η is in operation here, but η can be regarded as a limiting case of δ. As r rises the wage frontier initially shifts *outwards* along the wage line reaching its furthest position when $r = r'$. Further increases in r bring a retreat along the wage line, the speed of the retreat increasing as the wage frontier gets flatter. But when r passes r''' the wage frontier no longer intersects the wage line. This does not mean that the w–r relation terminates in mid-air since, from here on, we can regard technique ϵ as a limiting case of δ, so that the w–r relations for the two techniques coincide for $r > r'''$. For completeness, we may note that for η the wage at r^0 is the same as for δ but, as r rises, large disposals of unwanted product 1 accompany a very rapid fall in w.

We may summarise as follows: up to r'' (where the wage frontier becomes vertical), ϵ offers the highest wage; between r'' and r''', δ takes over; but beyond r''', ϵ reasserts itself, whether in its own right or as a limiting case of δ is of no real significance.

The lower panel of fig. 10.7 shows what is happening to relative prices (taking $p_1 = 1$). If products in excess supply have zero prices then for ϵ, $p_2 = 0$ from r^0 to r'''. Beyond r''' product 1 is in excess supply which means (since $p_1 = 1$) that the price of 2 is infinite. For δ, the upward slope of the wage frontier for r up to r'' means that $p_2 < 0$. It becomes zero at r'' and thereafter positive. But from r''' onwards, when δ and ϵ coincide, p_2 is infinite.

With this example in mind let us now reconsider Sraffa's statement that should a variation in r bring about a negative price it would also signal a change in technique. Suppose we start from somewhere between r'' and r''' with δ in operation and both prices positive. As r falls below r'', p_2 becomes negative and there is a change to technique ϵ. In the other direction, the rate r''' can also be considered as a switch-point, from δ to ϵ. (We have, in fact, an example of reswitching.) Were it not for his assertion that discarded processes 'make room for others', which implies no change in the number of processes, Sraffa's statement would be quite consistent with our illustration.

There is, however, more to our switch-points than just a change in the combination of processes used. On Steedman's definition they may also signal a change in the set of 'commodities'. As r decreases through r'', for example, product 2 loses this status; as r rises through r''', product 1 suffers this fate. According to Steedman, switch-points can correspond to three possible types of change:

> type (a) involves a change from one Sraffa-like system to another in which the set of products which are 'commodities' is unchanged but the set of methods used is different (a Method Switch); a switch of type (b) involves no change in the set of methods used but does involve a change in the set of products which are 'commodities' (a Commodity Switch); at a switch of type (c) both the set of methods and the set of 'commodities' change. (Sraffa's two discussions of switches under joint production ... would both seem to relate to what are here called Method Switches) (1976, p. 875).

The switches illustrated in our example are clearly both of type (c).

Our example has illustrated Steedman's contention that the number of processes will equal the number of commodities, appropriately defined, and that that number may change with variations in r. It can also be seen from fig. 10.7 that the $w–r$ frontier is downward-sloping, even though individual $w–r$ relations have positive ranges. A crucial assumption in this discussion is that commodities may be disposed of freely. If it does not hold the analysis has to be complicated by including specific 'disposal activities' and the profitability calculations must bear these in mind. In this case it may even make perfect sense to have negative prices for those products regarded as waste – 'bads' as opposed to 'goods'.

In conclusion, it seems that Steedman's analysis has undermined the view that Sraffa's treatment of joint production is inherently inferior to von Neumann's and even suggests that the two approaches 'may be closer than might at first appear' (Steedman, 1976, p. 876).

7 Identifying basics

In joint-production systems a non-basic commodity is not confined to a single process but may appear in any number of processes, some of which produce basics and non-basics and some of which may use basics and non-basics as means of production. Because of this basic commodities are more difficult to identify. Nonetheless, if the equations of the system can be re-arranged such that there remains a system capable of self-replacement without need of some commodities as inputs then such commodities may be defined as non-basic. This identification is accomplished by applying a set of multipliers to the equations of the actual system. This has the effect of removing non-basics, leaving a system of 'Basic equations'.

To see what is involved consider the following actual system (employing one unit of labour):

	Labour	1	2	3	4		1	2	3	4
1	0.325	$14\frac{3}{4}$	$4\frac{3}{4}$	$5\frac{1}{2}$	$8\frac{1}{2}$	$\longrightarrow$	$16\frac{1}{2}$	11	5	$6\frac{1}{2}$
2	0.2	2	$6\frac{2}{3}$	$\frac{2}{3}$	2	$\longrightarrow$	$4\frac{1}{6}$	$5\frac{11}{30}$	$1\frac{1}{3}$	2
3	0.4	9	27	14	26	$\longrightarrow$	18	22	16	22
4	0.075	9	$7\frac{1}{2}$	9	15	$\longrightarrow$	12	$10\frac{1}{2}$	9	12

Sraffa's argument is that it is possible, by linear transformations, to reduce this system to two rows in which all quantities of non-basic are eliminated. To see this form the following rows

$$\text{row } (i), \text{ consisting of} \qquad \begin{array}{l} + \, 2 \text{ units of row (1)} \\ + \, \frac{1}{2} \text{ unit of row (3)} \\ - \, 2 \text{ units of row (4)} \end{array}$$

+ 3 units of row (2)

row (*ii*), consisting of   − 1 unit of row (3)

+ $\frac{4}{3}$ units of row (4)

giving, respectively,

	Labour	1	2	3	4		1	2	3	4
(*i*)	0.7	16	8	0	0	$\longrightarrow$	18	12	0	0
(*ii*)	0.3	9	3	0	0	$\longrightarrow$	10.5	8.1	0	0

and, in aggregate:

	1	25	11	0	0	$\longrightarrow$	28.5	20.1	0	0

We are left, notionally at least, with a system using only commodities 1 and 2 as inputs and producing positive net outputs of the same commodities. Since all quantities of commodities 3 and 4 have been eliminated, (*i*) and (*ii*) may be considered as a two-commodity 'Basic system' and the associated price equations are the 'Basic equations'.

Let us consider this transformation in a little more depth. In the example, three rows from the actual system were multiplied by constants and added. As a result all the quantities of commodities 3 and 4 on the input side and the output side become zero. The same thing happened when a second set of three rows were chosen. Indeed, the same would happen with any other set of three rows. In other words, any three rows (of the input and output quantities of 3 and 4) are *linearly dependent*. If, however, we took any two rows we would find no set of multipliers which would eliminate the quantities of 3 and 4; that is, any two rows are *in*dependent. In the present example, then, we may say that two commodities are non-basic if, of the rows containing the inputs and outputs of those commodities, only two are independent. This definition is generalised by Sraffa as follows:

> In a system of *k* productive processes and *k* commodities (no matter whether produced singly or jointly) we say that a commodity or more generally a group of *n* linked commodities (where *n* must be smaller than *k* and may be equal to 1) are *non-basic* if of the *k* rows (formed by the 2*n* quantities in which they appear in each process) not more than *n* rows are independent, the others being linear combinations of these (*PC*, p. 51).[2]

Thus, suppose in our example we had suspected three commodities of being non-basic. To check we would take the four rows formed by the inputs and outputs of the three commodities and look for independence of any (and every) three rows. Failure to find three independent rows would eliminate our suspicions.

This rather abstract method of identifying basics lacks the intuitive appeal of our earlier discussions. But it is a completely general method and it is capable of embracing a type of non-basic not yet considered, namely something ('commodity' may not be the right word) which enters the means of production but which does not appear among the outputs. Land and other natural resources are the main examples of this type of non-basic.

A word of caution is necessary concerning the Basic system with joint production. Unlike the single-products case the Basic system here need not represent a potential way of organising production in an actual economy. Sraffa is careful to point out (pp. 52–3) that the Basic system is merely a *mathematical combination* of the original equations: the coefficients of this system are purely notional and do not (in general) represent an actual technique of production. In fact the Basic system (like the Standard system) may contain negative quantities.

It follows from these considerations that the rôle of the basic–non-basic distinction in joint-production systems is much less clear than it is for single-products systems. This is because the form of the Basic system is not independent of the conditions of production of non-basics. If, in the above example, the elements of the input columns 3 and 4 and the output columns 3 and 4 are changed in such a way that commodities 3 and 4 remain non-basic, the corresponding Basic system will differ from the one already derived. This is despite the fact that the input and output coefficients of the basic commodities 1 and 2 are unchanged. It follows that the corresponding $w–r$ relation will also be different. Thus it is no longer completely true to say, as Sraffa does on p. 54, that non-basics have no part to play in the determination of the rate of profits and the prices of basics. To quote Steedman (1977*b*): 'While it is perfectly true that Sraffa's basic *equations* suffice to determine basic prices and the rate of profits, one cannot deduce that only basic *commodities* play a rôle in that determination'. Nevertheless, Steedman does agree that 'the prices of basics have a logical priority over the prices of non-basics', for: 'It is still the case that, *given* the conditions of production (of both basics and non-basics), the relation between the prices of basics and the rate of profits can be considered independently of the relation between the prices of non-basics and the rate of profits, while the converse is not true'.

8 Summary

The clear message of this chapter is that however complex is the behaviour of single-product systems it is nothing compared to the behaviour of joint-product systems. Within any one technique, prices and the wage in terms of any arbitrary standard may be positive, zero or negative at rates of profits between O and R, while the real wage basket may rise or fall with r.

Such unexpected properties are the result of an attempt to analyse competitive price behaviour in a single isolated technique. This can be done in single-products systems where the analysis of technical choice may follow and be superimposed upon the analysis of the single technique. Indeed, if the number of available processes is equal to the number of products, only one technique can ever be used. But in joint-production systems this limitation is not enough to rule out technical choice: both processes and commodities (positively-priced products) may come and go as the rate of profits changes. It is this competitive need to change techniques that eliminates the peculiar behaviour of prices and wages.

The rôle of the basic/non-basic distinction has also become rather blurred, even within a single technique. A change in the production coefficients of a non-basic may convert it into a basic and may also affect the prices of other basics and the rate of profits. If techniques change with variations in r then the set of basics is also a function of the rate of profits. While this may also be true of single-products systems, in that case it is a more peripheral consideration. Basics do, as Steedman puts it, retain a 'logical priority' but there is now no question of simply putting non-basics aside to look after themselves.

FURTHER READING

There are very few introductory texts (possibly none) which deal more than cursorily with joint-production systems of the Sraffa type. Joint production is generally regarded as an advanced topic to be treated mathematically. At that level the natural starting point would be the first four essays reproduced in Pasinetti (1980). The first of these, Manara (1968), is fundamental. It does for joint-production systems what Newman did for single-products systems, which is to say that it provided the first rigorous mathematical treatment of the subject. Pasinetti's own contribution (1973) develops a concept called the 'vertically-integrated sector' which finds its application in, amongst other things, Steedman's essay (1977*b*) concerning the identification of basics. Pasinetti adds a further note on this subject. See also Pasinetti (1981). For a textbook treatment, see Abraham-Frois and Berrebi (1979).

Steedman's other contributions to the joint-production literature include his controversial (1975) paper in which he draws attention to the possibility that a technique perfectly viable at some rate of profits may require commodities to embody negative quantities of labour. This has important and destructive implications for Marxian value theory, enlarged upon in Steedman's (1977*a*) book, and drew many responses from the defenders of that theory. (See chapter 13, below.) The interchange between Wolfstetter and

Steedman (1976) is particularly interesting not so much for what was said about Marx and Sraffa as for what was said about von Neumann and Sraffa. Wolfstetter argues that there is an 'inherent weakness' in Sraffa's 'equations' approach. Steedman, as we have seen, responds by showing that a 'Sraffa-type' approach is not only robust but may even be compatible with von Neumann's. The issues are discussed in considerable depth in Schefold (1980*b*). Readers should also consult the work of Morishima; see, for example, Morishima and Catephores (1978), chapter 2.

Von Neumann's article, which dates from 1932, was published in English in 1945. Non-mathematical readers should look at Champernowne's (1945) commentary on the article. The brief account of von Neumann in this chapter is based on Dorfman *et al.* (1958) which, despite its age, is still one of the best introductions to the subject.

Appendix: The Standard commodity with joint products

1 Derivation

The principal features of the Standard system are not affected by the introduction of joint products. Outputs and inputs of the system consist of the same composite commodity and, for a given technique, the Standard ratio R defines the maximum rate of profits in the actual system. The Standard proportions are obtained in the usual fashion, by applying to each process of the Basic system a set of multipliers, such that for each commodity the Standard output is $(1 + R)$ times the Standard input. Thus, for commodity j,

$$\sum_i \phi_i C_{ji} = (1 + R) \sum_i \phi_i c_{ji} \quad (i, j = 1, \ldots, k) \tag{10.A.1}$$

or, in unit notation,

$$\sum_i \phi_i L_i A_{ji} = (1 + R) \sum_i \phi_i L_i A_{ji} \quad (i, j = 1, \ldots, k) \tag{10.A.2}$$

with, of course,

$$\sum_i \phi_i L_i = 1. \tag{10.A.3}$$

The Basic system, it will be recalled, may also be an imaginary construction, so that this method of deriving the Standard system may involve two separate applications of multipliers.

The main complication brought about by joint products is that it is no longer necessarily the case that the set of ϕ-multipliers is all positive.[1] As we saw in chapter 6, a necessary condition for the existence of all-positive multipliers is that there occurs some overlap between the ranges of variation of input and output proportions in the Basic system. If no overlap exists then it is necessary that some multipliers be negative. This is illustrated in fig. 10.A.1. Positive multipliers can only re-arrange inputs and (net) outputs along the segments $I_1 I_2$ and $\alpha_1 \alpha_2$, respectively. This means that linear dependence of the input and output vectors is impossible. But by applying a negative multiplier to process 2 and a large positive multiplier to process 1,

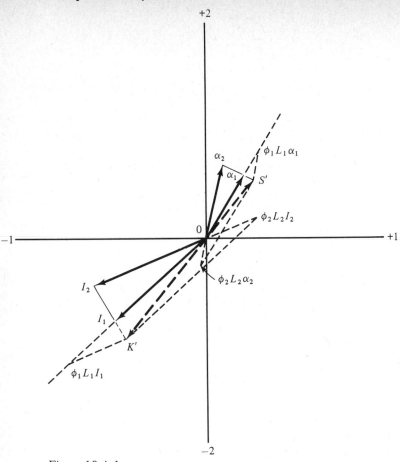

Figure 10.A.1

Standard proportions OK' and OS' can be obtained: K' is the sum of input vectors $\phi_2 L_2 I_2 + \phi_1 L_1 I_1$; and S' the sum of output vectors $\phi_2 L_2 \alpha_2 + \phi_1 L_1 \alpha_1$.[2]

It may help understanding of this to consider further the Basic system of section 7, reproduced here:

		Inputs			Gross outputs	
	Labour	1	2		1	2
Process 1	0.7	16	8		18	12
Process 2	0.3	9	3		10.5	8.1
	1	25	11		28.5	20.1

The ratio of the gross outputs of this system is free to vary from 10.5/8.1 to 18/12 (or 3/2). Similarly, the ratio in which commodities enter as means of production can vary from 16/8 (or 2/1) to 9/3 (or 3/1). It can be seen that the range of input proportions lies above the range of output proportions without there being any overlap. Standard proportions are given by the multipliers $\phi_1 = 2$ and $\phi_2 = -4/3$, the resulting Standard system being

	Labour	Inputs 1	2	Gross outputs 1	2
Process 1	1.4	32	16	36	24
Process 2	−0.4	−12	−4	−14	−10.8
	1	20	12	22	13.2

in which $20/12 = 22/13.2$ and

$$(1 + R) = 22/20 = 13.2/12 = (1 + 0.1)$$

The purpose for which Sraffa intends the Standard commodity is as a unit of measurement and, as he puts it, there is no reason why it should have 'bodily existence' (*PC*, p. 48). Although the existence of negative components makes it more difficult to visualise, the logic of its use as a measure of values is unaffected, at least so long as only one technique is considered. There remains, however, an important question. Equations (10.A.2) and (10.A.3) have k possible solutions; that is, k sets of multipliers and k values of R. In the single-products system it seemed natural to regard the relevant solution as the one involving all-positive multipliers. But was this decision justified? And if no all-positive Standard commodity exists, which of the several possible Standard commodities is the one that should be used as a unit of account?

2 Alternative systems

A two-commodity Basic system has two associated Standard systems. Although the Standard system illustrated in fig. 10.A.1 is obtained by applying a negative multiplier to the Basic system, the Standard commodity itself has all-positive components; that is, S' lies within the positive quadrant. We now wish to examine the properties of the second Standard system. We shall denote the systems as (*i*) and (*ii*), respectively, and distinguish their associated variables by the superscripts ' and ".

The important property of any Standard system is that aggregate inputs

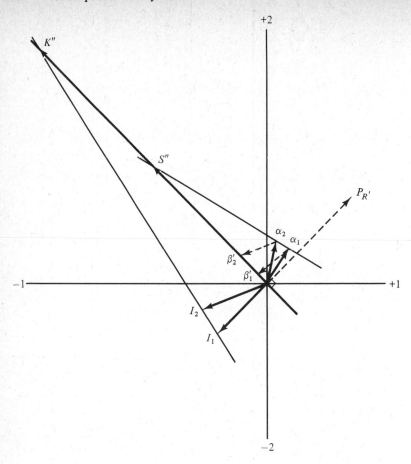

Figure 10.A.2

are in the same proportions as aggregate outputs. Thus the input and output vectors are linearly dependent and, of course, pass through the origin. The ϕ-multipliers can re-arrange the vectors anywhere along I_1I_2 and $\alpha_1\alpha_2$. It is possible to show (a proof is given at the end of this section) that the proportions of Standard system (*ii*) are, in fact, given by the slope of the line $\beta_1'\beta_2'$, the wage frontier which corresponds to the rate of profits R'. (See fig. 10.A.2, which refers to the same Basic system as fig. 10.A.1.) In other words, there exist multipliers ϕ_i'' such that $\phi_1'' > 1$ and $\phi_2'' < 0$ giving a Standard net output vector where $\alpha_1\alpha_2$ intersects $\beta_1'\beta_2'$ at S'', and a Standard input vector where I_1I_2 intersects $\beta_1'\beta_2'$ at K''. S'' and K'' lie on the same straight line through the origin and, therefore, have the same proportions. The normal to $\beta_1'\beta_2'$ is the price vector $P_{R'}$ associated with the rate of profits R'. In chapter 4 we saw that the scalar product of two vectors at right-angles is zero. Hence we have confirmation of Sraffa's proposition (*PC*, chapter V) that the Standard commodity of one Standard system has a value of zero when evaluated at the prices corresponding to the maximum rate of profits of another Standard system.

(The proof that the line $\beta_1'\beta_2'$ represents Standard proportions is as follows.[3] Let K'' be the Standard input vector and S'' the Standard output vector; that is, putting $\mu_i = \phi_i L_i$,

$$K'' = \mu_1 I_1 + \mu_2 I_2 \tag{10.A.4}$$

and

$$S'' = \mu_1 \alpha_1 + \mu_2 \alpha_2. \tag{10.A.5}$$

By definition, they are linearly dependent. Hence we may write

$$K'' = \theta S'' \tag{10.A.6}$$

where θ is a constant, equal to $1/R''$. Writing

$$\alpha_i = \beta_i' - R' I_i$$

S'' may be expanded as

$$S'' = \mu_1 \beta_1' + \mu_2 \beta_2' - \mu_1 R' I_1 - \mu_2 R' I_2$$

and, from (10.A.6),

$$K'' = \theta \mu_1 \beta_1' + \theta \mu_2 \beta_2' - \theta R'(\mu_1 I_1 + \mu_2 I_2).$$

From (10.A.4)

$$K'' = \theta \mu_1 \beta_1' + \theta \mu_2 \beta_2' - \theta R' K''$$

and

$$K'' = \frac{\theta}{1 + \theta R'} \cdot (\mu_1 \beta_1' + \mu_2 \beta_2') = \frac{1}{R'' + R'}(\mu_1 \beta_1' + \mu_2 \beta_2')$$

The μ_i are simple weights, so that the term $(\mu_1 \beta_1' + \mu_2 \beta_2')$ represents a vector on the extended wage frontier, of which K'', and hence S'', are constant multiples.)

3 The problem of multiple solutions

Whenever a Standard commodity is used as the measure of value the w–r relation is a straight line. Since this is true for all k Standard commodities, does it matter which one is used as the measure of value and, if so, which is the appropriate one? The Standard ratios corresponding to the various Standard systems are, in general, distinct numbers. Since the Standard ratio is also the maximum rate of profits in the actual system, it is clearly necessary to distinguish one, and only one, relevant Standard measure

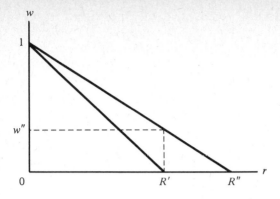

Figure 10.A.3

because the actual maximum rate of profits must be unique. According to Sraffa (*PC*, pp. 53–4), the Standard commodity 'eligible for adoption as unit of wages and prices' is the one associated with the lowest Standard ratio. His argument is as follows.

Let Standard system (*i*) be that with the lowest Standard ratio, R', and let (*ii*) be another Standard system with some higher ratio, R''. The corresponding w–r relations are shown in fig. 10.A.3. Remembering that *relative* prices in either Standard system are the same as those in the actual system, consider the consequences of basing a measure on system (*ii*). Assign to the economy a wage, w'', which is a fraction $1 - (R'/R'')$ of the net product of system (*ii*). This wage corresponds to a rate of profit $r = R'$ and a particular set of relative prices. But using Standard system (*i*) the wage appropriate to R' is zero. The wage thus appears to be positive using one measure and zero using another. This is as it should be: the wage is a positive *quantity* of Standard commodity (*ii*), but we know that if we value the Standard commodity of one system at the prices appropriate to the Standard ratio of another its value becomes zero. If this is so, then at R' the prices of actual commodities in terms of Standard commodity (*ii*) must be infinite which, as Sraffa says, is 'economically meaningless' and can be avoided by choosing system (*i*) as the Standard of value.

One way of confirming this choice would be to check whether in single-products systems the 'commonsense' measure (corresponding to all-positive multipliers) is also the one with the lowest value of R. That it is is demonstrated by Sraffa on pp. 29–31 of *PC*. Nevertheless, we should draw attention to the fact that Sraffa's contention is not universally valid in the case of joint-production systems. Steedman (1977c) has shown that the multipliers which yield the system with the lowest value of R may be such that (in a two-commodity example) $\phi_1 L_1 = -\phi_2 L_2$. Then, to quote Steedman, 'it is thus *not possible* to scale ϕ_1 and ϕ_2 so that employment in the Standard system is equal to that in the actual system. The derivation of the $w = (R - r)/R$ relation thus breaks down', and Sraffa's criterion becomes inappropriate.

11

Fixed capital

1 Introduction

Even a cursory consideration should be enough to convince anyone that models which include only circulating capital provide a rather inadequate representation of modern industrial economies, capitalist or otherwise. It is difficult, if not impossible, to think of a major industrial process that does not employ more or less durable or 'fixed' capital. But fixed capital includes not only the machinery, furnaces and mills of manufacturing and extractive industry. The warehouses, shops and offices of the retail and service sectors, together with the office machinery and computers that go in them, make up increasingly important parts of the stock of fixed capital. Trunk roads, railways and port facilities are essential parts of the industrial infrastructure, and so is modern telecommunications equipment. Power stations and gas pipelines provide the energy without which almost the entire economy would come to a halt. All of these are examples of fixed capital which can, in principle, come under private ownership for the purpose of making profits through the sale of their products or services. They may all, therefore, be included in our analysis. Other examples, such as city streets or houses, are either not privately owned or else not intended as a source of profits and do not fit comfortably into the analysis. In so far as they yield services which are either not used as inputs (as in the case of private housing, beyond basic needs), or else if used are not privately costed (as in the case of city streets), they may be regarded as non-basics, their provision being financed from the economy's surplus, privately or through taxation.

2 Fixed capital as a joint product

Consider an industry producing corn, the output of which, by the nature of the process, occurs during a brief period once a year. The means of production are seed and fertiliser, which are used up during the course of one year and renewed afresh the following year, and a tractor which may last, say, ten years. Over the course of its life the condition of the tractor deteriorates due to wear and tear until, at the end, all that is left is a heap of metal which may or may not have value as scrap. Does the fact that we have included among the means of production a piece of durable capital mean that we must now abandon the idea of a year-long production period? Not if we treat tractors of different ages as being different commodities so that, in the process of producing corn, a one-year-older tractor is also produced. This implies that, for each of the ten years of its life, a tractor is engaged in ten different processes: each process uses seed and fertiliser, but each uses a tractor of different age; each produces corn, but each produces a different joint product – again, a tractor of different age.

This way of treating fixed capital allows us to retain the framework of production periods used up to now and it allows Sraffa to say of joint production that it is 'the genus of which fixed capital is the leading species' (*PC*, p.63). But are we not perhaps being too hasty? The simple example of a tractor producing corn is one thing. But can we apply this treatment to the vast complex of processes employing fixed capital, many of which have production runs over different and overlapping periods, many providing a continuous flow of goods and services? The answer is 'yes', for we are not confined to choosing as a period of production the length of time of any actual production run. Suppose, for example, we pick on the week as our period. One year of corn production then consists of 52 processes, the first 51 of which produce one-week-older tractors plus a part growth of corn. In principle, we can make the period as short as we like so that it becomes the highest common denominator, as it were, of all actual production runs. We could in fact make it so small that the flow of periods approaches that of continuous time. Nothing, in principle, would be lost by this but it would mean dealing with an almost infinite number of processes so that, for quite practical expositional reasons, a 'lumpier' approach is preferred.

3 The price equations

If we are to try to represent real industrial economies then just about all of the processes in the model would have to involve fixed capital. But to begin at that point would present us with a hopelessly complicated task of analysis. Instead we make the smallest possible concession to reality by allowing just one process the use of fixed capital. Suppose we have altogether k basic final commodities (that is, k commodities excluding partly-used machines). The first $k-1$ of these directly use only circulating means of production and produce single products. The typical price equation for these commodities therefore looks very like that of the single-products system:

$$p_j = (1+r)\Sigma_i p_i a_{ij} + wl_j \quad (j = 1, \ldots, k-1; \ i = 1, \ldots, k)(11.1)$$

Suppose that the product of one of these $k-1$ industries, say industry m, is a machine. This machine is then employed among the means of production of process k. If this machine lasted for only one period the price equation

$$p_k = (1+r)\Sigma_i\, p_i a_{ik} + wl_k \quad (i=1,\ldots,k) \tag{11.2}$$

would be the same as in the single-products system – if a machine lasts for one period then it is no different from any piece of circulating capital. If, however, the machine lasts for, say, three periods, equation (11.2) needs modification and supplementing, for the production of k now involves three processes which can be run both consecutively (with a given machine) and side-by-side (with many machines of different ages). The process using the new machine has the following equation:

$$p_k + \pi_1\bar{m}_1 = (1+r)\Sigma_i\, p_i e_{i0} + w\lambda_0 + (1+r)\pi_0 m_0 \quad (i\neq m) \tag{11.3}$$

The right-hand side of equation (11.3) is essentially the same as that of (11.2), the apparent differences being the result of the following: (*i*) the machine has been separated from the rest of the means of production and given the symbol m_0, which is the quantity of machines per unit of process 0 (of the production of k); (*ii*) the price of the new machine is denoted by π_0; (*iii*) circulating capital input coefficients are denoted by e_{i0}; (*iv*) the labour coefficient is denoted by λ_0. These changes may seem confusing at first, but they are designed to minimise the use of sub- and superscripts in what follows. Since the first $k-1$ processes retain the original notation we can immediately drop the subscript k. The left-hand side of (11.3) shows that, along with one unit of finished product k, a quantity $\bar{m}_1$ of one-year-older machines is also produced. (In *numerical* terms $\bar{m}_1 = m_0$.) The book value of each one-year-old machine is π_1. These older machines then form part of the means of production for the next k-producing process:

$$p_h + \pi_2\bar{m}_2 = (1+r)\Sigma_i\, p_i e_{i1} + w\lambda_1 + (1+r)\pi_1 m_1. \tag{11.4}$$

It is possible that equations (11.3) and (11.4) are identical except for the ages of the machines and their book values. That is, the physical quantities of machines in the inputs and outputs of each unit process, the physical quantities of circulating capital of each type and of labour may all be the same. This would be so if the machine worked with constant efficiency throughout its lifetime, suddenly expiring at the end of its third year. It is much more likely, however, that the machine's efficiency varies during its lifetime. It may, for example, improve to begin with because of 'running in' and, in all probability, it will with older age become less efficient. These changes would be reflected in differences between the price equations (11.3) and (11.4). Thus, if, in numerical terms $m_1 > m_0$, more one-year-old machines are required per unit of k than are new machines. On the other hand, the productiveness of the machine may be maintained by the use of spares or repairs, or through more intensive operation, which would be reflected by changes in the circulating inputs and labour coefficients.

For the third and final period we have the equation

$$p_k + \pi_3 \bar{m}_3 = (1+r)\Sigma_i\, p_i e_{i2} + w\lambda_2 + (1+r)\pi_2 m_2. \qquad (11.5)$$

The remarks just made concerning variation in efficiency apply equally here. The only new consideration which arises with equation (11.5) concerns the term $\pi_3 \bar{m}_3$ on the left-hand side. At the end of the third period the machine is technically incapable of working any further. It is beyond repairs and main-tenance. The producer of k is thus left with a heap of metal and π_3 is the value of that heap. The simplest procedure is to suppose that the machine is worthless and can be disposed of at zero cost. In that case $\pi_3 = 0$, by assump-tion. Adopting that assumption to begin with, let us now look back at the system in its entirety, rather than process by process.

Choose some commodity, say i, as the standard of values (so $p_i = 1$), and let r be fixed exogenously. The system of equations (11.1) and (11.2), repre-senting a single-products basic system, then consists of k equations to solve for the $k-1$ relative prices and w. The properties of this system have already been thoroughly explored in Part II. Suppose now we replace (11.2) with (11.3). This does not change the number of equations but it does add one unknown: π_1. The system is therefore underdetermined. Adding equation (11.4) does not help since that brings another unknown with it, π_2. But help finally comes from (11.5), since $\pi_3 = 0$, by assumption. Thus, replacing (11.2) by (11.3)–(11.5) adds two equations and two unknowns so that the system as a whole is determinate.

What then is the consequence of dropping the assumption that $\pi_3 = 0$? π_3 may be non-zero for one, or a combination, of two reasons. First it may have positive value as scrap. This possibility is explicitly recognised by Sraffa, who notes two sub-cases (*PC*, p.64*n*). The first is where the scrap 'is interchangeable in use with some other material already accounted for', in which case, 'it simply assumes the price of the latter without need of an additional process'. This introduces an example of *pure* joint production with two processes producing the same product. But since π_3 is not an additional unknown the system is determinate. The second sub-case also introduces pure joint production but in a different way. If the scrap 'is not completely inter-changeable (for example, scrap iron as compared with pig iron), then there will be room for two processes, producing the same commodity (for example, steel)'. In this case the scrap forms an alternative input and π_3 is a separate unknown. The indeterminacy is resolved by introducing a new pro-cess (and hence equation) for producing a commodity already produced by other means.

The other reason why π_3 may be non-zero is that the worn-out machine may be costly to dispose of. Sraffa says nothing of this possibility but it can be handled in an obvious manner by explicitly specifying an additional process, d, called a 'disposal activity'. Let p_d be the price of an arbitrarily specified unit of d, determined by the prices of its means of production which consist of the k final commodities. This gives us one more equation and one more unknown but it also makes it possible to eliminate π_3. The number of units of d required per unit of the last k-process depends on the quantity of machines to be disposed of. If e_{dm} is the quantity of d per unit of $\bar{m}_3$, then this requirement is equal to $e_{dm}\bar{m}_3$. Thus the term $\pi_3\bar{m}_3$, can be replaced by $-p_d e_{dm}\bar{m}_3$, the negative sign indicating that it is a cost. More neatly, it could be transposed to the right-hand side and regarded as a cost of production.

Although they do not affect the determinacy of the system, positive scrap values and/or disposal costs do complicate the analysis so that, from now on, we shall assume that the end-of-period price of the oldest machine to be used is zero.

What we have just said may be satisfactory from the algebraic point of view but there are also economic considerations. The machines, we know, may be getting less efficient with age, so that more inputs may be required per unit of output. If that is so the later processes may not be profitable: at the given rate of profits they may not be able to pay a competitive wage. Competitive pressure then would ensure that the machine were scrapped after, say, just two years. Thus whereas the technical life-span of the machine is three years, the economic life-span is only two years; whereas three processes for producing k are possible, only two are actually operated. This limitation of the number of processes through the premature scrapping of a machine is known as a *truncation*. Thus, we may talk of a one-year truncation, a two-year truncation, and so on. What does this imply for the determinacy of the system? The same considerations apply to truncated as to non-truncated systems. On the zero scrap-value/free disposal assumption, for example, a two-year truncation would imply $\pi_2 = 0$, so that equation (11.4) is one equation with no additional unknowns.

As a convenient reference for what follows we conclude this section by writing out the price equations for a system of $k - 1$ commodities produced by circulating capital only, and for a kth machine-using industry having $N + 1$ possible truncations. We shall, however, make one change to our standard practice: instead of taking an arbitrary commodity as the standard of value we shall instead put $w = 1$.[1] With the nominal wage thus fixed variations in the real wage depend on variations in the prices of wage goods. The $k + N$ equations are as follows:

$$p_j = (1+r)\Sigma_i\, p_i a_{ij} + l_j \quad (j = 1, \ldots, k-1) \qquad (11.1)$$

$$(\pi_1 \bar{m}_1) + p_k = (1+r)\Sigma_i \, p_i e_{i0} + \lambda_0 \tag{11.0}$$

$$(\pi_2 \bar{m}_2) + p_k = (1+r)\Sigma_i \, p_i e_{i1} + \lambda_1 + (1+r)\pi_1 m_1 \tag{11.I}$$

$$(\pi_3 \bar{m}_3) + p_k = (1+r)\Sigma_i \, p_i e_{i2} + \lambda_2 + (1+r)\pi_2 m_2 \tag{11.II}$$

$$\vdots \qquad\qquad \vdots \qquad \vdots \qquad \vdots$$

$$0 + p_k = (1+r)\Sigma_i \, p_i e_{in} + \lambda_n + (1+r)\pi_n m_n. \tag{11.N}$$

The first $k-1$ equations, (11.1), include the price equation of industry m which produces the machine. (11.0) shows the price of k in the process using a new machine (the unit cost of which is included in the first terms on the right-hand side). If this is the only process to be used (truncation 0) then the term $\pi_1 \bar{m}_1$ is zero by the no scrap value/free disposal assumptions. It has been placed in parenthesis to remind the reader that its existence depends on the truncation adopted for the system. It will be clear that truncation 0 is nothing other than the usual single-products system. (11.I) refers to the process using a one-year-old machine of price π_1. This is shown explicitly by the coefficient m_1. There is, of course, no reason why the coefficients in (11.0) and (11.I) should be the same and, in particular, since process I does not use a new machine, $p_m e_{m1} = 0$. The other equations, $II, III, \ldots, X, \ldots, N$, may be similarly interpreted, except that in the last possible process (truncation N) our assumptions necessarily imply $\pi_{n+1} = 0$. There is one further complication: since the prices will depend on the truncation, even at a given rate of profits, they will need to be identified by an appropriate superscript. Thus p_i^2 refers to the price of final commodity i under truncation II.

4 Choice of technique

We noted in the last section that there is no reason why a machine must be operated over its entire physical life-span. If it is profitable to scrap prematurely then competition will ensure that scrapping occurs. The choice of truncation is a choice about which of the $k+N$ processes is most profitable. It is, in other words, a choice of technique. The system corresponding to each truncation is fully determinate, given r, and varying r allows us to trace out a real wage – rate of profits (real-w–r) relation for each. These real -w–r relations may be superimposed and the analysis of the choice of technique proceed according to the principles established in chapter 8. The properties of a fixed-capital system are not, however, as simple as those of a single-products system. We may, for example, find that for a given truncation the real-w–r relation is upward-sloping, at least in part, while machine prices may be negative. These features serve to remind us that we are in a joint-production world. But, in that case, we should expect the choice of technique to provide the means for relegating such behaviour into the zone of unprofitable practice. Confirmation of these expectations will occupy us in the following sections. Since the analysis is relatively involved it is worthwhile anticipating here our principal conclusions. We shall derive the following six propositions:

(1) The prices of final commodities are positive for all truncations, provided $r > 0$.

(2) Given r, extending the truncation by one process raises, lowers, or leaves unchanged the real wage, according as the price of the oldest machine used is positive, negative or zero.

(3) Given r, extending the truncation by one process raises, lowers or leaves unchanged the real wage, according as the prices of all younger machines are raised, lowered or unchanged.

(4) Given r, extending the truncation by *any* number of processes raises, lowers, or leaves unchanged the real wage, according as the price of all intermediate machines are positive, negative or zero.

(5) The real-w–r relation for a given truncation, other than 0, may slope upwards over some range of r.

(6) The real-w–r frontier is always downward-sloping.

The meaning of these propositions can be clarified by reference to the example in fig. 11.1, showing a system with three possible truncations. The real-w–r relation for truncation 0 is necessarily downward-sloping since this is just a single-products system. For the other two truncations the real-w–r relations may have upward-sloping parts (proposition 5). First, consider the

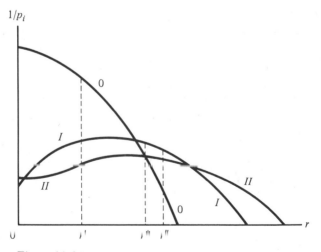

Figure 11.1

effect of switches occurring at the rate of profits r'. A switch from 0 to I reduces the real wage and implies from (2) that the value of the one-year-old machine used in truncation I is negative: $\pi_1^1 < 0$. We shall see that it is this negative price that allows I to have an upward-sloping real-w-r relation. A further switch, from I to II, reduces the real wage even further, so that $\pi_2^2 < 0$ and, by (3), makes π_1 even more negative. Again II has an upward-sloping relation. Next, consider switches at the rate r''. A switch from 0 to I raises the real wage so that $\pi_1^1 > 0$ and the new real-w-r relation must be downward-sloping. A switch from I to II implies $\pi_2^2 < 0$, but in this case the negativity is insufficient to cause an upward-sloping real-w-r relation. The real-w-r frontier consists only of those parts of the real-w-r relations that are downward-sloping (proposition 6). Finally, look at the rate r^* representing a switch-point between 0 and II. From (4), a switch from 0 to II implies that π_1^2 and π_2^2 are both zero. Yet a switch from 0 to I implies that $\pi_1^1 > 0$. This serves to illustrate the importance of relating prices to the truncation in use.

5 Analysis of switch-points

In this section we examine the properties of switch-points between successive truncations. We are not yet in a position to say whether these switch-points will occur on the real-w-r frontier.

We wish to prove the following: at a switch-point between any two successive truncations $X - 1$ and X, $\pi_x^x = 0$; that is, the value of the oldest machine used in the Xth truncation is zero. Consider the switch-point between truncations 0 and I. The price equations for process 0 for the two truncations are, respectively:

$$p_k^0 = (1+r)\Sigma_i\, p_i^0 e_{i0} + \lambda_0 \tag{11.0^0}$$

and

$$\pi_1^1 \bar{m}_1 + p_k^1 = (1+r)\Sigma_i\, p_i^1 e_{i0} + \lambda_0. \tag{11.0^1}$$

At the switch-point, r is, of course, the same for both truncations. Thus it is necessarily the case that $p_k^0 = p_k^1$, for otherwise the output of one process would never be purchased. If follows, from (11.1), that $p_j^0 = p_j^1$ for $j = 1$, $\ldots$, $k - 1$. The two equations above can, therefore, be consistent only if $\pi_1^1 = 0$.

The same reasoning can be applied to all other switches. Thus, consider the switch (I, II). For truncation I, π_2^1 in equation $(11.I^1)$ is zero, by assumption. Since r and $p_1, \ldots, p_k$ are the same for both, by the previous reasoning, it follows from a comparison of $(11.I^1)$ and $(11.I^2)$ that π_2^2 is also zero. And so on.

If the rate of profits is exogenous then comparative profitability of techniques is indicated by the real wage. At a switch-point the real wage should be the same for both techniques. That this is so follows from the fact that the prices of all final commodities remain constant. Thus the nominal wage $w = 1$ can buy the same bundle of wage commodities in either truncation.

To summarise, we may state the following: in extending the truncation by one period, at the switch-point rate of profits the price of the oldest machine to be used is zero.

6 Prices of final commodities

We now show that, no matter which truncation is adopted, the prices of final commodities are always positive, provided $r > 0$. The easiest way to do this is to start at truncation 0 and extend the argument along the succession of truncations. Truncation 0 is, of course, the single-products system and since, by assumption, all k products are basic then there is a unique set of all positive prices. This was shown in chapter 7 and it is worth repeating the argument briefly. To quote Sraffa, 'the price of no commodity can become zero until the price of at least one of the other commodities entering its means of production has become negative. Thus, since no price can become negative before any other, none can become negative at all' (*PC*, pp.27–8). What happens if we extend the truncation by one period? In that case, equation (11.0^1) could be written

$$p_k^1 = (1 + r)\Sigma_i\, p_i e_{i0} + \lambda_0 - \pi_1^1 \bar{m}_1$$

First examine the switch-point between 0 and I. Since $p_1, \ldots, p_k$ are positive with 0, they are positive with I. We also know that $\pi_1^1 = 0$. Now suppose we vary r away from its switch-point value and, operating truncation I, a negative π_1^1 emerges. In the above equation, that means that the last term, $-\pi_1^1 \bar{m}$ becomes positive. Then, on Sraffa's argument, it is clear that p_k can become negative only if one of the p_i do so first. Since that cannot happen, p_k remains positive. But if, as r changes, a positive π_1^1 emerges is it then possible for p_k to become negative? The answer is still no. Look at equation $(11.I)$ (with $\pi_2 = 0$). Starting at the switch-point $(0, I)$, everything on the right-hand side remains positive as r varies as, therefore, does p_k.

The argument may be extended along the entire list of truncations. Thus, so long as $r > 0$ so are all the final-commodity prices. This is proposition (1). It should be stressed, however, that nothing we have said here tells us how the prices of used machines behave. That is the next item on the agenda.

7 Prices of used machines

As a preliminary it is necessary first to establish some results in the context of the single-products system (truncation 0). Suppose that an alternative process becomes available for the production of k. Consider the effects of a change (*not* at a switch-point) to this second process. If, at the given rate of profits, p_k falls then, quite clearly, the initial prices of the other commodities cannot be sustained since k, being basic, enters into all the other processes. Thus, directly or indirectly, each of the terms $\Sigma p_i a_{ij}$ in equations (11.1) will be reduced and, directly or indirectly, each p_j will fall.

Now consider the relative magnitudes of these price changes. We intend to show that if the price change originates with commodity k then p_k changes proportionately more than the price of any other final commodity. Suppose that, as a result of the change in processes, p_k falls, and let h be that commodity among the remaining $k - 1$ commodities whose proportionate price fall is greatest. The price equation for h may be written as:

$$p_h = (1+r) \sum_i^{k-1} p_i a_{ih} + (1+r)p_k a_{kh} + l_h$$

By hypothesis, the fall in p_h is proportionately greater than the fall in the value of those means of production contributed by commodities $1, \ldots,$ $k - 1$. Since r is fixed, that means that p_h falls proportionately by more than the first term on the right-hand side. To maintain the balance of the equation, it follows that the second term must fall by proportionately more than p_h. And that must be because the fall in p_k is greater. (Note that a_{kh} is necessarily positive for, otherwise, some p_i would have to fall by more than p_h, contrary to our assumption.)

With these preliminaries completed we can now examine the behaviour of used machine prices. Once again, consider an extension of the truncation from 0 to I, this time at a value of r which is *not* a switch-point. Thus, p_k may rise or fall with the extension. With truncation 0, (11.0^0) is the relevant equation; with truncation I, (11.0^1) holds. What we have to do is consider the sign of π_1^1. To do this subtract (11.0^0) from (11.0^1) and rearrange slightly to give

$$\pi_1^1 \bar{m}_1 = (1+r)\Sigma_i e_{i0}(p_i^1 - p_i^0) - (p_k^1 - p_k^0). \qquad (11.6)$$

Suppose that $p_k^1 < p_k^0$. We know, from our preliminary discussion, that if, at a given rate of profits, the price of a basic final commodity (say p_k) falls because of a change in its process of production, the prices of all other final commodities will also fall. We also know that these other prices will fall less than in proportion to p_k. The same reasoning is fully applicable here, so that the term $(1+r)\Sigma_i e_{i0}(p_i^1 - p_i^0)$ falls less than in proportion to the term $(p_k^1 - p_k^0)$. Moreover, since (11.0^0) implies that

$$(1+r)\Sigma_i p_i^0 e_{i0} \leqslant p_k^0,$$

looking at the right-hand side of (11.6), the absolute magnitude of the second term must be greater than the absolute magnitude of the first. In other words, the right-hand side must be positive and so, therefore, must π_1^1.

Thus, if, in extending the truncation from 0 to I, $p_k^1 < p_k^0$, then $\pi_1^1 > 0$. Since the prices of *all* final commodities have fallen, the wage in terms of any of them has increased. A positive π_1^1 is accompanied by an increase in the real wage. By exactly the same reasoning it can be shown that an extension from 0 to I which results in a reduction of the real wage also results in a negative π_1^1. We already know, of course that $\pi_1^1 = 0$ at a switch-point when the real wage is constant.

Again, it is possible to extend this argument along the series of truncations. Comparing I and II, for example, the equations we need to compare are:

$$p_k^1 = (1+r)\Sigma_i\, p_i^1 e_{i1} + \lambda_1 + (1+r)\pi_1^1 m_1 \qquad (11.I^1)$$

and

$$\pi_2^2 \bar{m}_2 + p_k^2 = (1+r)\Sigma_i\, p_i^2 e_{i1} + \lambda_1 + (1+r)\pi_1^2 m_1. \qquad (11.I^2)$$

Subtracting the first from the second gives

$$\pi_2^2 \bar{m}_2 = (1+r)\Sigma_i\, e_{i1}(p_i^2 - p_i^1) + (1+r)m_1(\pi_1^2 - \pi_1^1) - (p_k^2 - p_k^1). \qquad (11.7)$$

The argument that was applied to equation (11.6) can also be applied to equation (11.7), except that the latter equation has an extra term on the right-hand side. We can determine the sign of the middle term by examining equation (11.0) when solved for $\pi_1 \bar{m}_1$:

$$\pi_1 \bar{m}_1 = -[p_k - (1+r)\Sigma_i\, p_i e_{i0}] + \lambda_0.$$

If, say, $p_k^2 < p_k^1$ then the expression in square brackets is also smaller for II than for I (because the reduction in the p_i is in lesser proportion to the reduction in p_k). In that case, it follows that $\pi_1^2 > \pi_1^1$. Thus, in (11.7) the middle term is positive and, by a repetition of our previous argument, so is π_2^2. Indeed, if we were to continue along the series of truncations, we would find that, for each extension, a rise in the real wage is accompanied by a positive price for the oldest machine used, and *vice versa*.

The last part of our argument showed in passing that an extension from I to II which raises the real wage also raises the price of the one-year-old machine. This again is a proposition which may be generalised along the entire series of truncations: an extension which raises the real wage raises the prices of *all* younger machines. This may be added to the main proposition of this section: in extending the truncation by one process (at a given rate of profits), the price of the oldest machine to be used is positive, zero, or negative, according as the real wage increases, remains the same, or falls. These are propositions (3) and (2), respectively.

We may, finally, generalise our results to include extensions to non-adjacent truncations; from 0 to III, for example. We can show that, in extending the truncation by any number of processes (up to N), if the real wage increases, the prices of the machines of all intermediate ages are positive: proposition (4). For π_1 this is easy: in equation (11.0^1) simply replace the superscript 1 by any superscript $2, \ldots, n$ and follow the same argument as above. The same goes for π_2: in equation $(11.I^2)$ replacing the superscript 2 by any superscript $3, \ldots, n$ allows us to show, in the same manner, that a reduction in p_i implies $\pi_2 > 0$.

8 The real-w–r frontier

Our last finding implies that if part of the real-w–r relation of any truncation X appears as part of the real-w–r frontier then, at the associated values of r, $\pi_x^x > 0$, as are all $\pi_1^x, \ldots, \pi_{x-1}^x$. We can show that this part of the frontier is downward-sloping.

Consider the price of some final commodity j. Since the nominal wage is fixed at unity, as r rises p_j can only fall if the price of at least one of its means of production falls. For truncation 0, described fully by the system of single-products equations, this is not possible since no price can fall before any other. Hence, for truncation 0, the real wage (whatever its composition) must fall as r rises. But for some truncation $X > 0$ it may be thought that p_j might fall through p_k falling faster. It is easy to show, however, that this is not possible. For $X = II$, say, it can be seen from equation $(11.II^2)$ that p_k^2 can fall only if π_2^2 falls; in turn, π_2^2 and p_k^2 can fall only if π_1^2 falls – equation $(11.I^2)$. But from (11.0^2), π_1^2 cannot fall. It follows that, as r rises, the prices of all final commodities rise so that the real-w–r relation is downward-sloping whenever it forms part of the frontier: proposition (6).

On the other hand, if part of the real-w–r relation for X does not appear on the frontier we cannot say for sure that that part will be downward-sloping: proposition (5). This is because the prices of some intermediate machines may be negative. Consider truncation I. If a switch from 0 to I reduces the real wage at a given r then π_1^1, we know, must be negative. (At this r the real-w–r relation for I cannot be on the frontier since it is dominated by 0, at least.) Looking at equation $(11.I^1)$, the term $(1 + r)\pi_1^1 m$ is negative and can become increasingly so as r rises (even if the absolute magnitude of π_1^1 is falling, provided it does not offset the increase in $(1 + r)$). This means that p_k^1 can now fall as a result of r rising. This is perfectly consistent with (11.0^1): it is true that if the fall originates with p_k, the right-hand side of (11.0^1) must fall in lesser proportion; but if π_1^1, on the right-hand side, is falling in absolute magnitude (that is, becoming more positive), this is possible. If p_k can fall then so can p_j and, indeed, the prices of any final commodities making up the wage basket.

9 Some generalisations

There are two obvious generalisations that can be made to the preceding analysis. The first is to extend the use of machines to other industries. The second is to allow commodities to be produced using a combination of machines.

The first is straightforward. Each machine-using industry will have available a number of processes equal to the number of periods that its machine can physically endure. If, say, two commodities are producible by machines lasting three and four years, respectively, then, in the absence of alternative technologies, there are twelve techniques for the system as a whole. It does not matter if the machines are the same *when new* (wearing out at different rates according to how they are used), provided that partly-used machines are not transferred from one industry to another (see below). This generalisation introduces the possibility that the machines are, themselves, the product of machinery. The principles established above can be adapted without difficulty to this case.

The second case, in its most general form, gives rise to considerable analytical difficulties. This is because the productivity of one of the machines may depend on the physical condition of the other machines with which it is worked. Roncaglia (1978, p.43) has shown that this interdependence may generate an infinite number of productivity combinations and, hence, an infinite number of processes for the production of a final commodity. To avoid these complications we shall assume that the productivity of each machine is independent of the ages and conditions of other machines.

Consider, then, an industry in which a final commodity is produced by combining two machines which last two and five years, respectively. These two machines may be said to comprise a composite machine or 'plant' whose physical lifespan is ten years (the lowest common multiple of two and five). Renewing the components of that plant every two and five years can then be considered as analogous to repair and maintenance. The decision to truncate the lifetime of the plant is made on the basis of profitability, as in the case of a single machine. This procedure can be illustrated by the simple example of a lorry. A lorry is often considered as a single machine, but it is, in fact, composed of many machines: engine, carburettor, battery, gearbox, and so on. Although the engine may last fifteen years, the battery may need replacing every four. Fitting a new battery can be regarded as routine maintenance, the replacement batteries entering the price equations on the same footing as circulating-capital inputs. Note that, with the lowest common multiple of the components' physical lifespan being at least sixty years, it is quite likely that at least *some* components will be scrapped before they are physically worn out.[2]

We noted above one other possible generalisation: the inter-industry sale of second-hand machinery. This brings with it the complication of pure joint production. As with positive scrap values it needs to be handled in a general joint-production framework.

10 Summary

We have seen that fixed capital is readily handled within the Sraffian framework as a particular case of joint production. (This is also true of the von Neumann approach.) The important conclusion to be drawn from the analysis is that, as in the case of pure joint production, competition ensures that the *system* behaviour is such that real wages fall whenever r rises. Potential transgressions of this rule are always seen to imply non-profitable behaviour. Thus, while a particular truncation may give rise to a positively sloped real-w–r relation, that relation will always lie below the real-w–r frontier. In this case capitalists are alerted to their unprofitable choice of truncation by the negative book values of used machines. In general, opportunities for improving profitability by changing the truncation are indicated by the increasing value of all used machines, and *vice versa*. It is worth recalling, however, that we have ruled out by assumption the possibilities of positive scrap values and costly disposal (not to mention second-hand sales). Even so, from what we have learned so far we should be surprised if any of these should present an exception to the rule that the real-w–r frontier is negatively sloped.

FURTHER READING

There is not a great deal available (in English) on this important subject. Roncaglia (1978) pp.36–48, is a good description of the production relationships of Sraffa's fixed-capital system. But for an analysis of its price-distribution properties it is necessary to turn to three papers included in Pasinetti (1980). These are Varri (1974), Baldone (1974) and Schefold (1980*a*), Part II. The first two were originally published in Italian (like so much of the work on Sraffa); the last is a compilation of previously published articles. These three papers are very good but very mathematical. Fortunately, we have been able to obtain most of their important conclusions in this chapter.

Sraffa's own discussion of fixed capital (*PC*, chapter X) is concerned much more with the treatment of depreciation than with the system behaviour of prices and distribution.

The approach to fixed capital adopted by Sraffa was, he says, first suggested by Torrens in 1808, and again in Torrens (1821). It was formalised mathematically by William Whewell in his *Mathematical Exposition of Some of the Leading Doctrines in Mr. Ricardo's Principles of Political Economy and Taxation* of 1831 (reprinted in Whewell, 1971). For a discussion of Whewell's contribution, see Campanelli (1982).

12

The theory of rent

1 Introduction

Rent is a consequence of scarcity. In the systems so far considered, in which all commodities are producible by labour and other commodities, the processes of production ensure that commodities are available in the required combinations and in the amounts necessary for these same processes to be repeated (in the case of proportional growth, on an enlarged scale). An obvious problem arises, therefore, if we wish to extend the analysis to cover cases of non-expandable means of production, of which land is the most important example. The use of a particular method of cultivation on land of a particular quality, and which is of limited availability, may not produce a sufficient amount of corn to satisfy demand. And in a growing economy not favoured with technological progress, the scarcity of that land will increase over time. The theory of rent is concerned with the mechanisms by which the supply of and demand for land and land-using commodities are brought into line.

On the face of it, the Sraffa–Leontief approach would appear to be ill-suited to handling the problem of resource scarcity. Traditionally, scarcity has been regarded as the province of neoclassical economics. In fact, however, non-expandable means of production can be dealt with in the Sraffian framework as a 'species' (to use Sraffa's metaphor) of joint production. In the 'commonsense' view, joint-production processes are those which produce more than one commodity. But complications similar to those of 'commonsense' joint production also arise where one commodity is simultaneously produced by more than one process. Joint production may, therefore, refer to joint commodities or joint processes, and joint processes are what will occur whenever there is a scarcity of some means of production. Suppose that the production of corn on land of the highest quality is insufficient to meet demand. Then poorer grades will have to be employed at the same time. To produce a unit of corn on the poorer grades will require more costly inputs. And so, to satisfy demand, the corn industry will have to consist of several technically different activities. But what happens if there is only a single quality of land available? In that case it is necessary that the land be subject to increasingly intensive exploitation: a more intensive process operating side by side with a less intensive process, with the former taking up more of the land area as demand increases. Positive growth therefore implies continual changes in the nature of land-using processes. Either there is a progressive extension to lands of poorer and poorer quality, or there is an increasingly intensive exploitation of land of a particular quality, or both. We consider these possibilities in turn.

2 Extensive rent with two grades of land

Suppose there are k final commodities, the first $k - 1$ of which are 'industrial' commodities whose land requirements are so small that they can be neglected. To keep things simple, the industrial sector is made up entirely of single-products industries and there is only one process available for producing each industrial commodity. The kth commodity is corn and it requires significant amounts of land of some quality. All k commodities are basic. Taking a unit of labour as the standard of value (that is, putting $w = 1$), the price equation for a typical industrial commodity is

$$p_j = (1 + r)\Sigma_i p_i a_{ij} + l_j \quad (j = 1, \ldots, k - 1; i = 1, \ldots, k). \quad (12.1)$$

When it comes to finding a price equation for corn, however, we have a problem. Even if there is only one process associated with each grade of land we cannot say *a priori* which of those processes will be used first. The ordering of grades according to fertility (which can, presumably, be measured beforehand) is of no help since fertility, in the biological sense, is not synonymous with 'profitability'. Suppose that two grades of land are available. One is a flat plain whose soil is not especially fertile but which is ideally suited to mechanisation. Whereas labour, using only simple tools, gets a scanty reward from this soil, irrigation, fertilisers, pesticides, tractors and harvesters together yield good crops. This plain gives way to steep volcanic slopes whose surface is rich in plant nutrients and requires no fertilisers. The steepness renders mechanisation impossible with the technology available. Maintaining the narrow terraces is therefore a labour-intensive operation and cultivation is carried on using hoes and other simple tools. If the complete cultivation of *one or other* of these grades is more than sufficient to satisfy demand for corn, then quite clearly we have a straightforward choice of technique. The alternative price equations for corn may be written

$$p_k = (1 + r)\Sigma_i p_i e_{i0} + \lambda_0 \quad\quad\quad (12.2)$$

$$p_k = (1 + r)\Sigma_i p_i e_{i1} + \lambda_1 \qu\quad\quad\quad (12.3)$$

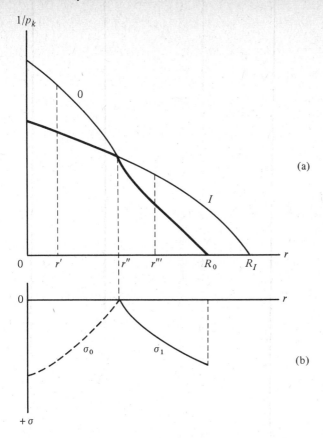

Figure 12.1

where 0, let us say, refers to the plain, 1 to the slopes. The notational changes are exactly as in the last chapter and are made for the same reasons: e_{i0} is the input of i per unit of k produced on land of grade 0, and so on. Because either grade is in excess supply, each is a 'free good' and there is no rent.

The choice of technique follows the usual criterion: derive the real-w–r relations for the two systems (12.1) with (12.2) and (12.1) with (12.3), superimpose them, and compare profitability at the exogenously given rate of profits or real wage. The top part of fig. 12.1 shows how the wage in terms of corn $(1/p_k)$ varies with r for each technique. At low rates of profits the more mechanised technique is the most profitable. At higher rates the labour-intensive technique is superior. Whilst reswitching is unlikely in our particular example there is nothing, in principle, to prevent this from occurring. The real-w–r relations may intersect several times. The general conclusion, therefore, is that the ranking of grades according to profitability depends on the value of the exogenous distributive variable.

All this follows directly from what we already know. If both grades of land are in excess supply the problem of scarcity does not arise and the choice of grades is a simple choice of technique. But suppose now that at, say, $r = r'$ the growth of the economy leads to the complete using up of grade 0. Further growth of corn requirements will require an extension of cultivation to the less profitable grade I, part of which, however, remains unused. Thus two processes are now operated simultaneously. The consequences of this extension can be seen by examining the nature of the price adjustments starting from the initial, 0-only, prices. Since grade I remains in excess supply it costs nothing to use. The labour and commodity input requirements mean, however, that corn from grade I is more costly: p_k must rise to cover these costs and pay profits at a rate r'. Since p_k is basic all other prices must rise too. But, as we know from chapter 11, section 7, they do not rise, in proportionate terms, by as much as p_k. This creates an imbalance in equation (12.2), where the left-hand side has risen by more than the right-hand side. The imbalance is restored by the rent which is now payable on the scarce land 0; (12.2) is thus modified as follows:

$$p_k = (1 + r) \Sigma_i p_i e_{i0} + \lambda_0 + \sigma_0 t_0 \qquad (12.4)$$

where t_0 is the number of acres of land of grade 0 needed to produce a unit of corn, and σ_0 is the rent per acre.

Because all prices have risen the wage in terms of any one of them has fallen, but its fall is greatest in terms of corn. The extent of the fall of $1/p_k$ is, in fact, indicated by the real-w-r relation for technique I, at $r = r'$. This is because in the new situation equation (12.4) is irrelevant to the determination of prices. (12.1) and (12.3) are k equations in k unknown prices (remember $w = 1$, by choice, and r is exogenous) and so are fully determinate. Together they form what may be called a 'price-distribution' subsystem of equations.[1] And the prices they yield are the same as those which would obtain in an economy in which all corn was produced on no-rent land of grade I quality. (12.4) provides an extra equation and an extra unknown, σ_0. It may be regarded as the 'rent' sub-system.

With an extension of cultivation an increase in the price of corn gives rise to a positive rent on superior quality land, that is, the land on which labour and capital costs are lower. A negative rent could arise only if the extension brought about a decrease in p_k: for example, if at r''' there were an extension from 0 to I. But under competitive conditions this could never be the case for, at r''', the use of 0 on its own is unprofitable. It would not be the first grade to be used. At this rate of profits the extension would be from I to 0 and a positive rent would ensue. At $r = r''$, the two processes are equiprofitable. Although the physical properties of the lands may differ, *in economic terms* it is as though the lands are of the same quality. The fact that some land is unused therefore means that rent is zero.

The distributional implications of extensive cultivation depend on the availabilities of the two grades of land relative to the demand for corn. There are three possibilities which we can consider: (*i*) where there is more than enough grade 0 to meet all corn demands on its own, whereas the acreage of grade *I* is insufficient to do so; (*ii*) the reverse situation of an abundance of grade *I* with a small amount of grade 0; (*iii*) where neither grade is sufficient on its own to satisfy demand but together they are more than enough. The real-w–r relationships for each of these cases can be seen in part (*a*) of fig. 12.1 and the σ–r relationships in part (*b*).

In case (*i*), for rates of profits between zero and r'', the abundant grade 0 is more profitable. With grade *I* completely unused no rent can arise. But above r'', grade *I* becomes more profitable and is now eagerly purchased by competing capitalist farmers. Because of its scarcity the result of this competition is to create a rent, σ_1 per acre. Since the real-w–r relationship over this range is determined by the 'price-distribution' equations (12.1) and (12.2), it remains the same as that for grade 0. The economy's maximum rate of profits is R_0. The 'rent' equation is (12.3) when the right-hand side is modified to include the term $+ \sigma_1 t_1$. Its sole function is to determine the behaviour of σ_1 which rises as p_k increases relative to the value of non-land costs on grade *I*. The relation between σ_1 and r is shown by the right-hand 'branch' in part (*b*).

Case (*ii*) is simply the reverse of case (*i*). (12.1) and (12.3) are the 'price-distribution' equations which means that the economy's real-w–r relation is the same as that for grade *I* on its own, and has a maximum rate of profits R_I. For rates of profits up to r'' there is a rent on grade 0 land, the relationship between σ_0 and r indicated by the left-hand branch in part (*b*).

The third case is a combination of the previous two. For rates of profits up to r'' equations (12.1) and (12.3) determine the real-w–r relation; grade 0 is scarce and has a positive rent. For $r'' < r < R_0$, (12.1) and (12.2) determine the real-w–r relation and I is the scarce grade with a positive rent. At r'' itself there is effectively a single quality of land, in excess supply, so that there is no rent at all at this rate. In case (*iii*), then, as r increases from zero, rent falls and then rises, as indicated by *both* branches in part (*b*) (each branch, of course, corresponding to a different grade).

It follows from these considerations that part (*a*) of fig. 12.1 no longer represents the standard choice-of-technique problem in which the real-w–r relations are superimposed to obtain an *outer* envelope or frontier. We have just derived three real-w–r relationships (in addition to the standard case) which combine parts of the individual relations in different ways, depending on the availability of each grade of land. Generally speaking, a growth in the demand for corn forces the use of inferior grades of land and thus forces an *inward* movement of the real-*w*–*r* possibilities. Thus, if it were necessary to use both grades of land the economy's real-*w*–*r* frontier would not be the outer envelope of the individual relations, but their *inner* envelope, and the maximum rate of profits would not be R_I but R_0. Quite clearly, distributional relationships depend on the level of demand for the scarce means of production. (A *contraction* in the economy would allow R_0 to be exceeded once grade 0 had become redundant.)

Before generalising the analysis of extensive rent it would be useful to summarise the argument so far. At a given initial rate of profits, an extension of cultivation to land involving higher capital and labour costs raises the price of corn. In a competitive world the price of corn must be uniform. The immediate impact of the extension is to give an advantage to the users of the less costly land. But that land is scarce, and capitalists striving to obtain the higher rate of return from its use will bid up the price of the land. The potential profits are reduced by competition, to the benefit of the landowners, until the rates of profits on the two grades of land are brought back into equality. (We are, of course, making a 'functional' distinction between landlords and capitalists. Since some capitalists are likely to be owners of land the social implications are less clear-cut.) The use of poorer land thus reduces 'profitability' (which in this case means a reduction in the real wage) but raises rent per acre on land of superior quality. It should, by now, be clear that 'superiority' cannot be defined independently of income distribution: at $r = r'$, grade 0 is superior, but at $r = r'''$ grade I has that status. Finally, we have seen that rents per acre need not be monotonically related to either r or the real wage.

3 Extensive rent with many grades of land

There is no difficulty in extending the equation system to include many grades of land. Suppose that there are, altogether, $N + 1$ types of land of which $X + 1$ are in use. The system is then described by the following $k + X$ equations:

$$p_j = (1 + r)\Sigma_i\, p_i a_{ij} + l_j \quad (j = 1, \ldots, k - 1) \tag{12.1}$$

$$p_k = (1 + r)\Sigma_i\, p_i e_{i0} + \lambda_0 + \sigma_0 t_0 \tag{12.0}$$

$$p_k = (1 + r)\Sigma_i\, p_i e_{i1} + \lambda_1 + \sigma_1 t_1 \tag{12.I}$$

$$\vdots \qquad \vdots$$

$$p_k = (1 + r)\Sigma_i\, p_i e_{ix} + \lambda_x. \tag{12.X}$$

The ranking $0, I, \ldots, X$ we may suppose to be a ranking according to profitability at some specified value of r. Provided the demand for X does not exceed its availability no rent is payable on that grade. The k equations (12.1) and (12.X) therefore allow for the determination of all prices. Equations (12.0), (12.I), etc. then determine their associated rent terms σ_0, σ_1, and so on. Since lands $X + 1, \ldots, N$ are not yet in use their equations are, for the time being, irrelevant. Sooner or later, however, the growth of the economy will lead to the complete using up of grade X. The latter will therefore pass on its 'marginal' status to $X + 1$ and the term $+ \sigma_x t_x$ will have to be added to the right-hand side of (12.X).

Each time the margin is extended the price of corn rises, not only relative to the nominal wage, but relative to other prices as well. With each extension, therefore, the rent of every infra-marginal grade rises. It does not, however, follow that the ranking of lands according to rent per acre is necessarily the same as the ranking according to profitability. The rent per acre on grade I, for example, is given by

$$\sigma_1 = [p_k - (1 + r)\Sigma p_i e_{i1} - \lambda_1]/t_1$$

The rate at which σ_1 rises with p_k depends, in part, on the *composition* of the means of production used on this land. The aggregate value of the means of production may vary in an extremely complex way, depending on the price changes of the individual commodities which, themselves, depend on the price changes of their own means of production, and so on.[2] Thus, as the rents on the infra-marginal grades rise with an extension of the margin, they may do so at different rates: σ_4 now overtaking σ_5, σ_5 now pulling back and overtaking σ_4, and so on. These possibilities are illustrated graphically in fig. 12.2 where the first column of numbers shows how σ_0 increases as the margin is extended from grade 0 to grade 9; the second column shows how σ_1 increases, etc. Thus, while the profitability ranking, for a given r, remains 1, 2, 3, ..., 9, the order or rentability is subject to a large number of changes. To take one example, when grade 9 is marginal, the order of rents (starting with the highest) is 2, 1, 3, 0, 6, 5, 4, 7, 8.

Nothing new, in principle, can be said about the relations between the real wage, the rate of profits and rents per acre in the present case, except that the functions relating the rents per acre, on particular grades, to r will now run side-by-side, overlapping and criss-crossing, according to availability of grades, and changes in the orders of profitability and rentability.

It remains to say something, briefly, about changes in distribution induced by the growth of the economy. With an extension of the margin production becomes less profitable. Whether this results in a falling rate of profits or a falling real wage depends, of course, on which of these is fixed from outside. Whether it is r or the real wage that is exogenous, and at what level it is fixed, depends on how the potential antagonisms between capitalists and

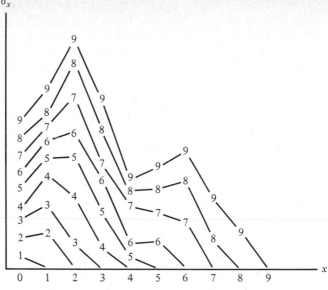

Figure 12.2

workers are resolved. With the appearance of extensive rent the possibilities for antagonism increase. Most obvious is the fact that landlords now take a slice of the surplus. Competition amongst capitalists weakens their own power and allows landlords a share of the surplus simply as a consequence of their ownership of land. Less obviously, as Quadrio-Curzio (1980) has pointed out, antagonism may arise between workers who have been employed for some time and those who have not. At a given rate of profits, the employed will suffer a fall in real wages with an extension of cultivation. But the previously unemployed may now find jobs which give them an income greater than the level of social security payments, if any. There thus arises the possibility of an alliance between unemployed workers and land-lords. Naturally, if the real wage is fixed this possibility does not arise. Here it is the rate of profits which falls, but *aggregate* profits may fall, stay the same, or rise, depending on whether or not the extension of activity out-weighs the reduction in r.

4 Intensive rent

In the previous sections a growth in the demand for corn has been satisfied by extending cultivation to poorer grades of land, it being supposed that there is always land of some quality available for further exploitation. We now turn to the case in which land is of a uniform quality but in limited supply. If with a given method of cultivation all of the available land becomes used up the only way to satisfy additional demand is to use another method which exploits the land more intensively.

Let us denote the less intensive process by 0, the more intensive one by *I*. Here t_0 and t_1 no longer refer to different grades of land but to acreages of the same grade cultivated by processes 0 and *I*. By definition $t_0 > t_1$; that is, more land is required to produce a unit of corn when using process 0 than when using process *I*. While method 0 is incapable of meeting demand on its own with the land available, it must be the case that *I* can do so. (Otherwise a third, even more intensive process will be required, a possibility which is discussed below.) An alternative would be to operate 0 and *I* side by side so as to use up the land available. There is, therefore, a choice of technique: technique (*I*) which uses process *I* on its own, leaving land in excess supply; and technique (0, *I*) where both processes are operated together and the land is fully used up. Clearly, only in the second case will a rent be established. But, because the land is of uniform quality, the rent per acre will be the same no matter which process is used. Thus $\sigma_0 = \sigma_1 = \sigma$.

The price equations for the two techniques obviously have in common the equations for industrial commodities (12.1). For corn, technique (*I*) is represented by

$$p_k = (1+r)\Sigma_i p_i e_{i1} + \lambda_1 \tag{12.5}$$

and technique (0, *I*) by two equations:

$$p_k = (1+r)\Sigma_i p_i e_{i0} + \lambda_0 + \sigma t_0 \tag{12.6}$$

$$p_k = (1+r)\Sigma_i p_i e_{i1} + \lambda_1 + \sigma t_1. \tag{12.7}$$

Combining (12.1) and (12.5) yields a single-products system in which scarcity does not arise; with, say, *r* given there are *k* equations in *k* unknowns. But with technique (0, *I*) there is competition for land. This generates a uniform rent per acre, σ, so that the system contains an extra equation with an extra unknown. When the two processes are operated together it can be seen that the one which is physically more productive (that is, the one which produces more corn per acre), *I*, also has the higher capital and labour costs. Since the price of corn must be the same for both processes then the right-hand sides of (12.6) and (12.7) must be equal. It follows that if $t_1 < t_0$, then

$$(1+r)\Sigma_i p_i e_{i1} + \lambda_1 > (1+r)\Sigma_i p_i e_{i0} + \lambda_0. \tag{12.8}$$

The analysis of the choice between the two techniques is discussed with reference to fig. 12.3. Consider the rate of profits r'. At very low levels of demand process 0 was able to cope and this was the most profitable way of producing corn. But as the land became used up a change in technique was

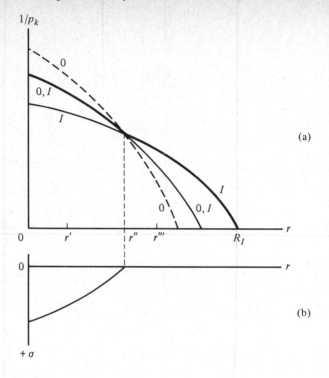

Figure 12.3

required. Although process I can satisfy the higher demand on its own its use involves a considerable reduction in profitability. In the case illustrated a more profitable course is to combine 0 and I such that together they just meet demand, while jointly occupying all of the land available. This gives rise to a rent for the following reason. If rent were zero then capitalists would have a straightforward choice between 0 and I. But since $p_k^1 > p_k^0$ at the rate of profits r' there could be no co-existence. Those capitalists who were operating I would switch to 0, but because 0 is more land-intensive this would imply competition for scarce land. All farmers would compete for larger acreages to operate process 0 and a rent would emerge. Although the rent is uniform it nevertheless succeeds in removing the differences in price (and profitability) of the two processes because process 0, being more land-intensive, has a higher charge for rent: $\sigma t_0 > \sigma t_1$.

Thus, at the rate of profits r', technique $(0, I)$ is associated with a positive rent. The size of σ depends on the extent to which p_k must rise to allow process I to co-exist profitably with process 0. (It does *not* depend on the proportions of land occupied by the two processes.) At r''', method I was

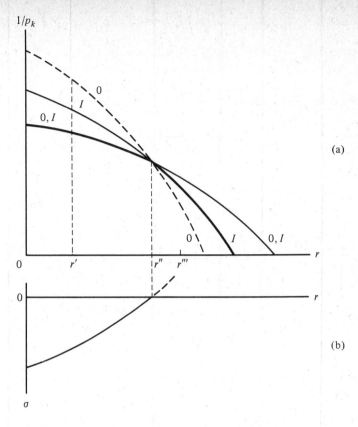

Figure 12.4

more profitable even at low levels of demand and it continues to be so as long as some land is in excess supply. Rent at r''' is, of course, zero. At r'', techniques (I) and $(0,I)$ are equiprofitable and here, too, rent must be zero, since any threat to the existence of surplus land can easily be rectified by operating I at a higher level. The behaviour of σ with respect to r is shown in part (b) of fig. 12.3.

The case illustrated in fig. 12.3 is relatively straightforward. We now consider two other cases which display somewhat more complex features. The first is illustrated in fig. 12.4. Whereas previously the real-w–r relation for technique $(0,I)$ was sandwiched between those for (0) and (I), in this case it lies outisde.[3] The resulting behaviour is somewhat paradoxical. Consider the rate of profits r'. At this rate the most profitable technique is (0), but this is incapable of satisfying demand. The next most profitable technique is (I) and since this can meet corn requirements it might be supposed that this is the technique that is adopted. The problem, however, is that if process I were used alone and land were in excess supply some capitalists would be tempted to get a higher return through using 0. And for a short period they might succeed. But competition would force other capitalists to do likewise until the supply of land became exhausted. A rent would emerge and profitability (as reflected in the real wage) would decline for both processes, but the rate of decline would be greater for 0, the more land-intensive one. This would continue until the two became equiprofitable at some lower real wage, indicated by the real-w–r relation for technique $(0, I)$. The paradox is that while (I) offers a higher real wage than $(0, I)$ it cannot be sustained under competitive conditions. There will always be an incentive for someone to introduce process 0. The search for individual profit appears to undermine the profitability of the system as a whole.

To resolve this paradox it is necessary to consider further the way in which we have been using the term 'profitability'. In chapter 8, it was argued that if the rate of profits were exogenous, action by capitalists to improve their profitability would, as the result of competition, have the consequence of increasing the real wage. Consequently, the profitability of the *system* could be reflected either in the rate of profits, as such, or in the real wage, depending on which was exogenous. In the case of rent we have a third claim on national income so that, with r given, it is possible that the striving for greater individual profitability could manifest itself in increased real wages *or* in increased rents or both. Up to now, no difficulty has arisen from our practice of using 'profitability' to refer solely to the real-w–r possibilities since no feasible technique has paid a higher real wage and a lower rent than some other feasible technique. But, in the present case, while technique $(0, I)$ is 'less profitable' than (I) as reflected in the real wage, it is 'more profitable' as reflected in the rent.

Similar considerations arise at r'''. Here technique $(0, I)$ yields a higher real wage than (I). But whereas rents are zero with (I), they are negative with $(0, I)$. Since negative rents make no economic sense, (I) is the only feasible technique.

The second case concerns the possibility of the rate of profits and the real wage rising and falling together. In single-products systems an increase in r needs to be compensated for by a fall in the real wage. But with positive rents it becomes possible for an increase in r to be accompanied by a rising real wage provided that they are both compensated for by a sufficiently large fall in rents. It is nevertheless the case that a positive relation between r and the real wage can only occur in the case of intensive rent.[4] The reason is that, in the case of extensive rent, the 'price-distribution' sub-system of equations does not include a rent term, whereas in the present case a real-w–r relation cannot be determined independently of σ. (This, of course, would not be the case if the produce of the land were a non-basic, non-wage commodity.)

To see, in more detail, how the real wage and the rate of profits may vary in sympathy, compare the single-products system (12.1) and (12.5) with the system (12.1), (12.6) and (12.7). For the first system we can recall the argument used in chapter 7, section 2 (adapted here to the case of 'labour-commanded' prices), to demonstrate the inverse relationship between r and the real wage. As r rises no price (in terms of labour) can fall. To see this, suppose, on the contrary, that some prices do indeed fall. Then consider the commodity whose price has fallen most, in proportionate terms, say commodity j. Since r has risen and all other prices have not fallen by as much, the price of j must have fallen below its cost of production, an outcome which can be rejected. But in the system with rent things are different. With a rise in r, p_k could fall, and its fall could be greater than that of other prices if there were, at the same time, a sufficient reduction in the value of σ. There is, of course, a limit to this movement, namely when σ has fallen to zero. Although, algebraically, it could continue through rents becoming negative this would not make sense economically. Within limits, then, a rise in r could be accompanied by an increase in the purchasing power of the nominal wage.

The case of a rising real-w–r relation is shown in fig. 12.5 which otherwise displays the characteristics of the previous case. The result is a real-w–r frontier consisting of an upward-sloping range for rates of profits up to r'' (associated with positive rent), and a downward-sloping range for higher rates of profits (when the economy has, in effect, returned to a single-products system). No problems arise from this if the rate of profits is exogenous since for each r there is only one real wage. But a problem does occur when the real wage is exogenous. Suppose it is fixed at $(1/p_k)'$. It is consistent with *either* a rate of profits r' and a positive rent per acre σ' *or* a rate of profits r''' and zero rent. It is possible to guess which of these two outcomes will be established. If capitalists have the freedom to choose their process of production they will choose I on its own and the rate r''' will be established. So, to avail themselves of any rent the landlords would have to try and force on the capitalists contracts which specify the processes to be used on the land. To satisfy corn demand it would be necessary to get the distribution of land, in each year, just right. In a world of many landowners that seems most unlikely.

To complete this section it would be natural to ask: what happens when the growth in demand has exhausted the possibilities of further expanding process I? In that case there will now be a need to introduce a yet more productive process, say II. If II was not previously considered it was because its costs were even higher than those of process I. The general

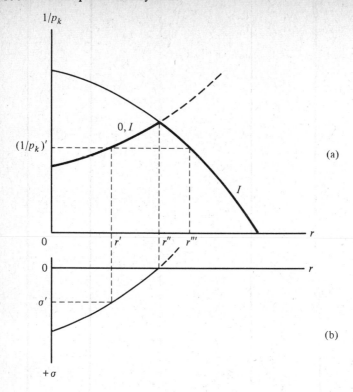

Figure 12.5

progress of agricultural methods is summarised by Sraffa on p. 76 of *PC* as follows:

> The increase [of production] takes place through the gradual exten-
> sion of the method that produces more corn at a higher unit cost, at
> the expense of the method that uses less. As soon as the former
> method has extended to the whole area, the rent rises to the point
> where a third method which produces still more corn at a still higher
> cost can be introduced to take the place of the method that has just
> been superseded. Thus the stage is set for a new phase of increase in
> production through the gradual extension of the third method at the
> expense of the intermediate one. In this way the output may
> increase continuously, although the methods of production are
> changed spasmodically.

Thus, with the introduction of *II*, p_k will have to rise and, with it, σ. Prices and rent remain stable for a period during which process *II* is expanded until, at some future date, it is found necessary to introduce yet another process.

It is important to stress that this succession of processes does not represent technological *advance*, merely the necessary adoption of known but more costly techniques. The progression just described is based on the absence of technological progress.

5 Generalisations

In the previous sections we have considered the cases of 'pure' extensive and 'pure' intensive rents. The two varieties of rent will be found side by side where there exist lands of different qualities the least profitable of which has been fully used up. Once all the land has become employed it is necessary to introduce a new process to operate alongside one of the existing ones. It is not possible to say on which grade the new process will be introduced but, normally, only one of the grades will be subject to a 'duality of methods', to use Sraffa's phrase.[5] When that grade is totally cultivated by the new process another process is introduced, either on that or some other grade.

A second complication arises where several commodities require land for production. In the case of land of uniform quality a rent emerges when the combined demand for land from the various industries equals the supply. In this case, normally one of the industries will be required to introduce a second process which will gradually expand to squeeze out the first. When that has happened a further new process will be introduced either in that or some other industry. The case of many industries using land of different grades is more complicated, but the general rule here, as it is in the preceding cases, is 'that the number of separate processes should be equal to the number of qualities of land plus the number of products concerned' (*PC*, p. 77).

Provided inputs are scarce their owners can command a rent. Rent theory can therefore be applied to many things apart from land. Ricardo noted in his *Principles* that the theory of extensive rent could be applied to mineral resources. A growing demand for, say, coal would lead to the opening up of more inaccessible and costly fields. Since these could only be worked profitably if the price of coal increased, the owners of more readily worked seams would receive rents.

In *PC* (p. 78) Sraffa says that 'machines of an obsolete type which are still in use are similar to land in so far as they are employed as means of production, although not currently produced.' Suppose that a newly-invested machine allows some commodity to be produced more cheaply than with the traditional machine. Some producers will find themselves encumbered with obsolete machines at various stages of wear. Since they have already been purchased the loss cannot entirely be made good but it can be minimised. So long as the value of the output from the continued operation of the obsolete machine is more than sufficient to pay labour and return profits on the *other* means of production used, then any surplus will help to offset the loss on the obsolete machines. The surplus is in the nature of a rent. It is determined by the difference between the price of the final commodity and the unit costs of labour and those means of production which are still being reproduced.

Industrial monopolies frequently exist because of limited access to raw materials, new technology, market information, etc. These things may be kept artificially scarce through ownership, patents or differences in the dynamism of firms. The scarcities confer rents, on those with access, which may be regarded as 'monopoly profits'. We said in chapter 1 that competition implies the weakness of 'barriers to entry'. In the present context, strong entry barriers are what protect and sustain scarcity. Viewed in this way, differences between individual profit rates and the natural rate can be regarded as rents whose permanency depends on the strength of entry barriers. Although there has been a number of attempts to adapt the Sraffian analysis to cope with the existence of monopoly, this way, which appears particularly promising, seems to have been rather neglected.

6 Scarcity and economic growth

Rent arises because the growth in demand presses on the availability of fixed resources. Clearly, scarcity and growth are not incompatible, even in a given state of technical knowledge. What are incompatible are scarcity and *continuous steady* growth, for there is a limit to the extent to which the processes described in this chapter can go. As rents rise profitability falls. If this is manifested in a reduction in the real wage the limit is set by the level of subsistence. If it is manifested in a falling rate of profits then before that rate reaches zero the sources of net investment will dry up. Even if landlords could be encouraged to invest their rents it is still the case that increasing output requires the use of more costly techniques. The economy's productivity is falling, and with it the potential for net investment.

Thus, in the absence of technological advance, the economy will, sooner or later, arrive at a stationary state. Continuous growth in the face of fixed natural resources requires a continual series of technological improvements; that is, the introduction of more productive but *less* costly techniques. These would work to reduce relative scarcity and the growth of rents. In a properly dynamic context it may well be the pressure on fixed resources and the threat of reduced profitability that stimulate the invention of new, more intensive but less costly processes. The stimulus or inducement to innovation would be even greater in the case of non-renewable natural resources. Whereas land is non-producible it is 'renewed' afresh each year. Oil, on the other hand, once burned is gone for ever. The development of less oil-intensive processes and of oil substitutes would be a natural response to the prospect of paying enormous and rapidly increasing rents to the owners of oil wells. But there is no reason why inducements to innovation should concern only zero and negative growth inputs. Scarcity is a relative concept. In the von Neumann model the limit to the system rate of growth is set by the slowest growing basic(s) (and products which grow at a faster rate become 'free goods'). There would be considerable returns from the invention of techniques which economised on the uses of the slowest-growing basics, or which increased the productivity of industries producing those basics.

Theories which stress scarcity and theories which stress continuous growth appear to be diametrically opposed. Induced technological change provides a nexus between the two and opens up the possibility of developing a framework for the study of irregular growth and economic crises.

7 Summary

In the case of pure extensive rent, growth in the demand for corn can be accommodated by the exploitation of higher-cost grades of land. Since this requires a rise in the prices of corn, owners of more favoured lands receive rents. In the case of pure intensive rent the increased demand is satisfied by exploiting land of uniform quality with more intensive but more costly methods. Again the price of corn must rise and with it rent per acre. Thus the price of corn (and all other prices, if corn is basic) depend in a direct way on the demand for corn resulting from a growth in population. Distributive relations in a world with scarcity are much more complex and, in the case of intensive rent, there exists the possibility that part of the real-w–r frontier may be positively sloped.

Scarcity and continuous steady growth are not compatible in the absence of technological improvements. The threat to profitability could provide the stimulus to such improvements.

FURTHER READING

Sraffa's discussion of rent (*PC*, chapter XI) is terse even by his standards, the entire subject being covered in just four and a half pages. It is a pity, therefore, that there exist (to my knowledge) only three papers in English on Sraffian rent theory. Montani (1975) is a thorough account of the properties of two-commodity models and the more difficult mathematics are confined to footnotes. We have relied heavily on his discussion of intensive rent. Quadrio-Curzio (1980) is a very mathematical discussion of extensive rent only. Both these writers have also published in Italian on the subject.

Kurz (1978) is probably the easiest of the three articles. It is additionally useful in that it relates Sraffa's theory to statements of Ricardo and Marx on the subject.

Taking up the historical theme, the precursors of Sraffa's theory were Malthus, whose views were published in his 1815 pamphlet *Inquiry into the Nature and Progress of Rent*, and Ricardo who elaborated the theory in chapter II of his *Principles*. Essentially the same theory was discovered independently by J. H. von Thünen in his book *Der Isolierte Staat* published in 1826. (See von Thünen, 1966.) In his theory, however, the profitability of different grades of land is not primarily a function of their physical properties but of their distances to major centres of population, since additional costs have to be incurred in transporting commodities to and from more distant lands. Marx's views are to be found in *Capital*, vol. III (Marx, 1972).

A theory of 'induced' technical progress was formalised by Kennedy (1964), but the idea has not been properly incorporated into the Sraffa–Leontief model.

PART IV

Some broader issues

13

Some broader issues

1 Introduction

The principal purpose of this book, a purely expository one, is now complete. But the reader, having come this far, may wish to know in what ways this approach to the understanding of capitalism differs from the more orthodox schools of Marxism and neoclassicism. *PC* was intended as a critique of neoclassical theory in its 'aggregate capital' guise and while it is true that the aggregate production function 'is still hovering about in countless text-books, resembl[ing] in this the Flying Dutchman, who has perished many times and cannot die' (Schefold, 1980*a*, p. 190), the issues involved may nevertheless be regarded as formally settled. But that is certainly not true of the relationship between the Sraffa–Leontief[1] approach and the more sophisticated 'General Equilibrium' version of neoclassical theory. Nor is it true of the relationship between Sraffa and Marx. These are the subjects of current debate with the arguments being conducted at an advanced level. It is impossible, therefore, in a few concluding pages to an introductory text, to do anything like justice to the views expressed on all sides. To avoid attempting the impossible we shall simply state what we regard as the major issues and express our own view on each.

The chapter begins with an evaluation of Marxist value theory in the light of *PC*. It is argued that Marx's labour theory of value has been rendered redundant by Sraffa's work. Nevertheless, the question of whether capitalists 'exploit' workers is left open – indeed, it is argued that there is nothing in the formal value theory of either Sraffa or Marx which says anything about this matter. The question is postponed till section 4, after a brief outline of neoclassical General Equilibrium theory, where it is argued that if exploitation exists, in an ethically meaningful sense, then it is because of the determinants of capitalists' savings behaviour. Rather than being an immediate 'sacrifice' as they are portrayed by neoclassical theory, savings must actually be a means of gratification. This is consistent with Marx's wider views on capitalist behaviour. The Sraffa–Leontief theory, however, says nothing formally about this issue and so it is open to incorporate either view. But if it is to be the basis of a wholly distinct approach rather than just a special case or a minor revision of neoclassical theory, then it is essential that it is accompanied by the Marxian view of savings. As an illustration of the importance of this issue, a consideration is given, in section 6, of the question of the gain from trade, discussed previously in chapter 9. It is shown that, while the conclusion that the gain may be negative is easily sustainable on the Marxian view of savings, it is undermined by the neoclassical view.

2 Sraffa and Marx

There are few explicit references to Marx in *PC* and those that exist are not related to the issues we wish to discuss here. Even so, as is evident from the recent literature, Sraffa's work has far-reaching implications for Marx's value theory. Initially, it was widely believed that Sraffa had successfully removed many of the logical deficiencies of Marx's theory whilst leaving the structure substantially intact. But more mature reflection has led to the view (though not one which is universally shared) that *PC* has destroyed the whole basis of Marx's approach to value. We do not propose to become heavily involved with the technical details of recent controversy in this area (see the Further Reading guide) but the central issues appear straightforward enough.

As a first approach to the understanding of value and distribution in a capitalist economy Marx operated within the framework of the pure labour theory of value in which prices are proportional to the labours embodied in commodities. We saw in chapter 2, section 2, that, under the assumptions of the labour theory of value (and when wages are advanced), the w–r relation could be written as

$$r = (1 - w)/w \tag{2.4}$$

where w is the number of units of labour embodied in the wage basket. The equation was interpreted as saying that the rate of profits is positive if each labourer is paid a quantity of commodities which require less than one unit of labour to produce. This is commonly discussed in terms of the division of the working day between 'necessary' labour and 'surplus' labour. If the working day is eight hours and it requires six hours to reproduce the daily wage goods consumed by the worker, then those six hours are necessary labour and the remaining two surplus labour – labour which is performed by the worker but the produce of which is appropriated by the capitalist.

It is upon this distinction that Marx bases the notion of 'exploitation'. The worker is said to be exploited because he or she is performing work solely for the benefit of the capitalist. The 'rate of exploitation' is the ratio of surplus to necessary labour which, in our example, is $1:3$, and is the outcome of many conflicting and interacting forces which can be grouped under the general term 'the class struggle'.

A problem with this approach arises when we drop the assumptions underlying the pure labour theory of value. If there are differences in the capital : labour ratios of each industry (in the terminology of chapter 2, differences in the 'time profiles of production'; in Marx's terminology, differences in the 'organic compositions of capital') then prices are no longer proportional to quantities of labour embodied. (The latter, in Marxian theory are referred to as 'labour values' or just plain *values*.[2]) Moreover, the expression for the $w–r$ relation is rather more complex in this case and it is no longer obvious that it can be given an interpretation similar to that of (2.4). That is, it cannot be immediately taken for granted that a positive rate of profits implies and is implied by the expenditure of surplus labour. Marx's view is that the divergence of prices from *values* does not alter the nature of 'surplus *value*' (the produce of surplus labour) or the process by which it is created, but merely redistributes the economy's total surplus *value* among the various industries:

> Now, if the commodities are sold at their *values*, then, as we have shown, very different rates of profit arise in the various spheres of production, depending on the different organic composition of the masses of capital invested in them. But capital withdraws from a sphere with a low rate of profit and invades others, which yield a higher profit. Through this incessant outflow and influx, or, briefly, through its distribution among the various spheres, which depends on how the rate of profit falls here and rises there, it creates such a ratio of supply to demand that the average profit in the various spheres of production becomes the same, and *values* are, therefore, converted into prices of production. (Marx (1972), p. 195, italics added.)

Thus, it is Marx's view that aggregate surplus *value* and aggregate profits are one and the same thing and that the divergence of prices from *values* is the mechanism by which they are redistributed to ensure that profits bear a uniform proportion to the capital employed in each industry.

The implication of Marx's argument is that a positive rate of profits can obtain only if surplus *value* is positive; if, that is, there is something to redistribute. Thus, according to Marx, a positive rate of profits is a necessary and sufficient condition for a positive rate of exploitation, a proposition which has subsequently become known as the Fundamental Marxian Theorem (FMT). To demonstrate his proposition, Marx attempted first, to show how *values* were 'transformed' into prices and secondly, to construct an 'average' commodity whose production process could be regarded as a microcosm of the whole economy. There are a number of reasons why he was not successful in either of these tasks. (See, for example, Meek (1961).) What is interesting, however, is that Sraffa appears to have accomplished both of them. First, the Sraffian price equations show how prices vary with variations in r, beginning with proportionality to *values* when $r = 0$; and secondly, the Standard commodity looks very much like the average commodity that Marx was seeking. (Recall, however, that any Standard commodity is valid only with respect to one technique of production.) The Standard equation, remembering that wages are no longer advanced, is

$$r = R(1 - w).$$

If, then, the wage is measured in terms of Standard commodity, $(1 - w)$ can be interpreted as the proportion of the working day whose produce goes to capitalists and is positive if, and only if, $r > 0$.

On the face of it then, Sraffa seems to have cleared up some of Marx's problems. Not only has he solved the so-called 'transformation' problem of relating *values* to prices, he has also provided a formally rigorous explanation of the FMT along Marxian lines, *for a one-technique economy*. At the same time, however, the Sraffian analysis completely undermines the significance of either of these problems. Sraffa's price equations can be solved directly for prices without need of first determining *values*. *Values* may be relevant when $r = 0$, but we do not even have to think about them when $r > 0$. So far as exploitation is concerned, there is again no need to go through an elaborate exercise to relate profits to surplus *value*,[3] either through the construction of the Standard commodity or by any other method, since the essential point can be seen directly in physical terms. If $r > 0$, then the vector of wage commodities can have no element greater than the corresponding element of the net output vector, and at least one must be smaller. Thus, it must be the case that workers produce commodities appropriated by capitalists.

But if the use of labour *values* and the transformation procedure are quite unnecessary, they are also inconsistent once a multiplicity of techniques is admitted. When there are many techniques, each is associated with a different set of *values* and it is not possible to say which set prevails until the choice is known. But the choice cannot be known independently of the determination of distribution and prices. It seems, therefore, that we have to know prices before we can find the *values* that have to be transformed into prices!

Worse is to come. It was noted in chapter 10 that a joint-production technique, perfectly viable at some positive rate of profits, may be associated with a negative ratio of labours embodied (that is, negative *values*). Steedman (1975) has shown, in this case, that aggregate surplus *value* may also be negative when $r > 0$, thus contradicting the FMT. Yet, of course, in physical terms there is a surplus product. It seems that Sraffa's analysis has undermined any attempt to develop a theory of exploitation on the basis of Marx's labour theory of value.[4]

This brings us to a perhaps more fundamental question. What precisely does exploitation mean in this context? Why, in Marxian terms, is surplus labour exploitative? Or, in physical terms, why is the production of commodities not consumed by labour exploitative? For 'exploitation' to have any real ethical significance it needs to be shown why capitalists do not deserve their share in production: that profits are not a just reward for any effort or sacrifice on their part. We shall return to this issue in section 4, having first considered the explanation of profits in neoclassical theory.

Finally, it should be stressed that the Sraffa-based critique of Marx relates only to value theory. It does not extend to the rest of Marx's work, particularly on the dynamics of capitalist development. In fact, the replacement of Marx's cumbersome and inconsistent value procedures by the more elegant and logically superior Sraffian approach could place Marx's dynamic analysis on much sounder footings.

3 Neoclassical general equilibrium theory

As we saw in chapter 8, there is a branch of neoclassical theory which relies on the concept of aggregate capital. That theory is logically sound in a world in which there exists a single type of capital good but its conclusions do not generalise to more realistic cases. It would be wrong, on those grounds alone, to condemn neoclassical theory as irrelevant or uninteresting. For there exists a much more sophisticated and powerful theory of price determination within the neoclassical tradition to which these criticisms do not apply. This is usually known as Walrasian General Equilibrium theory (hereafter WGE), after Leon Walras, though reference is also commonly made to two modern exponents, Arrow and Debreu. The purpose of this section is to give a *brief* sketch of WGE theory.

In WGE theory, the economy consists of a number of *agents* who are functionally divided into two groups: households and firms. The former has a set of *endowments*, including an ability to work (labour) and perhaps some property and shares in firms. These may be exchanged with firms or other households to obtain a consumption basket which is most preferred, subject to the value of the initial endowments. In a more popular terminology, a household is said to maximise utility subject to its budget constraint. The firm's objective is to maximise profits, the difference between its receipts and its expenditures on labour, raw materials and capital equipment, subject to the technology available. Of course, the amounts of commodities and labour bought and sold by the various agents depend on relative prices. It is thus possible to describe supplies and demands as functions of all commodity prices and the wage:

$$S_i = S_i(p_1, \ldots, p_n, w) \text{ for commodities } i = 1, \ldots, n$$
$$S_L = S_L(p_1, \ldots, p_n, w) \text{ for labour}$$

and

$$D_i = D_i(p_1, \ldots, p_n, w)$$
$$D_L = D_L(p_1, \ldots, p_n, w).$$

Equilibrium is characterised by equality of supply and demand in those markets where price is positive and by positive or zero excess supply in those markets where price is zero. (One commodity may be chosen as *numéraire* provided, of course, that it belongs to the first category.) Thus, in equilibrium,

$$p_i > 0 \text{ implies } D_i = S_i$$

and

$$p_i = 0 \text{ implies } D_i \leqslant S_i.$$

Commodities of the second type are 'free goods'. These conditions apply equally to labour which may be regarded as a commodity like any other. (The distinction is maintained here simply to permit a comparison with Sraffian theory.) There thus arises, theoretically at least, the possibility of labour being a 'free good' (the wage being zero) whenever there is excess supply.

The existence of an equilibrium price vector can be guaranteed on certain conditions among which are that production and consumption 'sets' are 'convex'. In straightforward terms this means that production is subject to decreasing or constant *but not* increasing returns: and that indifference maps allow diminishing or constant but not increasing marginal rates of substitution. In general, it is necessary to know both demand and supply functions to determine equilibrium prices but, in the particular case where production possibilities are characterised by constant returns, only supply conditions are relevant to the determination of goods prices. (This is analogous to the case in partial equilibrium analysis where the supply curve is horizontal.)

The equations which we have just noted and the exchange process which they underlie may refer to a purely timeless economy with production and consumption taking place instantaneously. But this highly abstract interpretation is not necessary and several other characterisations are possible. The most relevant for us is the 'intertemporal' variety in which production takes place in time and commodities are specified not only according to their physical characteristics but also according to their dates of delivery/receipt. The dates run from the present period (0), which agents begin with a set of initial endowments, through any finite number of periods into the future. Thus, if there are k physically different commodities (other than labour) and T periods, then $n = kT$, and there are also T types of labour. Households and firms are assumed to have perfect foresight in that each of the former knows its own preferences and each of the latter knows the technological possibilities for each of the T periods. Thus, contracts relating to the exchange of commodities in each period can be made in period 0. There are, therefore, $k + 1$ 'spot' markets for immediate deliveries, and $(k + 1) \times (T - 1)$ 'forward' markets on which future deliveries are contracted. The equilibrium vector of $n + T$ prices can be written as:

$$\{p_1^0, \ldots, p_k^0, w^0; p_1^1, \ldots, p_k^1, w^1; \ldots; p_1^t, \ldots, p_k^t, w^t; \ldots;$$
$$p_1^{T-1}, \ldots, p_k^{T-1}, w^{T-1}\}$$

where p_i^t is the price of the commodity with physical characteristic i in period t. Provided that it is positive, any one of these prices, say p_1^0, can be chosen as a *numéraire* with which to express the remaining prices.

There is nothing, in principle, to stop the price of physical commodity i varying from period to period. The relationship between the prices of the same physical commodity in succeeding periods defines the 'own' rate of interest of that physical commodity between those two periods. Thus, the own rate of interest for physical commodity i between periods 0 and 1 is

$$\rho_i^{01} = \frac{p_i^0 - p_i^1}{p_i^1} = \frac{p_i^0}{p_i^1} - 1 \tag{13.1}$$

and indicates the additional amount of commodity i that could be obtained by purchasing it in period 1 rather than period 0. For example, if $p_i^0 = 1$ and $p_i^1 = \frac{2}{3}$ then an additional 50 per cent of commodity i could be obtained by postponing purchase till period 1.

In the most general case, with changing patterns of demand and changing technology, own rates of interest will vary between physical commodities and, for the same physical commodity, from period to period. But where demand patterns and technology are constant the structure of relative physical commodity prices is also constant from period to period; that is to say,

$$p_i^0/p_j^0 = p_i^t/p_j^t, \text{ for all } t = 1, \ldots, T-1.$$

However, the constancy of demand patterns refers only to the relative demand for physical commodities at each set of prices within each period and not to the intensity of demand for commodities in general, period by period. If this intensity changes, then the price of the physical commodity which acts as *numéraire* will, in general, differ from unity in all periods other than period 0. This variation in demand intensity over time is known as *time preference* and if the 'rate of time preference' is constant then the rate of change of price is also constant as, therefore, is the own rate of interest.

Thus unchanging demand patterns, unchanging technology and a constant rate of time preference will mean that all own rates of interest are equal and constant. In this instance we may justifiably talk of *the* rate of interest, ρ. There is nothing, in principle, which says that this interest rate must be positive but the general positivity of interest rates in reality is explained on the basis of *positive* time preference, that is, a general preference for higher consumption at earlier rather than later dates. We shall return to the subject of time preference in the following section.

Consider now an intertemporal-WGE system in which there exists one physical commodity (called i), other than labour, which is produced by means of itself and labour subject to constant returns. The system can be represented by price equations which relate end-of-period (output) price to start-of-period (input) price and to wages, which we shall assume are paid at the end of the period. For period 0, the equation would, in our usual notation, be

$$p_i^1 = p_i^0 a_{ii} + w^1 l_i. \tag{13.2}$$

That is, inputs of i are purchased at the beginning of period 0 on the 'spot' market while, simultaneously, contracts are drawn up for the delivery of i, one period hence, on the 'forward' market, at the 'forward price', p_i^1. (If, for example, we set $p_i^0 = 1$, then p_i^1 is the quantity of i paid *now* in return for a unit of i to be received in a period from now. The end of period 0 is, of course, the start of period 1.) Wages, by assumption, are also contracted for forward payment. The prices in (13.2) are known as 'present value' prices (where 'present' refers to the beginning of period 0), since they are prices paid now for present and future deliveries. Equation (13.2) could, however, be equivalently expressed entirely in period 0 prices if these are *discounted* by the appropriate own rates of interest. From (13.1),

$$p_i^1 = p_i^0 / (1 + \rho_i^{01}).$$

This may be interpreted as saying that a unit of i delivered in one period's time can be valued in terms of the spot price p_i^0, provided that this value is discounted by a factor of $1/(1 + \rho_i^{01})$ to give its present value p_i^1. (13.2), which is expressed in ready-discounted prices, could therefore be rewritten in undiscounted period 0 prices, as follows:

$$p_i^0 / (1 + \rho_i^{01}) = p_i^0 a_{ii} + w^0 l_i / (1 + \rho_L^{01})$$

Similarly, (13.2) can be rewritten in terms of the prices of *any* other period, provided that the correct discount factor is introduced. Thus, in period 1 prices, we have

$$p_i^1 = (1 + \rho_i^{01}) p_i^1 a_{ii} + w^1 l_i. \tag{13.3}$$

In this case, since the quantity a_{ii} is being delivered one period ahead of the price in which it is valued, that value must be *multiplied* by $(1 + \rho_i^{01})$ to obtain the present value.

What is true of this simple one-physical-commodity economy applies equally to a many-physical-commodity world. Corresponding to (13.2) and (13.3) we could, for some period t, write

$$p_i^{t+1} = \Sigma_j \, p_j^t a_{ji} + w^{t+1} l_i \qquad (i, j = 1, \ldots, k) \qquad (13.4)$$

and

$$p_i^{t+1} = (1 + \rho)\Sigma_j \, p_j^{t+1} a_{ji} + w^{t+1} l_i \quad (i, j = 1, \ldots, k) \qquad (13.5)$$

where ρ is the uniform rate of interest appropriate to the case of unchanging demand patterns, unchanging technology and constant time preference. From (13.5) it can be seen that, if we drop the time superscripts (which are all the same), and if we replace ρ with r, then we arrive at the familiar Sraffian price equations. The Sraffian price equations are, therefore, *formally* identical to the particular case of intertemporal WGE in which demand patterns, technology and time preference are unchanging. From a Walrasian point of view, the rate of profits r can be interpreted as nothing other than the rate of interest which arises in this particular case.

4 'Abstinence' versus 'animal spirits'

We have just seen that 'interest' in the neoclassical theory bears a formal similarity to 'profits' in the classical/Sraffian theory. The purpose of this section is to see whether the similarity extends beyond the formal level.[5]

In intertemporal WGE the existence of a positive rate of interest is the consequence of positive time preference. Essentially the same point has been put by earlier neoclassicals in the form of 'abstinence' and 'waiting' theories. These theories emphasise the fact that saving is an abstention from present consumption and, hence, a sacrifice on the part of the saver. Unless there is some form of compensation, postponing consumption till a later date involves a reduction in utility. Thus, when people save in order to lend, or to invest in their own enterprises, repayment with interest is merely compensation for the sacrifice involved. The interest arises from the fact that the savings are invested in productive activities which allow future consumption possibilities to be expanded. So, although consumption is postponed, the waiting is offset by a higher level of future consumption than would otherwise have occurred. In equilibrium, the magnitude of the interest rate measures the 'impatience' of savers in general. A higher rate of interest is required to induce more impatient individuals to abstain from present consumption. The interest rate is, therefore, commensurate with the sacrifice being made.

Neoclassical theory (in all its variants) thus regards consumption as, ultimately, the only satisfying or utility-yielding activity. If that is so, then interest, the means of attaining enlarged consumption possibilities at later dates, may be considered as nothing more than compensation for sacrifices made. There are thus two ways to contribute to production: through labour and through abstinence. Wages are payment for the former, interest for the latter. There is no room in this story for the concept of exploitation.

There is, however, an alternative view of savings and investment, more closely associated with neo-Keynesian, classical and Marxian economists, in which saving is not entirely a sacrifice. Mrs Robinson (1962), for example, sees accumulation as arising out of the 'animal spirits' of the capitalist, a phrase defined by Keynes (1936, p. 161) as a 'spontaneous urge to action rather than inaction'. For Marxists, however,

> It is not at all a question of innate human propensities or instincts; the desire of the capitalist to expand the value under his control (to accumulate capital) springs from his special position in a particular form of organisation of social production. A moment's reflection will show that it could not be otherwise. The capitalist is a capitalist and is an important figure in society only in so far as he is the owner and representative of capital. Deprived of his capital, he would be nothing. But capital has only one quality, that of possessing magnitude, and from this it follows that one capitalist is distinguishable from another only by the magnitude of the capital which he represents. The owner of a large amount of capital stands higher in the social scale than the owner of a small amount of capital; position, prestige, power are reduced to the quantitative measuring rod of dollars and cents. (Sweezy (1942), p. 80.)

Thus the motive for accumulation is accumulation itself; the reward is not the *product* of capital but its possession. There is clearly a difference between this view and that of Mrs Robinson, but the end result is pretty much the same. What it amounts to (though Marxists may not like this way of expressing it) is that capitalists get utility not only from consumption but also from accumulation. Of course, investors and savers are not necessarily the same people, but this argument is not confined to owner-managers investing their own savings. So long as wealth is a measuring rod of prestige it is irrelevant whether the saver is in control of the physical capital or not. It is to be emphasised that wealth enters the utility function not as an indirect measure of consumption possibilities but because people desire wealth for its own sake, without any intention of ever converting the larger part of it into consumption.[6]

To the extent that saving is motivated by a desire for wealth *per se* it can hardly be considered a sacrifice; nor can interest/profits be justified as compensation. That leaves room for an interpretation of profits as representing, at least in part, the exploitation of workers by the class which has a monopoly of capital.

We may now relate this discussion to the issues that arose at the end of section 2. The very existence of surplus labour/*value*/product does not imply 'exploitation' in any ethical sense, and the use of that term by many Marxists to describe such a surplus is unfortunate. A surplus product (defined, simply, as net output in excess of wages) is as compatible with the 'abstinence' view of the world as it is with, say, the 'animal spirits' view. If exploitation has any meaning, therefore, it is because of the nature of the subjective aims of capitalists and not, simply, because workers produce more than they are paid. Of course, if profits are not a consequence of time preference in consumption then the rate of profits has to be explained either by the level of the wage (which itself will need explaining), or by some other means. (See the Further Reading guide for chapter 5.)

5 Comparing the Sraffa–Leontief and Walrasian General Equilibrium approaches

It was shown in section 3 that if r were taken as a discount rate for converting future values into their present equivalents then the Sraffian price equations could be recast in present-value form. Since the resulting system could be regarded as a special case of intertemporal WGE it would be tempting to infer that the Sraffa–Leontief model is merely a particular case of WGE. Precisely that inference has been drawn by many neoclassical economists (and some Marxists) and we shall now consider whether it is justified.

If the Sraffa–Leontief model is nothing more than a special case of WGE then it should be possible to arrive at the former by placing suitable restrictions on the latter. Restrictions which have been suggested are:

(1) That agents are grouped into classes, defined by the type and quantity of initial endowments and by the nature of demand (including savings) behaviour.
(2) That the nature of demand, technology and time preference is such as to generate constant period-by-period relative prices of physical commodities and a constant rate of interest.
(3) That production possibilities are subject to constant returns.
(4) That techniques of production are 'discrete' in that they do not allow continuous substitution between inputs.

Taking each of these 'restrictions' in turn, we now consider whether they are, indeed, an accurate representation of the relationship between the two approaches and, if so, to what extent the restrictiveness can be regarded as a weakness of the Sraffa–Leontief approach.

(1) *Social classes*

In so far as Walrasian agents could, but do not need to, be grouped into social classes, this is a genuine restriction. Unfortunately, few neoclassical economists ever bother to consider seriously the implications of such a grouping and, as a consequence, the conclusions derived from WGE are often far *too* general to be related in any meaningful way to the particular institutional context of capitalism. (In fact, and perhaps a little ironically, many economists have found WGE more helpful in formulating the means of efficient economic planning than in clarifying the workings of capitalists economies.) Class division must be in the foreground of any theory explicitly concerned with capitalist economies. This restriction can hardly be considered a weakness, therefore.

(2) *Steady growth*

The focus on steady growth in the Sraffa–Leontief approach is a deliberate attempt to discover the conditions for the smooth and continuous functioning of capitalist economies, as both a starting point and a point of reference for the analysis of more complex dynamic behaviour. Although intertemporal WGE may share some of the formal properties of classical steady growth, it is, in fact, approached in a quite distinct manner. Despite its analytical division into 'periods', conceptually the intertemporal WGE apparatus is quite static. The economic characteristics of every period are fully known by all agents in period 0: they have 'perfect foresight'. Thus contracts for exchange can be concluded in period 0, with future deliveries and payments taking place for all commodities (including labour) in perfect forward markets. The whole point of this exchange is to convert the initial endowments (with the help of productive transformations) into a preferred consumption time stream. But in so far as decisions are taken instantaneously, time enters the picture only in the most notional way.

In classical steady growth there is no suggestion, and certainly no necessity, for production to be geared towards a preferred time-profile of consumption. The two approaches, therefore, do not even have a common basis in terms of individual motivation. Moreover, the Sraffa–Leontief economy is viewed as proceeding in historical time with the *possibility* of events occurring in history that upset the conditions for continued steady growth. It is true that the transitional analyses of, say, technical change, or changes in tastes, or the opening of international trade, have not yet been worked out in full, but we have claimed only that the Sraffa–Leontief model is a starting point.

(3) Constant returns

Unlike the Sraffa–Leontief approach, WGE is able to admit diminishing returns in production, the existence of which gives rise to rents (or 'pure' profits). Diminishing returns are the result of an inability to increase inputs in proportion, and rents are commanded by the owners of relatively scarce inputs. We saw in chapter 12 that scarcity is inconsistent with continuous steady growth. The problem was, however, amenable to analysis in the Sraffian framework in terms of a comparison of different long-run positions. Since, as we have just argued, WGE is essentially static in conception, it is not clear that, on this issue, it is on any stronger ground. Moreover, while the Sraffian approach is *suggestive* of an analysis involving scarcity, induced technical progress and discontinuous growth, this possibility is much more elusive in WGE. If the state of the world in all periods is fixed in period 0, then there can be no such thing as 'induced' technical progress.[7]

(4) Discrete technology

This cannot properly be considered as a restriction. In simple WGE models, production possibilities usually allow continuous substitution between inputs but there is no necessity for this and discrete technology is possible (provided that any two techniques can be combined in any proportions). The difference is that, in the Sraffa–Leontief model, it is usual to consider discrete techniques (which may be combined at switch-points) but continuous substitution could be also allowed. It would simply require the existence of an infinite number of techniques each differing in an infinitesimal way from its 'neighbour'. Although neither can be regarded as a special case of the other, the discrete approach is certainly more relevant to modern industrial economies. Moreover, because Sraffa considered the discrete case he was able to say something illuminating about the nature of technical choice and to show the limitations of that branch of neoclassical theory based on the concept of aggregate capital. It has since been argued that reswitching and capital reversing are implicit in a fully specified WGE model but this new awareness appears to be a consequence of Sraffa's discovery.

These considerations suggest that assumptions which are often considered as 'restrictive' are simply 'different'. There is one further difference that is worth drawing attention to, and that concerns the treatment of wages in the two approaches. The concept of subsistence is not formally incorporated into WGE. Although assumptions can be introduced to avoid the possibility of zero wages, the supposition that any positive wage will satisfy subsistence requirements is hardly satisfactory. This problem does not arise in Sraffian analysis since the rate of profits can always be effectively constrained by a minimum real wage (as suggested by Sraffa himself, on p. 10 of *PC*). Nor, given the essentially historical character of the Sraffa–Leontief model, is there any need for all wage contracts to be agreed at the beginning of time. Complete and perfect forward markets for labour are inconsistent with the very nature of wage bargaining under capitalism.

Clearly then, the Sraffa–Leontief analysis is not simply a special case of WGE theory, even at a formal level, and conceptually it represents a quite distinct view of the world. The WGE view is of a generally classless set of agents arranging consumption over time and exploiting mutual gains from exchange. (After all, those who do not gain always have the option of sticking with their initial endowments.) Even if a class structure is imposed on this picture, so that only capitalists have non-labour resources to exchange, they still do so in order to obtain a preferred time-distribution of consumption. Interest is simply the price borrowers must pay lenders for the sacrifice of giving up current consumption, and the uniformity of interest rates arises only under a particular set of conditions, *analogous to* steady growth.

In the Sraffa–Leontief or, more generally, the classical view, the class distinction is made from the beginning. Workers may, of course, share in the surplus and consequently have scope for saving but, by and large, their concern is to maximise present consumption. Capitalists on the other hand are largely concerned to increase their wealth which implies maximising the rate of growth of the capital in their possession and that, in turn, means a continuous searching for those activities where profit rates are highest. Thus, outside of steady growth, it is still sensible to talk of a *tendency* towards a uniform rate of profits. It is the result of competitive processes initiated by the motivations of capitalists. (None of this is inconsistent with capitalists requiring a certain standard of consumption including, perhaps, a 'conspicuous' element as an advertisement of their wealth.) Since, for a given technique, profit rates are higher where wages are lower, the aims of the two classes are generally antagonistic. (A qualification is needed to the extent that the working class, as a whole, benefits from economic growth.) Incorporating the wealth-maximising view of capitalist behaviour explicitly into the formal Sraffa–Leontief analysis creates a powerful revision of Marxism without the labour theory of value, but with a meaningful concept of exploitation.

6   The gain from trade and the Golden Rule

In chapter 9, section 4, it was concluded that a capitalist economy may lose from international trade in the sense that the level of consumption per worker (p.w.) might be lower with trade than without. It has been argued that conclusions of this sort, reached by a comparison of alternative steady growth paths, are illegitimate since no account is taken of the path of transition from autarky to trade. It is said that whenever a country appears, on the basis of comparisons, to lose from trade, the transition involves a reduction in the value of its capital stock. The unwanted capital thus released may then be transformed into consumption goods, so giving a transitional consumption boost. The transformation may occur directly, where capital goods are also consumption goods, or through the transitional employment of the capital in those consumption industries still operating at home, or through the exchange of the unwanted capital for foreign consumption goods. (These possibilities are themselves problematic but we shall not pursue that matter here.) Thus, the argument goes, one should not compare the two levels of consumption p.w. which relate to the steady growth paths represented, in fig. 13.1, by N (no-trade) and W (with-trade). What should be compared are paths N and T (the transition-plus-trade path), and their associated intertemporal patterns of consumption.

The matter can be considered further by reference to fig. 13.2 which reproduces the essentials of fig. 9.3(a). In the top quadrant the curve $c_b eh$ is the autarky dual $w–r$ and $c–g$ relation, and the straight lines refer to alternative with-trade relations when country B specialises in commodity 2. The line de is the relation which prevails when international prices are given by $p_I = p_I'$ and the line fh is that which holds when international prices are equal to the autarky price ratio, p_b. (Although capitalists would, in the latter circumstance, be indifferent to trade, a consideration of this case is analytically useful.) In the interests of simplicity it is assumed that the rates of growth in trade and autarky are both zero. Thus, following the argument of chapter 5, section 5, the value of capital p.w. in autarky is given by the slope of the straight line $c_b h$ and, with trade, by the slope of the appropriate straight-line relation.

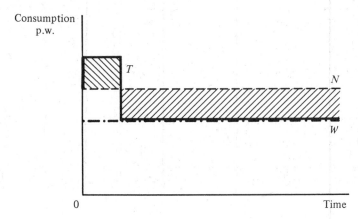

Figure 13.1

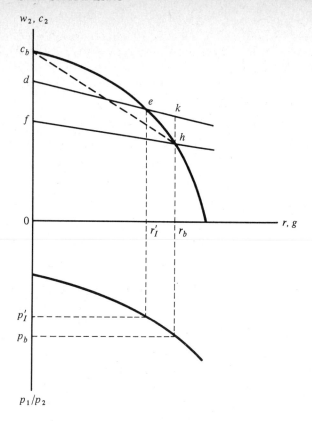

Figure 13.2

Consider trade occurring at prices $p_I = p_b$. The loss of consumption p.w. is the amount $c_b f$ which, since the wage is unchanged, is borne entirely by capitalists. At the same time the value of capital p.w. has fallen and, according to the previous argument, this de-cumulation is converted into the transitional consumption boost that is shown, somewhat schematically, in Fig. 13.1. It is easy to show that this boost exactly offsets the present value of the 'comparative loss' (the difference between N and W for all future periods) *when the latter is discounted at the rate of profits, r_b*; in other words, that the present values of the two shaded areas in fig. 13.1 are equal. If ΔK is the reduction in the value of capital p.w., then the loss of profits p.w. is $r_b \Delta K$ for each succeeding period to infinity. If this is discounted at the rate r_b then the present value of the loss is ΔK which, by assumption, is equal to the transitional consumption boost. In this case, therefore, the present value of the p.w. consumption streams N and T are identical. In the more likely case in which $p_I < p_b$ the argument needs modification. As before, the de-cumulation gives capitalists a temporary boost equal to the present value of their future losses. But there is, in addition, a relative price effect which increases wages (by hk in fig. 13.2). Thus the net effect on the gain from trade is the increase in the wage, which is always positive.

We may summarise the argument so far as follows: using the rate of profits as the rate of discount, the gain from trade is always positive in the sense that the present value of the transition-plus-trade p.w. consumption stream is greater than the autarky consumption stream (except in the unlikely case when $p_I = p_b$ and the gain is zero). The next, and crucial question is whether any significance can be attached to the present value calculations.

From the neoclassical viewpoint, in which the rate of profits is conceptually identical to the rate of interest which, itself, is equal to society's rate of time preference, the present value calculations indicate accurately society's preferred consumption profile. A high interest rate indicates a preference for more consumption in the present so that a shortlived consumption boost can offset eternally higher consumption in the future. As Smith (1976) puts it: 'An 'impatient' high-interest-rate country uses trade to obtain more of its more preferred goods: it sacrifices future consumption for present consumption'.

On the classical view however, the conclusions reached on the basis of these present-value calculations may be quite meaningless since the rate of profits has little to do with the appropriate social rate of discount. If, for example, society deems the welfare of future generations to be as important as that of the present, the rate of discount will be very low (and possibly negative) and path N might easily be preferred to path T. The analysis of chapter 9 is thus quite right to conclude that the gain from trade *may* be negative.

Finally, it may be recalled that the argument concerning the gain from trade is simply a particular case of that concerning the Golden Rule of Accumulation. In fig. 13.2, the frontiers $c_b eh$ and he may refer to *any* two techniques in, say, an autarkic economy. (*de* would not normally be a straight line, but that is of no relevance here.) With a low growth rate, consumption p.w. is greatest with the technique represented by frontier $c_b eh$, but profit maximisation leads to the choice of the technique represented by *de*. In switching from the latter to the former there would be need of transitional capital accumulation which, it may be argued, offsets the future p.w. consumption gains. But, again, the argument depends on the rate of profits being a measure of time preference in consumption, and where this is not the case, it breaks down.

7 Sraffa and constant returns

In the preface to *PC* Sraffa remarks that 'No changes in output and (at any rate in Parts I and II) no changes in the proportions in which different means of production are used by an industry are considered, so that no question arises as to the variation or constancy of returns'. Obviously, when the Sraffa price-distribution analysis is combined with the Leontief growth model the basis of this argument is removed and there can be no doubt that an assumption of constant returns is essential. But some purists would argue that the Sraffa–Leontief approach is an illegitimate extension of the analysis of *PC* since that analysis is intended to view price-distribution relations 'much like a photograph at an instant of time'. (Roncaglia (1978), p. 21.) But is Sraffa's position acceptable even then? The first point to note is that, as Sraffa is clearly aware, his argument does not apply to consider-ations of technical choice (which are discussed in Part III of *PC*). That fact alone considerably diminishes the value of an analysis which forswears any assumption on returns. In the consideration of single-technique economies however, it is true that there is no need to assume constant returns provided that an even less attractive assumption is employed instead; namely, that commodities are purchased in exactly the same proportions out of profits and wages. This is the only other way in which output levels can remain constant in the face of changes in distribution. Yet, in any economy which has a positive rate of accumulation, a portion of capitalists' demands will be for commodities (investment goods) which are very unlikely to appear in the wage basket.

It may be that the need to assume constant returns would gain more widespread acceptance were it not for a belief that this would sterilise Sraffa's achievement by reducing his analysis to a special case of WGE. As we argued in section 5, however, the Sraffa–Leontief approach is quite distinct, and Sraffa's contribution to this approach is a major accomplish-ment.

8 Conclusion

Sraffa's analysis in *PC* has effectively destroyed Marx's labour theory of value but it is not of direct relevance to the rest of Marx's work. Yet, in combination with the Leontief growth model, it provides a new and power-ful basis for the Marxian theory of capitalist development. Although the Sraffa–Leontief approach considers only capitalist economies in steady growth it is, nevertheless, a starting point for the analysis of discontinuous growth and crises which are characteristic of capitalism.

Neoclassical theory, in any of its guises, views savings as a reduction in current utility since utility is seen as attainable only from consumption.

Accordingly, 'interest' is regarded as repayment for the sacrifice of fore-going consumption. In the Marxian/classical view, capitalists also get satisfaction from the mere possession of wealth. Classical 'profit' is, there-fore, conceptually distinct from neoclassical 'interest' in that it cannot be considered as compensation for some sort of effort on the part of the capitalist. Thus, the appropriation by the capitalist of commodities produced by labour can reasonably be said to constitute 'exploitation'.

This Marxian/classical view of savings is consistent with the assumption that capitalists attempt to maximise their rates of profit and this, in turn, is sufficient to render a classical theory based on the Sraffa–Leontief approach quite distinct from any neoclassical theory. Since, moreover, the Sraffa–Leontief approach focuses on those features which are most charac-teristic of capitalist societies, it is of greater relevance to an understanding of the mechanics of capitalist development. It is clear, however, that to attain a fuller picture of capitalist economies a lot of work remains to be done, particularly in the study of non-steady behaviour. Reactions to technical progress, scarcity and changes in demand must be incorporated into a historical rather than a comparative analysis and, for this to be achieved satisfactorily, it will certainly be required to bring money properly into the picture. The analysis of steady growth, with which this book has been largely concerned, is simply a beginning.

FURTHER READING

Despite its age, Sweezy (1942) is still one of the best introductions to Marxian economics. Of the earlier writings which investigated the relation-ship of *PC* to Marx, Meek (1961) is by far the best. The more recent con-troversial re-examination of this relationship was sparked off by the article on negative surplus value in joint-production systems by Steedman (1975) and this critical theme was developed much further in his (1977*a*) book. For a relatively dispassionate review of this book, see Kurz (1979), but for a fuller range of views consult the essays collected in Steedman and Sweezy (1981). For Marxian criticism of Sraffian economics, the classic reference is Rowthorn (1974).

For an introduction to Walrasian General Equilibrium theory, see Gravelle and Rees (1981); a standard reference at an advanced level is Arrow and Hahn (1971). The original source is Walras (1954), first published in 1874. More directly related to the issues discussed here are, at an introductory level, Howard (1979) and, somewhat more advanced, Walsh and Gram (1980).

The concept of 'abstinence' is generally associated with Nassau Senior (1836), 'waiting' with Alfred Marshall (1890) and 'time preference' with

Irving Fisher (1907). For an account of alternative views on saving which are more consistent with those of Marx, see Steedman (1981).

The view that *PC* (and *a fortiori* the Sraffa–Leontief approach) is just a special case of WGE is forcefully expressed by Hahn: there 'is not a single formal proposition in Sraffa's book which is not also true in a General Equilibrium model constructed on his assumptions' (Hahn (1975), p. 362). For a further elaboration, see Hahn (1982). This view is also consistent with that of certain Marxist writers, notably Medio (1977) and Nuti (1974). In relation to specifically capital-theoretic issues it is also developed by Bliss (1975) and Dixit (1977). Arguments against this view, based on a conceptual distinction between 'interest' and 'profits' may be found in Garegnani (1976), Harcourt (1982) and Walsh and Gram (1980). None of these, however, particularly emphasises the importance of subjective savings behaviour which we consider crucial. A good summary of the various arguments (coming down on the neoclassical side) is Howard (1979).

The views expressed in this chapter are given a different perspective in Mainwaring (1983) in which two Marxian/classical assumptions (capitalists get satisfaction from accumulating, and there exists a subsistence minimum to wages) are inserted into a simple General Equilibrium-type model to obtain explicitly Marxian conclusions. This confirms our view that these two assumptions are critical in distinguishing, at a formal level, between the two broad approaches.

On the gain from international trade, see references cited in chapter 9; of direct relevance to the present discussion are: Metcalfe and Steedman (1974), for an initial statement of the issue; Samuelson (1975) and Smith (1979), for a neoclassical rationalisation; and Mainwaring (1979a), for a critique of the latter on the basis of the difficulty of transforming capital into consumption goods. The present argument relating to the appropriate rate of discount has not previously been pursued with any vigour.

For a defence of Sraffa's position on returns, see Roncaglia (1978). Eatwell (1977) develops the defence further against the attacks of Burmeister (1975 and 1977). The viewpoint taken in this chapter is explained more fully in Mainwaring (1979b) where it is also shown that if no assumption is made on returns, or on the class composition of demand, then the standard properties of the single-products w–r relation (inverse monotonicity and finite maximum rate of profits) no longer hold.

The most notable attempt to date to generalise the Sraffian approach in a more dynamic direction is Pasinetti (1981).

Notes

1 A simple theory of distribution and prices

1 *On the Principles of Political Economy and Taxation* 1817, p. 5. The *Principles* is reprinted in Vol. I of *The Works and Correspondence of David Ricardo*, edited by Piero Sraffa and Maurice Dobb (Sraffa and Dobb, 1951).
2 *Principles*, p. 5; in Sraffa and Dobb (1951), Vol. I.
3 Reprinted in Sraffa and Dobb (1951) Vol. IV; hereafter referred to as the *Essay*.
4 In a letter to J. R. McCulloch; Sraffa and Dobb (1951) Vol. IV.
5 Introduction to Sraffa and Dobb (1951) Vol. I p. xxiii.
6 *Production of Commodities*, p. 93; hereafter abbreviated to *PC*.
7 Introduction to Sraffa and Dobb (1951) Vol. I pp. xxxi–ii.
8 An economy which is incapable of producing profits is incapable of sustaining a capitalist class structure based on the restricted ownership of capital and the hiring of wage-labour. This is not to deny the possible existence of subsistence economies where individuals work, with or without capital, to produce just sufficient to provide for their own consumption requirements. A fuller analysis of a subsistence economy is given in chapter 3.
9 The singular form 'profit' is used to refer to the rate obtained by an individual capitalist. The plural form refers to the rate when applied to a sector of social aggregate.
10 *The Wealth of Nations*, Smith (1961) Vol. I p. 65.

2 The labour theory of value

1 See the editors' Introduction to the *Principles* in Sraffa and Dobb (1951), Vol. I, pp. xxxi–ii.
2 While, in general, the equality of equations and unknowns is neither necessary nor sufficient to ensure a solution, in the systems we shall be dealing with it nevertheless provides a useful preliminary guide. We shall alert the reader whenever there is a danger of being misled.
3 Putting $l_1 = 1$, then $w = 1/(1 + r)$ and

$$p_2 = l_2[1 + (1 + r)] = 2l_2 + 2r$$

Since l_2 is constant, p_2 varies directly with r.

3 A subsistence economy

1   Algebraically, this addition is performed by adding the corresponding elements of the two vectors. Geometrically, it is performed by 'completing the parallelogram' K_1OG_1 .... Readers unsure of this basic operation should practise with some simple numerical examples. Much of the geometry of the rest of the book relies on this operation.

2   Note that the negative slope reflects the fact that *more* of one commodity implies *less* of another. Individual prices are more properly defined by a vector having (in this case) all-positive elements. (See chapter 4, section 4.)

4 Production with a surplus

1   A little later in this chapter, however, we shall allow the possibility of workers sharing part of the surplus. The reader is reminded that rent is still being abstracted from.

2   Whereas equations (3.4′) allow for a unique determination of prices, equations (4.2) allow up to k separate solutions for the $k-1$ prices. Mathematically, this is because (4.2) reduces to a kth degree polynomial in r. To each of the k solutions for r there corresponds a set of p_i/p_j ratios. We shall see, however, that only one of these solutions consists of all positive values and is, therefore, the only one of economic interest.

3   In fact, the surplus economy with zero profits and a subsistence economy have identical logical properties. When $r = 0$ equations (4.3) are identical to equations (3.7′).

4   As we may have expected from our considerations in chapter 2, section 4.

5 Consumption versus growth

1   Since we are considering a growing economy, the workforce can no longer be fixed at unity. Figures such as 5.1 therefore have to be interpreted as showing magnitudes *per worker*. Consumption of commodity i per worker is the total consumption of commodity i (including capitalists' consumption) divided by the number of workers.

2   This section can be skipped without loss of continuity.

3   See Pasinetti (1962).

6 The Standard system and basic commodities

1   To complete this proof it is also necessary to consider the case in which process 1 uses up proportionately more of commodity 2; that is, the case in which the input vectors in fig. 6.1 are switched around, the output vectors remaining where they are. In this case the movement from ϵ_1 to ϵ_2 would be in the *same* direction as that from α_1 to α_2. But since the distance $\alpha_1\alpha_2$ is greater than the distance $\epsilon_1\epsilon_2$, the α-vector must move at a

greater rate than the ϵ-vector. Thus the ϵ-vector can only be 'overtaken' once, at which point the Standard proportions are defined.

2 For a general proof see *PC*, chapter V.

3 A non-basic which enters, directly or indirectly, into its own production (as does commodity 4) is known as a 'self-reproducing' non-basic. These give rise to certain theoretical problems which are not considered here (see guide to further reading).

4 Introduction to Sraffa and Dobb (1951) Vol. I, p. xxxi.

7 Relative prices and the rate of profits

1 These are the 'self-reproducing' non-basics referred to in chapter 6, note 3.

2 This merely confirms what we have already established in chapter 4. It may be noted that it cannot be the case that there is some rate of profits at which industry 1 switches from surplus to deficit and industry 2 from deficit to surplus. At such a rate the trade-offs would have to coincide, implying a system with equal capital:labour ratios, in which event (as we see in section 6) surpluses and deficits could not occur at any rate of profits.

3 This possibility finds its expression in Ricardo where all processes use only labour and last for a single period. (In Marx's *Capital*, the analogous case is that in which the 'organic compositions of capital' are the same in all industries; Marx (1970).)

8 Many techniques

1 It is possible, by sheer coincidence, that three $w-r$ relations pass through the same point. In that case two commodities will have equiprofitable alternative processes. We shall ignore this fluke possibility.

2 p_i then measures the amount of labour that can be purchased by one unit of commodity i, and is known as the 'labour commanded' price.

9 An application to international trade

1 Though some historians would say that this honour properly belongs to Torrens (1808).

2 Obviously, if we replaced Ricardo's assumption by the assumption that r is exogenously fixed, the benefits would be manifested entirely in increased wages.

3 Most people would argue that in an analysis of 'steady-state' growth (such as this) it is necessary that $g_a = g_b$. (If not, one country will eventually become so much larger than the other that the ability to specialise will break down.) In that case, country B necessarily has lower consumption p.w. with trade. Whether the model needs to be interpreted quite so literally is another matter.

4 It can be seen by inspection, however, that this possibility only arises
   when the $w-r$ relation is convex in one country and concave in the other.

10 Pure joint production

1 These diagrams correspond to the numerical example in Steedman
   (1975).
2 Sraffa's definition is a little imprecise. The n commodities are, in fact,
   non-basic if *exactly* n rows are independent. See Manara (1968).

Appendix

1 Another complication, which does not arise in the single-products case is
   that there may be no real solution (in the algebraic sense) for R. (Manara
   (1968) gives an example of a perfectly viable system for which this is
   true. In this case 'it is not even possible to construct the Standard product – at least, if we remain in the field of real numbers.')
2 It follows, incidentally, that there is no longer any correspondence
   between the Standard system and an actual system at maximum growth.
   In the economy illustrated in fig. 10.A.1, growth at the rate $G = R$ is
   simply not possible. The von Neumann path would involve a lower
   growth rate with the discarding of some of product 2.
3 Readers willing to take this proof for granted can skip immediately to
   the next section.

11 Fixed capital

1 These 'labour-commanded' prices have already been introduced in chapter 8, section 5.
2 In this case further complications arise if scrap values and/or disposal
   costs are non-zero, since these have now to be considered for every year
   of the plant's physical life. In the example, a used-up battery has to be
   sold or otherwise disposed of after only four of the lorry's possible sixty
   years.

12 The theory of rent

1 Not to be confused with Sraffa's 'sub-systems' discussed in Appendix A
   of *PC*.
2 This complex pattern of price behaviour was discussed in chapter 7,
   section 4.
3 Intuitively it may be thought that the real-$w-r$ relation for $(0, I)$ is a
   weighted average of those for (0) and (I), but the former contains the
   land coefficients t_0 and t_1, whereas the latter do not.
4 It is being assumed that no element of joint production, apart from that
   arising out of land, is present.

5 An exception to this would occur where by complete fluke two (or more) new methods were equiprofitable. This is just a particular case of the theorem, noted in chapter 8, section 3, that techniques 'normally' differ in only one process.

13 Some broader issues

1 The epithet 'Sraffian' is used to refer to the price-distribution relationships of *PC*, while 'Sraffa–Leontief' refers to the steady-growth model which combines these with the consumption-growth relationships of chapter 5. Comparisons will sometimes be made with the one, sometimes with the other, and the distinction should be borne in mind.

2 To avoid ambiguity in what follows, *value* will be italicised whenever it is used in this sense.

3 When wages are no longer advanced, Sraffa defines 'surplus' in such a way that part of it may go to labour. 'Surplus *value*', however, is the *value* of net output less the *value* of wage payments. 'Surplus product' and 'surplus labour' are defined in an analogous fashion.

4 It should be pointed out that Morishima has developed, on the basis of the von Neumann analysis, an alternative definition of exploitation such that surplus labour implies and is implied by a positive rate of profits. Here, surplus labour is defined in relation to those processes which produce steady-growth investment and consumption requirements with the minimum use of labour. However, they are not, in general, the processes chosen by competitive capitalists. See Morishima and Catephores (1978).

5 In neoclassical theory there exists a category of income called 'pure' profits which is distinct from interest. These pure profits, which are actually a form of rent, have no counterpart in the Sraffa–Leontief model since they are the result of diminishing returns in production. The discussion in this section does not concern pure profits.

6 As F. H. Knight ((1921), p. 133) puts it: 'Men save in large measure with no thought of ever consuming the capital, or *even the income* which it yields' (italics in the original).

7 There exists an alternative interpretation of WGE which incorporates uncertainty about the future. But this interpretation 'is designed to handle uncertainty about events independent of the action of economic agents (e.g., the weather) and not uncertainty about events resulting from the combined action of economic agents' (Nuti (1972), p.231).

References

Abraham-Frois, G., and Berrebi, E. 1979. *Theory of Value, Prices and Accumulation*, Cambridge: Cambridge University Press.

Arrow, K. J., and Hahn, F. H. 1971. *General Competitive Analysis*, Edinburgh: Oliver and Boyd.

Bain, J. S. 1956. *Barriers to New Competition*, Cambridge, Mass.: Harvard University Press.

Baldone, S. 1974. 'Fixed Capital in Sraffa's Theoretical Scheme', in Pasinetti, (ed.) (1980). (First published in Italian.)

Bharadwaj, K. 1963. 'Value Through Exogenous Distribution', *Economic Weekly* (Bombay), Aug. 1963, 1450–4.

1970. 'On the Maximum Number of Switches between Two Production Systems', *Schweizerische Zeitschrift für Volkswirtschaft und Statistik*, 106, 409–29.

1978. *Classical Political Economy and the Rise to Dominance of Supply and Demand Theories*, Calcutta: Orient Longman.

Bliss, C. J. 1975. *Capital Theory and the Distribution of Income*, Amsterdam: North-Holland.

Böhm-Bawerk, E. von. 1891. *Positive Theory of Capital*, London: Macmillan.

Bortkiewicz, L. von. 1952. 'Value and Price in the Marxian System', *International Economic Papers*, 2, 5–60.

Bradley, I., and Howard, M., (eds.) 1982. *Classical and Marxian Political Economy*, London: Macmillan.

Broome, J. 1978. Review of Pasinetti (1977), *Economica*, 45, 413–14.

1983. *The Microeconomics of Capitalism*, London: Academic Press.

Bruno, M., Burmeister, E., and Sheshinski, E. 1966. 'Nature and Implications of the Reswitching of Techniques', *Quarterly Journal of Economics*, 80, 526–53.

Burmeister, E. 1975. 'Comment: the Age of Leontief . . . and Who', *Journal of Economic Literature*, 13, 454–7.

1977. 'The Irrelevance of Sraffa's Analysis without Constant Returns to Scale', *Journal of Economic Literature*, 15, 68–70.

Campanelli, G. 1982. 'W. Whewell's Contribution to Economic Analysis: The First Mathematical Formulation of Fixed Capital in Ricardo's System', *The Manchester School*, 248–65.

Caves, R. E., and Jones, R. W. 1981. *World Trade and Payments*, Boston: Little, Brown.

Champernowne, D. G. 1945. 'A Note on J. von Neumann's Article "A Model of Economic Equilibrium" ', *Review of Economic Studies*, 33, 10–18.

Clark, J. B. 1899, *Theory of Distribution of Wealth*, New York: Macmillan.

Deane, P. 1978, *The Evolution of Economic Ideas*, Cambridge: Cambridge University Press.

Dixit, A. 1977. 'The Accumulation of Capital Theory', *Oxford Economic Papers* (New Series), 29, 1–29.

Dmitriev, V. K. 1974. *Economic Essays on Value, Competition and Utility*, (ed.) D. M. Nuti, Cambridge: Cambridge University Press.

Dobb, M. 1973. *Theories of Value and Distribution since Adam Smith*, Cambridge: Cambridge University Press.

Dorfman, R., Samuelson, P. A., and Solow, R. 1958. *Linear Programming and Economic Analysis*, New York: McGraw-Hill.

Eatwell, J. 1975a. 'The Interpretation of Ricardo's "Essay on Profits" ', *Economica*, 42, 182–7.

1975b. 'Mr. Sraffa's Standard Commodity and the Rate of Exploitation', *Quarterly Journal of Economics*, 89, 543–55.

1977. 'The Irrelevance of Returns to Scale in Sraffa's Analysis', *Journal of Economic Literature*, 15, 61–8.

1982. 'Competition', in Bradley and Howard, (eds.) (1982).

Evans, D. H. 1980. 'Unequal Exchange and Economic Policies', in I. Livingstone, (ed.) *Readings in Development Economics and Policy*, London: George Allen and Unwin.

Fisher, I. 1907. *The Rate of Interest*, New York: Macmillan.

Garegnani, P. 1970. 'Heterogeneous Capital, the Production Function and the Theory of Distribution', *Review of Economic Studies*, 37, 407–36.

1976. 'On a Change in the Notion of Equilibrium in Recent Work on Value and Distribution: a Comment on Samuelson', in M. Brown, K. Sato and P. Zarembka, (eds.) *Essays in Modern Capital Theory*, Amsterdam: North-Holland.

1982. 'On Hollander's Interpretation of Ricardo's Early Theory of Profits', *Cambridge Journal of Economics*, 6, 65–77.

Goodwin, R. M. 1970. *Elementary Economics from the Higher Standpoint*, Cambridge: Cambridge University Press.

Gravelle, H., and Rees, R. 1981. *Microeconomics*, London: Longman.

Hahn, F. H. 1975. 'Revival of Political Economy: The Wrong Issues and the Wrong Argument', *Economic Record*, 51, 360–4.

1982. 'The Neo-Ricardians', *Cambridge Journal of Economics*, 6, 353–74.

Hahn, F. H., and Matthews, R. C. O. 1964. 'The Theory of Economic Growth: A Survey', *Economic Journal*, 74, 779–902.

Harcourt, G. C. 1972. *Some Cambridge Controversies in the Theory of Capital*, Cambridge: Cambridge University Press.

1982. 'The Sraffian Contribution: An Evaluation', in Bradley and Howard, (eds.) (1982).

Harcourt, G. C. and Massaro, V. G. 1964. 'Mr. Sraffa's Production of Commodities', *Economic Record*, 50, 442–54.

Harcourt, G. C., and Laing, N. F., (eds.) 1971. *Capital and Growth*, Harmondsworth: Penguin.

Harris, D. J. 1978. *Capital Accumulation and Income Distribution*, London: Routledge and Kegan Paul.

Hollander, S. 1973. 'Ricardo's Analysis of the Profit Rate, 1813–15', *Economica*, 40, 260–82.

  1979. *The Economics of David Ricardo*, London: Heinemann.

Howard, M. C. 1979. *Modern Theories of Income Distribution*, London: Macmillan.

Hunt, E. K., and Schwartz, J. G., (eds.) 1972. *A Critique of Economic Theory*, Harmondsworth: Penguin.

Jevons, W. S. 1871. *Theory of Political Economy*, London: Macmillan.

Kaldor, N. 1955. 'Alternative Theories of Distribution', *Review of Economic Studies*, 23, 83–100.

Kalecki, M. 1971. *Selected Essays on the Dynamics of the Capitalist Economy*, (ed.) D. M. Nuti, Cambridge: Cambridge University Press.

Kennedy, C. 1964. 'Induced Bias in Innovation and the Theory of Distribution', *Economic Journal*, 74, 541–7.

Keynes, J. M. 1936. *The General Theory of Employment, Interest and Money*, London: Macmillan.

Knight, F. H. 1921. *Risk, Uncertainty and Profit*, Boston: Houghton Mifflin.

Kregel, J. A. 1971. *Rate of Profits, Distribution and Growth: Two Views*, London: Macmillan.

Kuczinski, M., and Meek, R. L. 1972. *Quesnay's Tableau Economique*, London: Macmillan.

Kurz, H. 1978. 'Rent Theory in a Multisectoral Model', *Oxford Economic Papers* (New Series), 30, 16–37.

  1979. 'Sraffa after Marx', *Australian Economic Papers*, 18, 52–70.

Leontief, W. 1951. *The Structure of the American Economy*, New York: Oxford University Press.

Mainwaring, L. 1974. 'A Neo-Ricardian Analysis of International Trade', *Kyklos*, 27, 537–53.

  1976. 'Relative Prices and "Factor Price Equalisation" in a Heterogeneous Capital Goods Model', *Australian Economic Papers*, 15, 109–18.

  1977. 'Monopoly Power, Income Distribution and Price Determination', *Kyklos*, 30, 674–90.

  1979a. 'On the Transition from Autarky to Trade', in Steedman, (ed.) (1979a).

  1979b. 'The Wage-Profit Relation Without Constant Returns', *Metroeconomica*, 31, 335–48.

  1982. 'A Long-Run Analysis of International Investment', *Metroeconomica*, 35, 11–25.

  1983. 'A Geometrical Analysis of Exchange and Accumulation in Marx', *Australian Economic Papers*, 23, 454–66.

Malthus, T. R. 1970. *An Essay on the Principle of Population*, (ed.) A. Flew, Harmondsworth: Penguin.

1815. *Inquiry into the Nature and Progress of Rent*, London.

1820. *Principles of Political Economy*, London.

Manara, C. F. 1968. 'Sraffa's Model for the Joint Production of Commodities by Means of Commodities', in Pasinetti, (ed.) (1980). (First published in Italian.)

Marshall, A. 1890. *Principles of Economics*, London: Macmillan.

Marx, K. 1970. *Capital*, Vol. I, London: Lawrence and Wishart.

1972. *Capital*, Vol. III, London; Lawrence and Wishart.

Medio, A. 1972. 'Profits and Surplus-Value: Appearance and Reality in Capitalist Production', in Hunt and Schwartz, (eds.) (1972).

1977. 'Neoclassicals, Neo-Ricardians, and Marx', in Schwartz, (ed.) (1977).

Meek, R. L. 1961. 'Mr Sraffa's Rehabilitation of Classical Economics', *Scottish Journal of Political Economy*, 8, 119–36.

1973. *Studies in the Labour Theory of Value*, London: Lawrence and Wishart.

Metcalfe, J. S., and Steedman, I. 1972. 'Reswitching and Primary Input Use', *Economic Journal*, 82, 140–57.

1973. 'Heterogeneous Capital and the Heckscher-Ohlin-Samuelson Theory of Trade', in J. M. Parkin, (ed.) *Essays in Modern Economics*, London: Longman.

1974. 'A Note on the Gain from Trade', *Economic Record*, 50, 581–95.

Milgate, M. 1982. Review of I. Steedman and P. Sweezy (1981), *Contributions to Political Economy*, 1, 104–6.

Miliband, R. 1969. *The State in Capitalist Society*, London: Weidenfeld and Nicolson.

Montani, G. 1975. 'Scarce Natural Resources and Income Distribution', *Metroeconomica*, 27, 68–101.

Morishima, M. 1976. 'Marx from a von Neumann Viewpoint', in M. Brown, K. Sato and P. Zarembka, (eds.) *Essays in Modern Capital Theory*, Amsterdam: North-Holland.

Morishima, M., and Catephores, G. 1978. *Value, Exploitation and Growth*, London: McGraw-Hill.

Napoleoni, C. 1975. *Smith, Ricardo, Marx*, Oxford: Basil Blackwell.

Neumann, J. von. 1945. 'A Model of General Economic Equilibrium', *Review of Economic Studies*, 13, 1–9.

Newman, P. 1962. 'Production of Commodities by Means of Commodities', *Schweizerische Zeitschrift für Volkswirtschaft und Statistik*, 98, 58–75.

Nuti, D. M. 1970*a*. 'Capitalism, Socialism and Steady Growth', *Economic Journal*, 80, 32–57.

1970*b*. 'Vulgar Economy in the Theory of Income Distribution', *De Economist*, 118, 363–9.

1972. 'Postscript' to Nuti (1970*b*), in Hunt and Schwartz, (eds.) (1972).

1974. 'On the Rates of Return on Investment', *Kyklos*, 27, 345–69.

O'Brien, D. P. 1975. *The Classical Economists*, Oxford: Clarendon Press.

1981. 'Ricardian Economics and the Economics of David Ricardo', *Oxford Economic Papers* (New Series), 33, 352–86.

Parrinello, S. 1973. 'Distribution, Growth and International Trade', in Steedman, (ed.) (1979*a*). (First published in Italian.)

Pasinetti, L. L. 1959. 'A Mathematical Reformulation of the Ricardian System', *Review of Economic Studies*, 27, 78–98.

1962. 'Rate of Profit and Income Distribution in Relation to the Rate of Economic Growth', *Review of Economic Studies*, 29, 267–79.

1973. 'The Notion of Vertical Integration in Economic Analysis', *Metroeconomica*, 25, 1–29.

1974. *Growth and Income Distribution. Essays in Economic Theory*, Cambridge: Cambridge University Press.

1977. *Lectures on the Theory of Production*, London: Macmillan.

(ed.) 1980. *Essays on the Theory of Joint Production*, London: Macmillan.

1981. *Structural Change and Economic Growth*, Cambridge: Cambridge University Press.

Phelps, E. S. 1961. 'The Golden Rule of Accumulation: A Fable for Growthmen', *American Economic Review*, 51, 638–43.

Quadrio-Curzio, A. 1980. 'Rent, Income Distribution and Orders of Efficiency and Rentability', in Pasinetti, (ed.) (1980).

Robinson, J. 1953. 'The Production Function and the Theory of Capital', *Review of Economic Studies*, 21, 81–106.

1961. 'Prelude to a Critique of Economic Theory', *Oxford Economic Papers* (New Series), 13, 53–8.

1962. *Essays in the Theory of Economic Growth*, London: Macmillan.

Roncaglia, A. 1978. *Sraffa and Theory of Prices*, Chichester: John Wiley.

Rowthorn, R. 1974. 'Neo Classicism, Neo-Ricardianism and Marxism', *New Left Review*, 86, 63–87.

Rymes, T. K. 1971. *On Concepts of Capital and Technical Change*, Cambridge: Cambridge University Press.

Samuelson, P. A. 1966. 'A Summing Up', *Quarterly Journal of Economics*, 80, 568–83.

1975. 'Trade Pattern Reversals in Time-Phased Ricardian Systems and Intertemporal Efficiency', *Journal of International Economics*, 5, 309–63.

Schefold, B. 1976. 'Different Forms of Technical Progress', *Economic Journal*, 86, 806–19.

1980*a*. 'Fixed Capital as a Joint Product and the Analysis of Accumulation with Different Forms of Technical Progress', in Pasinetti, (ed.) (1980).

1980*b*. 'Von Neumann and Sraffa: Mathematical Equivalence and Conceptual Difference', *Economic Journal*, 90, 140–56.

Schwartz, J. G. (ed.) 1977. *The Subtle Anatomy of Capitalism*, Santa Monica: Goodyear.

Schwartz, J. T. 1961. *Lectures on the Mathematical Method in Analytical Economics*, New York: Gordon and Breach.

Senior, N. 1836. *Outline of Political Economy*, London.

Smith, A. 1961. *An Enquiry into the Nature and Causes of the Wealth of Nations*, (ed.) E. Cannan, London: Methuen.

Smith, M. A. M. 1976. 'Trade, Growth and Consumption in Alternative Models of Capital Accumulation', *Journal of International Economics*, 6, 371–84.

1979. 'Intertemporal Gains from Trade', *Journal of International Economics*, 9, 239–48.

Spaventa, L. 1970. 'Rate of Profit, Rate of Growth, and Capital Intensity in a Simple Production Model', *Oxford Economic Papers* (New Series), 22, 129–47.

Sraffa, P. 1960. *Production of Commodities by Means of Commodities*, Cambridge: Cambridge University Press.

Sraffa, P. and Dobb, M. 1951. *The Works and Correspondence of David Ricardo*, Vols. I–X. Cambridge: Cambridge University Press.

Steedman, I. 1975. 'Positive Profits with Negative Surplus Value', *Economic Journal*, 85, 114–23.

1976. 'Positive Profits with Negative Surplus Value: A Reply to Wolfstetter', *Economic Journal*, 86, 873–6.

1977a. *Marx after Sraffa*, London: New Left Books.

1977b. 'Basics, Non-basics and Joint Production', *Economic Journal*, 87, 324–8.

1977c. 'A Note on the Standard System with Joint Production', *mimeo*.

(ed.) 1979a. *Fundamental Issues in Trade Theory*, London: Macmillan.

1979b. *Trade Amongst Growing Economies*, Cambridge: Cambridge University Press.

1981. 'Time Preference, the Rate of Interest and Abstinence from Accumulation', *Australian Economic Papers*, 20, 219–34.

Steedman, I., and Metcalfe, J. S. 1973a. 'The Golden Rule and the Gain from Trade', in Steedman, I., (ed.) (1979a). (First published in French.)

1973b. 'On Foreign Trade', *Economia Internazionale*, 26, 516–28.

Steedman, I., Sweezy, P., *et al.* 1981. *The Value Controversy*, London: New Left Books.

Sweezy, P. 1942. *The Theory of Capitalist Development*, New York: Monthly Review Press.

Sylos-Labini, P. 1962, *Oligopoly and Technical Progress*, Cambridge, Mass.: Harvard University Press.

Thünen, J. H. von. 1966. *Von Thünen's Isolated State*, (ed.) P. Hall, London.

Torrens, R. 1808. *The Economists Refuted*, London.

1821. *An Essay on the Production of Wealth*, London.

Vaggi, G. 1982. Review of Bradley and Howard (1982), *Contributions to Political Economy*, 1, 101–4.

Varri, P. 1974. 'Prices, Rate of Profit and Life of Machines in Sraffa's Fixed-Capital Model', in Pasinetti, (ed.) (1980). (First published in Italian.)

Walras, L. 1954. *Elements of Pure Economics*, (ed.) W. Jaffé, London: Allen and Unwin.

Walsh, V. and Gram, H. 1980. *Classical and Neoclassical Theories of General Equilibrium*, Oxford: Oxford University Press.

Weizsäcker, C. C. von. 1971. *Steady State Capital Theory*, Berlin: Springer Verlag.

Whewell, W. 1971. *A Mathematical Exposition of Some Doctrines of Political Economy; Second Memoir*, Farnborough: Gregg International.

Wicksell, K. 1934. *Lectures on Political Economy*, Vol. I, London: Routledge.

Wolfson, M. 1978. *A Textbook of Economics*, London: Methuen.

Wolfstetter, E. 1976. 'Positive Profits with Negative Surplus Value: A Comment', *Economic Journal*, 86, 864–72.

Author index

197

Subject index